DEVOTIONS®

***B*ecause he himself suffered . . . he is able to help those who are being tempted.**

—Hebrews 2:18

JANUARY

Photo © Stocksnapper / Dreamstime.com

Gary Allen, Editor

DEVOTIONS® is published quarterly by Standard Publishing, Cincinnati, Ohio, www.standardpub.com. © 2009 by Standard Publishing. All rights reserved. Topics based on the Home Daily Bible Readings, International Sunday School Lessons. © 2006 by the Committee on the Uniform Series. Printed in U.S.A. All Scripture quotations, unless otherwise indicated, INTERNATIONAL VERSION®. NIV®. Copyri Used by permission of Zondervan. All rights res lowing, used with permission of the copyright h (NASB), © The Lockman Foundation, 1960, 196 James Version (KJV), public domain.

W9-CHX-550

Maxed Out by Sin?

The ax is already at the root of the trees, and every tree that does not produce good fruit will be cut down and thrown into the fire (Matthew 3:10).

Scripture: **Matthew 3:7-10**
Song: **"Come, All Christians, Be Committed"**

We woke before dawn, on a cold December morning, to the sound of loud popping and cracking. A heavy ice storm had coated the trees, and instead of gunshots, we heard limbs breaking. The damage was so severe that our entire town had no electrical power for several hours. Many people had to seek shelter in community buildings for days until they could safely return to their homes.

After the worst was over, storm-damaged trees remained. It took weeks of work with chainsaws, tractors, and loaders, to haul away broken limbs. Many of the trees simply had to be uprooted and burned.

Some of our trees survived the storm and put out new leaves in the spring. But the ones we cut down and threw into the fire remind me of Jesus' solemn warning. Unlike the trees, we have a choice. If we repent of our rebellious ways, we can produce fruit. But if sin does its destructive work to the max in us, what then?

Father, I want to produce fruit for You! My prayer is that I will be like those trees that put out new leaves, the ones that will live and blossom again. Thank You, God, for giving me that choice. In Jesus' name, amen.

January 1–3. **LeAnn Campbell** is a mother, grandmother, and retired special education teacher. She has taught children in church for more than 40 years.

Already Wrapped in Love

What shall we say, then? Shall we go on sinning so that grace may increase? (Romans 6:1).

Scripture: **Romans 6:1-11**
Song: **"Jesus Lives, and So Shall I"**

When I taught at the Center for Children with Developmental Disabilities, it seemed that some of the kids were constantly looking for ways to get into trouble. Although our staff gave them much attention and love, these boys and girls sought more notice by misbehaving. They seemed to crave any recognition at all, even if it came in the form of discipline.

They didn't need to misbehave to win our greater out-pourings of attention and concern. And, of course, good behavior would have pleased us more! But these children didn't reason that way.

The same is true for us after we become Christians. Paul stressed this: by no means should we go on sinning so grace could increase. With our baptism, we died to sin, so it just doesn't make sense to go on sinning.

The word to us is: "Count yourselves dead to sin but alive to God in Christ Jesus" (v. 11). Why should we crave attention for bad behavior? We already have God's full attention, all wrapped up in His infinite love and grace.

Father, sometimes I feel You aren't paying attention, especially when my prayers seem to go no higher than the ceiling. But help me to know and feel that seeking Your ways, in daily faithfulness, is the best way through. And do keep me from temptation today. In Jesus' name, amen.

Hear the Great Preacher!

John's clothes were made of camel's hair, and he had a leather belt around his waist. His food was locusts and wild honey (Matthew 3:4).

Scripture: **Matthew 3:1-6, 11-17**
Song: **"I Love to Tell the Storyt"**

When I taught this lesson to my Sunday school class of preschoolers, I served pretzels and honey. The children enjoyed crunching on their salty "locusts." And then I told them about John, the real locust-and-honey eater who proclaimed the coming of the Lamb of God. The little meal of pretzels and honey was a great attention-getter.

But let's picture how John got people's attention in his day. This desert man showed up in camel skins and leather belt. He was thoroughly outspoken, probably a bit loud and brash. And he had one main theme: Repent, get baptized, and get ready for the Messiah!

People came from the whole region and listened to him. Many confessed their sins, and John baptized them in the Jordan River.

John must have been a great preacher, but there is something more important here for me. As nineteenth-century missionary George Dana Boardman once said: "The world is dying for want, not of good preaching, but of good hearing." How much of this great preacher's message am I hearing—and taking to heart?

Father, thanks for this great witness to Christ. Help me believe John's message with all my heart, and share it with others too. In Jesus' name, amen.

Keeping On

Blessed is the man who perseveres under trial, because when he has stood the test, he will receive the crown of life that God has promised to those who love him (James 1:12).

Scripture: **James 1:12-16**
Song: "Never Gonna Stop"

"God has a purpose for me today," Ardith often says. "I am His messenger." Her eyes sparkle with joy; she smiles.

Ardith lives in a county nursing home in Rockford, Illinois. At 91, she has lived a full life of service to God. She might be tempted to think that her work for Christ is done, but she perseveres in her mission.

While sitting in her wheelchair, she shuffles her feet down the halls of the home looking for people to whom she can minister. She holds their hands, smiles, leans forward to listen, fills out menus, prays. And by her love she leads fellow residents to Christ. Neither pain, discouragement, or loneliness keep her from this service to God. She knows that very soon she will see Jesus, and then she will receive the crown of life He promised.

Are we tempted to give up because the road is hard? God is faithful. Like Jesus, let us focus only on the joy set before us.

God of strength, *You give grace to endure amidst every trial. Help me persevere in faith and witness, one day at a time. In Jesus' name, amen.*

January 4–10. **Julie Kloster** is a regular contributor to ChristianBibleStudies.com. She lives in Sycamore, Illinois, with her husband and three daughters.

Reach for the Light

The seed on good soil stands for those with a noble and good heart, who hear the word, retain it, and by persevering produce a crop (Luke 8:15).

Scripture: **Luke 8:5-8, 11-15**
Song: **"Heavenly Sunshine"**

In the rainforests of Costa Rica, two hundred climbing plants may grow up a single tree trunk to reach the light at the top of the canopy. Lush vegetation has good soil and plenty of rain, but ground-level plants struggle to receive enough sunlight.

No doubt this is why plants growing on the rainforest floor have broad leaves, some more than 12 inches long. This large surface area absorbs the filtered light that seeps through thick foliage above. They are then able to make the chlorophyll necessary for their survival. We might say that, for these plants, it's a daily struggle to strive toward the light.

In the parable of the seeds and the soil, Jesus compared a fruitful spiritual walk to seeds that fall on good soil. So I must ask myself today: What is the soil of my heart? What large or subtle sins are choking my growth these days? And am I reaching, reaching, reaching for the light of Christ each day?

Father of Light, You alone can produce a noble and good heart in me. Soften the soil of my heart to receive Your Word. Help me to retain its message and persevere, that I might offer a life well lived to You. In the name of the Father, the Son, and the Holy Spirit, I pray. Amen.

Gentle Restoration

Brothers, if someone is caught in a sin, you who are spiritual should restore him gently. But watch yourself, or you also may be tempted (Galatians 6:1).

Scripture: **Galatians 6:1-5**
Song: **"Create in Me a Clean Heart"**

"The coach blew up at me again." Anna's eyes brimmed with hurt, and her chin quivered in frustration. "Her yelling makes somebody cry almost every week."

Anna's mother, Beth, knew this coach was a sister in Christ. After much prayer, Beth made a kind but direct plea: Could she exhibit a little more gentleness and patience with her team?

Repentant tears rolled down the red face of the coach as she told Beth some painful secrets that had contributed to her anger. Married in mid-life, she longed for a child, but she'd suffered repeated miscarriages. Between the raging hormones and grief, she was barely keeping things together. The coach acknowledged her fault, asked for prayer, and promised to seek God daily for grace to control her anger. And through this process of restoration, God provided the coach with a new friend in Christ.

God calls us to seek gentle restoration of one another when we're caught in sin. In this case, it worked wonderful results.

*Help Me, **Lord,** to accept restoration when there are areas in my life that require repentance. And give me the grace and courage to bear the burdens of my brothers and sisters too. In Christ's name, amen.*

Awake to His Presence?

Then he returned to his disciples and found them sleeping. "Could you men not keep watch with me for one hour?" he asked Peter (Matthew 26:40).

Scripture: **Matthew 26:36-46**
Song: **"Come, Thou Fount of Every Blessing"**

". . . and to his astonishment, he found his beard had grown a foot long!" When Rip Van Winkle awoke from a nap in the Catskill Mountains of New York, he didn't realize he'd been asleep for 20 years. When he returned to his village, the results of his slumber became apparent. "He found the house gone to decay—the roof fallen in, the windows shattered, and the doors off the hinges." In the tale of "Rip Van Winkle," Washington Irving details the life and trials of a man, prone to lethargy, who slept through the American Revolution.

In the Garden of Gethsemane, Jesus' disciples just couldn't stay awake. The Lord pleaded with them to keep watch and pray; they slept on, abandoning their master in His last hours on earth.

Have you ever fallen into a spiritual slumber? Ever found the things of God a bit boring? Let us recall: Christ calls us to rest in Him, but not to grow oblivious to His presence. He is there, always, offering vibrant life, with purpose and mission. It is for us to turn our attention, daily, to all this goodness.

Lord, help me stay awake to Your presence, that I may diligently run the race You have set before me. In Christ's name I pray. Amen.

Prayer Prompts

This, then, is how you should pray: "Our Father in heaven, hallowed be your name" (Matthew 6:9).

Scripture: **Matthew 6:9-15**
Song: **"Give Thanks"**

"God, this is Chelsey," my 3-year-old daughter prayed. She hesitated. "Tell Him what you are thankful for," I prompted. "Why is He such a great God?"

This nudge was all she needed. "Thank You for sunshine. Thank You for windows. Thank You for crayons. Thank You that You love me. Thank You for . . . ," Chelsey named everything she could remember.

Her heartfelt prayer opened my eyes. How many times had I thanked God for windows? Chelsey gave thanks for things that I took for granted.

Jesus prompted His disciples with a special form of prayer. Reciting it from a heart that cherishes its meaning is precious. But I believe that Jesus also meant for this prayer to be an example of *how* to pray, even when we use other words. That is, He outlined certain essential components here: praise, submission to God's will, requests and intercessions, confession and the seeking of grace to forgive others, and praying for protection from temptation. In other words, let us converse with the openness, intimacy, and honesty of a child—His child.

*Prompt me, **Lord,** to remember that You are the author of all good things. Teach me to pray with the heart of a child about everything that comes to mind. In Christ's name I pray. Amen.*

Escape Route

God is faithful; he will not let you be tempted beyond what you can bear. But when you are tempted, he will also provide a way out so that you can stand up under it (1 Corinthians 10:13).

Scripture: **1 Corinthians 10:6-13**
Song: **"Deliver Me from Evil"**

I was cheerful when I answered the phone, but that quickly changed. The caller immediately attacked with harsh words and bitter accusations. Caught by surprise, I felt my anger rise at the unjustified assault. Just as I was about to respond in an equally uncontrolled manner, the phone went dead.

I laughed. God had made a quick way of escape for me. Humbled by His grace, I asked Him for wisdom and discernment. So when the phone rang again, I was prepared. Renewed by the Spirit, I listened and responded calmly.

All of us fall short of God's glory. In our Scripture today, the apostle Paul listed the sin of grumbling right alongside sexual immorality and idolatry. Clearly, we must guard our hearts with diligence, even against the so-called little things. Even when we think we're standing firm, temptation may suddenly surprise us. But God is faithful—let us watch for the inevitable escape route and take it quickly.

Heavenly Father, *thank You for providing the grace to endure temptation. Help me diligently guard my heart, seeking Your wisdom, discernment, and guidance in all situations. In the name of Your Son I pray. Amen.*

Only One to Worship

Jesus said to him, "Away from me, Satan! For it is written: 'Worship the Lord your God, and serve him only' " (Matthew 4:10).

Scripture: **Matthew 4:1-11**
Song: **"You Alone"**

"Lottery winners often wind up wishing they hadn't been lucky," said Mark Meltzer in the *Atlanta Business Chronicle.* Many people think that if they had more money they would be happier. Lottery winners prove this just isn't true. Striking it rich brings on a whole new set of problems: lawsuits, fear of theft, loss of friendships, and strained family relationships, for example.

The devil tempted Jesus with a "get rich quick" scheme. He took Christ to a high mountain and promised to give Him all the kingdoms of the world if He would just bow and worship him. Clearly, though, the prince of darkness could hardly offer anything to the Light of the world—anything He did not already own!

Christ knew the tricks of the deceiver. I want to learn them too, so I can stay constantly on guard. And the next time I'm offered instant satisfaction, may I recall the words of King Solomon, who said: "Here is the conclusion of the matter: Fear God and keep his commandments, for this is the whole duty of man" (Ecclesiastes 12:13).

God of all, You alone are worthy of worship. You are all I need. And Your grace and strength are my only hope to withstand temptation. I give You praise and glory, praying in the name of Your precious Son. Amen.

I'm One of Them

The Pharisees and the teachers of the law who belonged to their sect complained to his disciples, "Why do you eat and drink with tax collectors and 'sinners'?" (Luke 5:30).

Scripture: **Luke 5:27-32**
Song: **"I Have Decided to Follow Jesus"**

Jesus offered a great response to the question posed in today's key verse. "It is not the healthy who need a doctor, but the sick," He said. "I have not come to call the righteous, but sinners to repentance."

That answer ministers to me, because I once was as lost as any tax collector. But Jesus took me in, just as He did Levi. Through the gentle call of His gracious Holy Spirit, He invited me to follow Him, and I did. I opened the doors of my heart and held a great spiritual banquet for my new Lord, and He came. And the most wonderful thing: He was undeterred by the social damage that might be done to His reputation . . . by identifying with me!

I think there's a lesson in this passage for all of us. Let us never shy away from ministering to the "sinners" we encounter each day. We are one of them. If He made a difference for us, He can make a difference for anyone.

Lord, I want to thank You so much for the work You have done in my life. Thank You for inviting me to follow You and for demonstrating Your love for me, just as I am. I owe You a life of gratitude, and I ask Your help to live a life worthy of a child of the king! In Jesus' name, amen.

January 11–17. **Von Mitchell** is a public high school teacher/coach in Cedaredge, Colorado. She also works as a freelance writer and songwriter.

His Healing Words

He sent forth his word and healed them; he rescued them from the grave (Psalm 107:20).

Scripture: **Psalm 107:17-22**
Song: **"Healing Waters"**

Has your life ever been changed as you meditated on the Scriptures? Has your attitude ever been adjusted by a Bible passage?

For most of us, I suspect the answer to both of these questions is "Yes." God's Word is "living and active. Sharper than any double-edged sword, it penetrates even to dividing soul and spirit, joints and marrow; it judges the thoughts and attitudes of the heart" (Hebrews 4:12). His Word is powerful.

I'm reminded of the Scripture, "You will keep in perfect peace him whose mind is steadfast, because he trusts in you" (Isaiah 26:3). There have been times in my life when that trust took the form of reciting a psalm or meditating on a Scripture I had memorized. I'd speak the words aloud, and God brought me comfort, peace, healing.

I invite you today to open the Psalms with me and read them aloud. See and feel the difference it will produce in your own life. Then you can join with the psalmist in declaring: "Give thanks to the Lord for his unfailing love and his wonderful deeds for men" (v. 21).

Lord, thank You for the healing power of Your Word. It brings such comfort and peace to my very soul. May You be glorified today and exalted with songs of joy. In the name of Jesus, my Savior, I pray. Amen.

The Power of Prayer

Hezekiah turned his face to the wall and prayed to the LORD, "Remember, O LORD, how I have walked before you faithfully and with wholehearted devotion and have done what is good in your eyes." And Hezekiah wept bitterly (2 Kings 20:2, 3).

Scripture: **2 Kings 20:1-7**
Song: **"The Weapon of Prayer"**

"One thing I know: God is still on the throne, and prayer changes things." A youth minister at a Denver church spoke those words more than once. I always liked that phrase, and furthermore, I believe he was speaking a great truth.

Hezekiah surely knew this truth. After all, the 20th chapter of 2 Kings beautifully illustrates the power of prayer, the value of heartfelt petition. The king lingered at death's door—until he prayed. Then God had mercy and granted 15 more years of life.

Over and over in God's Word we see examples of the power of prayer. When Nehemiah encountered opposition, he added prayer to his own defense (see Nehemiah 4:9). And in the New Testament, Peter miraculously escaped from prison because the church was "earnestly praying to God for him" (Acts 12:5).

When has God answered your prayers? Why not make a list? And may God encourage your heart as you remember all the times He has proved surpassingly faithful.

Lord, You know my needs even before I ask, and You know what is best for me. Thank You for Your faithful answers to prayer. In Jesus' name, amen.

Must Have Been a Good Boss

The centurion replied, "Lord, I do not deserve to have you come under my roof. But just say the word, and my servant will be healed" (Matthew 8:8).

Scripture: **Matthew 8:5-13**
Song: **"I Am Not Worthy, Holy Lord"**

Obviously, a major theme of today's passage is uncommon faith. But I'd like to submit a few other observations regarding the centurion's leadership.

One, the centurion cared about the needs of his servant. The fact that his servant was "paralyzed and in terrible suffering" troubled him. Compassion moved him to lead with concern. I'm sure we all appreciate bosses who genuinely care about us.

Two, the centurion sought help from the best possible source. He didn't mess around with makeshift solutions; he sought Jesus. Again, I'm sure we all value bosses who get us the best possible help to solve our problems.

Finally, it's clear that we are dealing with an extremely faithful leader who had drawn spiritual truth from his own station in life. He recognized the authority of Jesus and understood that all Jesus had to do was speak the word, and his servant would be healed. What well-placed faith sprung from the depth of his own experience!

Father, I am reminded today to pray for our leaders everywhere—at work, at church, and in our government. Please give them wisdom to govern according to Your will. Thank You for Your Word and the lessons therein. All praise to You, in Christ's name. Amen.

The Pain He Must Feel

But the more I called Israel, the further they went from me (Hosea 11:2).

Scripture: **Hosea 11:1-4**
Song: **"Alas! and Did My Savior Bleed?"**

As a public high school teacher and coach, I observe plenty of parent/child relationships. And I've seen dozens of situation in which the child is pulling away, despite a parent's efforts to improve the relationship. Why? Sometimes the child has been hurt by a painful divorce. Sometimes he or she has simply entered a rebellious phase. But understanding such things hardly lessens the heartache for any parent.

How it must hurt God to have one of His loved ones pull away from Him! It's clear throughout the Bible that He loves us more than any parent ever could. Furthermore, God has never violated our trust. In fact, He leads us "with cords of human kindness, with ties of love" (v. 4). So, why would we ever pull away from Him?

I'm not sure why, but I know there's a remedy that might even ease some of God's pain. We can spend some time today drawing closer to Him. We can bring some joy to His heart by praising and thanking Him for all He's done in our lives.

Lord, *thank You for loving me. Thank You for investing in our relationship, even when I have neglected it. I praise You for all You've done. Please forgive me for the ways I have grieved Your Spirit in the past. In the name of the Father, the Son, and the Holy Spirit, I pray. Amen.*

Give It Away

Heal the sick, raise the dead, cleanse those who have leprosy, drive out demons. Freely you have received, freely give (Matthew 10:8).

Scripture: **Matthew 10:1-8**
Song: **"Lord, I Want to Be Like Jesus"**

I love to read. It is one of my passions in life. Some might even say I'm obsessive about it, but that's OK with me.

Why do I love reading so much? It's not just the physical act of holding a book and taking in the words. It's not just the accumulation of knowledge, though I always enjoy learning new things. No, now that I think about it . . . maybe it's the joy of being able to *share* what I've learned. As a high school and Sunday school teacher, I am blessed regularly with that opportunity. Yes, I dearly love to share great stories and anecdotes from books that I read.

I guess that's it: I wouldn't love reading nearly as much if I couldn't give it away. Everything I gain from a book isn't worth much to me if it just sits in my mind like a stagnant pool gathering moss.

Giving is one of the great, joyous mysteries of life. I'm thankful for the opportunity to give any gift I have so happily received. How about you?

Dear Father, *today I want to thank You for all Your good gifts. I am so blessed! May You be pleased with my life as I give away small portions of what You have given me. And I pray for more faith, love, and hope to shine through my life as well. In Jesus' wonderful name, amen.*

There's Always a Critic

The Pharisees said, "It is by the prince of demons that he drives out demons" (Matthew 9:34).

Scripture: **Matthew 9:27-34; 11:2-6**
Song: **"These Things Are True of You"**

The Pharisees were the ultimate Monday morning quarterbacks. No matter what Jesus did, they found fault with it. *Did You heal someone on the Sabbath? Oops, wrong day. Drove out a demon, huh? Must've done it by the prince of demons.* They twisted their analyses to try and bring Him down, but they just couldn't do it. The truth trumped the critics.

And what was the truth? "The blind receive sight, the lame walk, those who have leprosy are cured, the deaf hear, the dead are raised, and the good news is preached to the poor" (11:5). That was the truth. Jesus never changed His story; furthermore, He never let the critics stand in His way of doing the Father's will.

Now if Jesus was criticized when He did miracles, what would make any of us think we are immune to criticism as we go about our daily lives? There will always be critics, but their opinions don't change the truth. So let us cling to God's power in the face of dubious criticisms. After all, in the words of Henry Longfellow, "The strength of criticism lies in the weakness of the thing criticized."

Heavenly Father, please help me recognize and apply the truths of Your Word. And may my critics never deter me from seeking to do Your will. I give You praise today, in the precious name of Jesus. Amen.

Why Pray Aloud?

I knew that You always hear Me; but because of the people standing around I said it, so that they may believe that You sent Me (John 11:42, *New American Standard Bible*).

Scripture: **John 11:38-44**
Song: **"My Faith Looks Up to Thee"**

Why do we ask others to pray? If God answers one person's prayer, is there any benefit in asking 50 people to pray? John answers those questions in today's Scripture.

Mary and Martha suffered overwhelming grief after the death of their brother, Lazarus. Many Jews had come to comfort them, but the one who could have spared them this grief was four days late. And they let Him know it as soon as He arrived: "Lord, if You had been here, my brother would not have died."

They didn't know Jesus had something better in mind than healing a dying man. He planned to raise a dead man. But, of course, Jesus didn't need to pray. He already had the power to do whatever He wanted. But He *did* pray—so that everyone present could hear and have the opportunity to believe.

You see, when we pray aloud we put our prayer-answering God on display. When we ask others to pray with us, we're letting everyone in on the blessing.

O Lord, please give me opportunity to pray with someone today. May my petitions be a spotlight for Your grace and glory. In Jesus' name, amen.

January 18–24. **Kathy Hardee,** of Mendota, Illinois, loves the truth of Psalm 29:2. She hopes to give God the glory due Him through her writing.

Our Prayer, God's Provision

"So do not be like them; for your Father knows what you need before you ask Him" (Matthew 6:8, *New American Standard Bible*).

Scripture: **Matthew 6:5-8**
Song: **"I Know Who Holds Tomorrow"**

I couldn't believe what I was hearing. A close friend confided in me that her husband was abusing her. "Just pray that he breaks my arm," she said. "Then I'll know I should leave."

"No way!" I cried. "I won't pray for you to get hurt." I told Amy I'd be asking God to give her a safe way out. And I begged her to be looking for that way.

Two nights later, while Amy and her husband were out for the evening, he did the unthinkable. He handed Amy the car keys and told her to go to a local hotel bar. He wanted her to seduce another man! Amy remembered that I was praying she would escape without being hurt. She recognized that moment as the answer to those prayers.

So she took the keys and drove away, leaving her husband temporarily stranded without the car. But instead of going to the hotel, she went home, packed her things, and got to a safe place. I smile as I consider: God knew exactly when and how He'd rescue Amy, long before I prayed.

Dear Father, I'm so glad You know my needs, and how You'll meet them, even before I begin to pray. Thank You for loving me that much. I pray this prayer in the name of Jesus, my merciful Savior and Lord. Amen.

Keep Your Eyes on Him

But seeing the wind, he became frightened, and beginning to sink, he cried out, "Lord, save me!" (Matthew 14:30, *New American Standard Bible*).

Scripture: **Matthew 14:22-33**
Song: **"Turn Your Eyes upon Jesus"**

Imagine how much more fun Peter could have had in his water-walking experience. If he would have kept his eyes on Jesus, he could have walked directly into his master's happy embrace. But Peter didn't keep his eyes on Jesus. He turned to his left and saw the crashing waves. He jerked to the right at the sound of the howling wind—and he began to sink.

I sometimes do something similar. It seems the longer I pray for a certain thing, the harder it is for me to trust God with it. Doubts come in waves, crashing into my confidence. And I begin to sink, questioning the very thing I believe most: Does God really answer prayer? Will He ever answer mine?

After studying today's Scripture, I realized that doubts only come when I focus on my dire circumstances rather than the power of my Savior. Doubts fill my mind every time I take my eyes off the Lord of all. O, how much more fun when I keep my eyes on Jesus!

Almighty and ever-living God, forgive me for sometimes looking away from You, sinking into worry and doubt. Please, quickly grab my attention every time I look in the wrong direction. In the name of Jesus, Lord and Savior of all, I pray. Amen.

Childlike, Come to Him

Jesus said, "Let the little children come to me, and do not hinder them, for the kingdom of heaven belongs to such as these" (Matthew 19:14).

Scripture: **Matthew 19:13-15**
Song: **"It's Just Like His Great Love"**

I remember the many times my 2-year-old grandson asked, "Can we read this one again, Gram?" His favorite book was *The Pokey Little Puppy.* I'd quit whatever I was doing and gather Tyler up in my arms. For the next 10 minutes we'd laugh about that bouncy little beagle. I loved those times we shared together, and I couldn't imagine turning Tyler away.

When the disciples saw children brought to Jesus, they thought it was a waste of His time. Maybe they considered the more important matters coming before them that day—like whether a couple could get divorced (19:3-9), or what a person must do to inherit eternal life (19:16-21). However, when Jesus saw the children, He opened His arms, gathered them up, and blessed each one.

And therein lies our hope, our promise of blessing. Anyone who comes to Christ, like a child, with no resources of his own, will be accepted into the kingdom of Heaven. Do you need a blessing today? Come to Christ. He won't turn you away.

Dear God, *thank You for the assurance that I can come to You anytime, like a child, and be wrapped in Your loving embrace. I am ready, just now, Lord! All praise to You, in Christ's name. Amen.*

On Loving and Praying

I say to you, love your enemies and pray for those who perse-cute you (Matthew 5:44, *New American Standard Bible*).

Scripture: **Matthew 5:43-48**
Song: **"They'll Know We Are Christians by Our Love"**

The meeting was called to order. The question: Should we continue having Sunday evening worship services? Attendance was low, so we were considering home Bible study groups instead. A vote was taken: Sunday night church would continue.

The man sitting behind me bristled. The decision didn't please him, and he didn't hold back his feelings. (I thought about telling him he needed a serious attitude adjustment, but I kept quiet.)

I couldn't forget about his comments. The next time he taught Sunday school, I thought: *How can you preach to me about holiness?*

I held onto my contempt, though, until God showed me that I was the one sinning. Jesus said, "Love your enemies," but I was holding a grudge against my brother in Christ. Jesus said, "Pray for those who persecute you," but I wasn't even praying for a man who had been kind to me. I realized I'd never be able to love my enemies, if I couldn't even love those who were more than willing to be a friend.

Dear Lord, *please bring to my mind those whom You would like me to love, and for whom I ought to pray. In this way, may I become more like You, through the inner workings of Your Spirit. I pray in Jesus' name. Amen.*

On Believing and Praying

If you believe, you will receive whatever you ask for in prayer (Matthew 21:22).

Scripture: **Matthew 21:18-22**
Song: **"Only Believe"**

I learned at a very young age that when Mom said "No" she meant. "No." Therefore, we did very little begging at our house.

I figured that if Mom didn't like it when I begged, God probably didn't like it either. So, after asking God for something, I usually didn't bother Him again with the same request. It took me a while to figure out that there's a difference between "begging" God and faithfully bringing my requests before Him.

You see, "begging God" implies that I have to talk Him into giving me something good. However, when I continually pray in faith, I'm demonstrating my daily reliance on His promise to care for me (Psalm 84:11). I've been praying for the spiritual well-being of several loved ones for many years. I haven't seen all of the answers yet, but I keep bringing those same people before the throne of God. And this is why I know He will answer: I haven't given up! Only God can give someone like me the faith to persevere in prayer for almost 30 years.

My almighty Lord and God, I gladly trust You and look forward to seeing how You will display Your glory through the answers to my prayers—in this world or in the world to come. In the name of the Father, the Son, and the Holy Spirit, I pray. Amen.

Our Rest in Christ

Take My yoke upon you and learn from Me, for I am gentle and humble in heart, and YOU WILL FIND REST FOR YOUR SOULS (Matthew 11:29, *New American Standard Bible*).

Scripture: **Matthew 11:25-30**
Song: **"Resting in You"**

"Can you come and sit with Harold?"

He was dying and alone, so Harold's nurse called me. His room was small: just the bed, one chair, and a tiny dresser. Harold smiled as I took his hand. I didn't say much. Everyone thought Harold would die that day.

Nursing home employees came in, one by one, to say good-bye to a man they had grown to love. Sadness pervaded the atmosphere in the small room.

Then Mary came in. She gave Harold a hug and told him how much she enjoyed taking care of him. Harold held onto her arm and asked, "Mary, do you think I'll go to Heaven?"

"Harold," she said, "you're one of the kindest men I've ever met. I'm sure you'll make it!" Harold shook his head and closed his eyes as Mary left the room. Mary's words didn't bring him comfort. And I knew why.

I scooted my chair close to his bed. "Harold," I whispered, "I know the way to Heaven—as the Bible tells it." Then I told him about Jesus and His atoning grace. "Harold, only Jesus can offer eternal rest for your soul."

Dear Jesus, thank You for Your death and resurrection on my behalf. I praise You for giving me eternal life. In Your precious name, amen.

Colors Tell the Story

All of us like sheep have gone astray, Each of us has turned to his own way; But the Lord has caused the iniquity of us all to fall on Him (Isaiah 53:6, *New American Standard Bible*).

Scripture: **Isaiah 53:1-9**
Song: **"Come, Ye Sinners, Poor and Needy"**

Tucked away in my child evangelism resources are 4 x 5 cards of various colors. I used these to teach Isaiah 53:6 to children who learned easily, not only the words, but the verse's meaning. To name a few colors: brown meant the path sheep (children) take when going astray (green for grass). The color purple was for iniquity, and red for Jesus' sacrifice on the cross.

As I held up each colored card, the children recited the memory verse. It was more than saying words; the colors connected words with meaning.

Even as an adult, I can be led astray by what looks like greener pastures. I may think someone else has all the advantages. (Perhaps he was "born with a silver spoon in his mouth.") So quickly, envy can lead me once again into forbidden territory. Just as sheep nibble their way from the flock, I may not notice that I'm headed toward a much less satisfying existence.

Gracious God, I am thankful for Christ's sacrifice that washes away my sin and makes me pure. May even these colors remind me of Your gift and my response. I pray through my deliverer, Jesus. Amen.

January 25–31. **Ann L. Coker** has continued working part-time at a crisis pregnancy center after her husband retired from ministering in Terre Haute, Indiana.

Knowledge Is Power

My people are destroyed for lack of knowledge. Because you have rejected knowledge, I also will reject you (Hosea 4:6, *New American Standard Bible*).

Scripture: **Hosea 4:1-6**
Song: **"O Breath of Life"**

Several years ago a slogan was popular—"Knowledge Is Power"—and the acronym was KIP. A counselor at the crisis pregnancy center where I worked tried one evening to empower her client by imparting knowledge. The college coed could use this know-how to keep herself safe and bring about a positive change in her life. That positive power could have lasting, good results.

Ashley, the counselor, practiced what she taught. She knew that true knowledge was found in the Bible, and that living this truth brought the power of the Holy Spirit to bear upon all her thoughts and actions. Ashley's client was not unfamiliar with the way of truth; she chose not to follow it.

How differently lives unfold when they allow the Word of God to direct them. How different also are the consequences! I ask myself whether my daily life reflects the knowledge of the holy. That is, does God's power ignite His truth in my life, day by day?

Holy God, with Your knowledge I gain understanding, then wisdom, which is the application of knowledge. As You speak to me through Your Word, I want to understand Your truth. But help me take the next step and live Your truth. In Christ's name I pray. Amen.

Value Exchange

Laying aside the commandment of God, ye hold the tradition of men (Mark 7:8, *King James Version*).

Scripture: **Mark 7:5-13**
Song: **"Dear Lord and Father of Mankind"**

"What will you take for this?" the dealer asks. If the object in question is a true treasure, the asking price will be high. But if it's something of little worth, you might accept the first reasonable offer.

The exchange of goods is just that: What good is it? What is its value? I'm not writing here of a material object, but of a treasure more valuable. That is, how about your commitment to purity? What value do you place on your reputation or your good name? (You probably wouldn't consider exchanging it for anything. It's not for sale, at any price.)

God's commands are not to be exchanged for mere traditions, the "way we do things around here." Of course, the tradition of the faith—the body of doctrine by which we interpret the Bible—is to be handed down to each generation (see 2 Thessalonians 2:15; 3:6, *KJV*). We return to this treasury of truth to discover the worth of everything else. So how would you answer the dealer? It depends on what "this" is, right? The owner determines its value. Who owns you and your reputation?

*Help me, **Lord,** not to value my own ways of doing things above what You have established as good and right—for my good and for Your righteousness. In the name above all names I pray. Amen.*

God's Way Is Best

In all your ways acknowledge Him, And He will make your paths straight (Proverbs 3:6, *New American Standard Bible*).

Scripture: **Proverbs 3:5-12**
Song: **"I Know Whom I Have Believed"**

In the records of Judah's kings, Hezekiah stands out as one of the few good kings. He tore down the places of idol worship and reformed their spiritual festivals. He followed the commandments of God and did not make alliances with pagan nations.

If you tour historical sites in Israel, your guide will most likely include Hezekiah's tunnel. It was built as a provision and a defense. To prevent the armies of Assyria from getting a needed water supply, Hezekiah built the tunnel to divert the Gihon Springs, making it flow into Jerusalem at the Pool of Siloam.

The remarkable part of this undertaking was that crews worked from both ends and met in the middle. They made only a few false turns, for the work was guided by the men shouting to each other through the rock.

You can't call the tunnel "straight," because of the twisted layout. But the work was done right. Could it be because of how Hezekiah "acknowledged" his God in righteous living? So . . . how is God guiding your own paths these days?

Holy Spirit, continue to be my true guide. Although my life takes its twists and turns, I depend on You to keep me straight. I trust not in my own understanding, but in Your truth. Through Christ, amen.

How Can This Be?

All were speaking well of Him, and wondering at the gracious words which were falling from His lips; and they were saying, "Is this not Joseph's son?" (Luke 4:22, *New American Standard Bible*).

Scripture: **Luke 4:16-22**
Song: **"Living for Jesus"**

A few months after I was married, my mother came for an extended visit. One day I drove around town taking care of errands, such as dropping off my husband's suits at the dry cleaners. After returning to our home, mother remarked about how well I handled the day's tasks. She was actually amazed at my driving skills, how I found my way around so easily. To me, it was like she was asking, "Can this be my daughter?"

Similarly, people may often be amazed at how we handle life's circumstances after beginning our walk with the Lord. Before conversion, we may have buckled under the pressures, and now we tend to trust God to handle what life throws at us.

When God's Son read God's Word in God's house, the people asked how this could be. Even though they spoke well of Jesus' reading abilities, they left wondering about His authority. But for us, let it be different: We can enter our places of worship expecting to meet Jesus. We can hear the living Word speak through the written Word.

O Christ, while I stand amazed at Your wonderful acts of mercy and grace, I know You are God Incarnate, the true Son of God. In Your name, amen.

His Way Wins Out

Passing through their midst, He went His way (Luke 4:30, *New American Standard Bible*).

Scripture: **Luke 4:23-30**
Song: **"His Way with Thee"**

Have you ever been in a crowd and later found out that a celebrity had been close by? He or she had passed by unnoticed?

A couple we know was in a jewelry store when the wife looked around and thought she recognized a famous person. She ventured out and spoke to him—and, sure enough, he was the one she suspected him to be. He didn't escape her notice.

As a teenager attending a youth retreat, I looked around and saw Cliff Barrows, song leader for Billy Graham's crusades. He was visiting that resort. I had a notebook with me and asked him to sign it. He was a "celebrity" whom I respected.

Jesus passed through the crowd, escaping those who wanted to throw Him off a cliff. Their way was thwarted; He went His way. Jesus is in our midst, not visible but evident. When we face Jesus, will we recognize Him? Yet He wants more than to be noticed. An autograph isn't sufficient. He wants to have His way in all of our lives.

Dear Father, Your Son laid down His life for me, and I know what You want. You delight to live in me so that I may live for You. Help me to surrender my will to Yours this day, and give me Your guidance in each decision I will face. I ask in the precious name of Jesus. Amen.

Self-Focused?

Nevertheless I say to you that it shall be more tolerable for the land of Sodom in the day of judgment, than for you (Matthew 11:24, *New American Standard Bible*).

Scripture: **Matthew 11:20-24; 13:54-58**
Song: **"Great Giver of All Good"**

Perhaps it's more prevalent in women than in men, but we tend to judge ourselves by comparison with others. One author called it "compare-itis." The condition can manifest itself in one of two directions: We either put ourselves down, or we think more of ourselves than we ought. Either, "I'm better than she is," or "I just don't measure up." Either way, it's a comparing disposition, a matter of pride.

I hear a news story about an athlete who confesses to taking steroids, and I'm disappointed in her. I judge her actions without knowing her heart. The story goes on to quote her as being repentant. Then I have to evaluate my own attitude. Or I see a friend of years past, and she recounts her accomplishments. I may not envy her position, but mentally I focus on my lack of opportunities. This is not productive, nor honoring to God.

What is the antidote for such self-focus? It's refocusing our affections on God and all that He has given us. Yes, it takes practice. But it's worth the effort.

Creator God, *all I have comes from You. In fact, it is all on loan from You. So help me to be gracious and generous, not judgmental or prideful, no matter how I may compare with someone else. For Your name's sake, amen.*

DEVOTIONS®

Gary Allen, Editor

"**M**y sheep
listen to my
voice; I know
them and they
follow me."

—John 10:27

FEBRUARY

Photo
© Steve Clark | Dreamstime.com

DEVOTIONS® is published quarterly by Standard Publishing, Cincinnati, Ohio, www.standardpub.com.
© 2009 by Standard Publishing. All rights reserved. Topics based on the Home Daily Bible Readings,
International Sunday School Lessons. © 2006 by the Committee on the Uniform Series. Printed in the
U.S.A. All Scripture quotations, unless otherwise indicated, are taken from the HOLY BIBLE, NEW
INTERNATIONAL VERSION®. NIV®. Copyright © 1973, 1978, 1984 by International Bible Society.
Used by permission of Zondervan. All rights reserved. Where noted, Scripture quotations are from the
following, used with permission of the copyright holders, all rights reserved: *The Message,* by Eugene
H. Peterson. Copyright © 1993, 1994, 1995, 1996, 2000. Used by permission of NavPress Publishing
Group.

Wait, Wait, Wait

There was a man in Jerusalem called Simeon, who was righteous and devout. He was waiting for the consolation of Israel, and the Holy Spirit was upon him (Luke 2:25).

Scripture: **Luke 2:25-35**
Song: **"God of Our Life"**

It's so hard to wait. "Type A" people constantly push to *make things happen*. They just can't pause. For them, nothing worthwhile is worth waiting for

That attitude is the hallmark of our age. Thankfully, God seems to think that life's best really is worth waiting for. So, for years, the world awaited a coming Messiah. Now we find ourselves only a few weeks from Good Friday, the day of Christ's death. Again, we wait . . . for resurrection, for ascension, for a coming again.

As we wait, we discover that we're not unlike Jesus' followers. They had their own ideas of who the coming Messiah would be and what He would do, including the type of leadership He'd provide. They knew what they wanted, and they wanted it *now*.

But wait a minute. This isn't our time; it's God's time. God knew then—and God knows now—that we must wait for the right moment, for "the fullness of time." (Be assured that the right time is coming.)

God, *slow me down as I continue life's journey. May Your Holy Spirit guide me, like Simeon, through times of waiting. In Jesus' name, amen.*

February 1–7. **Drexel Rankin** served as a minister for more than 35 years. He and his wife Patty live in Louisville, Kentucky.

Doing Good, Nevertheless

To those who by persistence in doing good seek glory, honor and immortality, he will give eternal life (Romans 2:7).

Scripture Romans 2:1-11
Song: **"Make Me a Blessing"**

The old Southwest rancher spotted the scorpion floundering in the water. He decided to save it by stretching out his finger. Rather than crawl onto the finger, the scorpion stung him. The old man tried a second time to get the scorpion out of the water but, once again, the scorpion stung him.

A man standing nearby told the old rancher to stop trying to save the little critter that just wouldn't cooperate. But the rancher said: "It is the nature of the scorpion to protect itself and to sting. It is my nature to love. Why should I give up my nature to love just because it is the nature of the scorpion to sting?"

Christ calls me to replicate His nature of love, to do good, and not to sting. Even when others delight in cutting, stinging, hurting, abusing, Jesus calls me to love. He encourages me to do good, to show love and mercy—even if, once in a while, I get stung. After all, I am dealing with the souls of my neighbors. As the great Christian apologist G. K. Chesterton said: "The way to love anything is to realize that it might be lost."

God of love, give me the courage and the kindness to follow Jesus' example and to go about doing good in His name. May I keep in mind that Your message goes out to those who are lost without it. In Jesus' name, amen.

Lighting the World

This is what the Lord has commanded us: "I have made you a light for the Gentiles, that you may bring salvation to the ends of the earth" (Acts 13:47).

Scripture: **Acts 13:44-49**
Song: **"Lighten the Darkness"**

Early in the day, I arrived at the hospital to visit with a worried mother; her little girl was scheduled for high-risk cardiac surgery the following morning. In the afternoon, I phoned a friend who was entering the final stages of life with a terminal disease. Before going home, I rushed to the hospital again to be with a family whose teenage son lay in a coma following a near-fatal auto wreck. It was a draining, blessed, day of ministry.

My wife and I had tickets to a performance that evening of Margaret Edson's powerful, harrowing play *Wit*. The play is about an accomplished woman with stage four cancer. During her monologue, the actress tells the audience: "There is no stage five."

The events of the day reminded me just how fragile life is. And I thought once again about what a *gift* life is—a grace to be cherished, enjoyed, and shared with others. To understand this is to find a freedom in life, a freedom to be a light to the end of the earth.

Generous God, save me from attempting to save myself and keeping life closed in about me. Set me free to share life with others that they would know the glory of living life with You in Christ. I pray in the name of this same Lord Jesus Christ. Amen.

Arise

Arise, shine, for your light has come, and the glory of the Lᴏʀᴅ rises upon you (Isaiah 60:1).

Scripture: **Isaiah 60:1-5**
Song: **"Holy Spirit, from on High"**

In the animal kingdom there is a very small, strange critter known as a tardigrade. It has been spotted on mountaintops and in the deepest oceans, in tropical forests, and in the Antarctic.

He's tiny—only about 1 millimeter (the thickness of a dime) in length. He can endure temperatures from minus 328 degrees to plus 324 degrees, survive a lack of oxygen and water, or continue to exist under the pressure of a vacuum. He has been revived after a decade of a death-like sleep without water; when he's moistened, he immediately springs back to life.

Why am I telling you all this? Well, sometimes I feel like a tardigrade. I allow my life to become dull, flat, and death-like. Occasionally, I'm even tempted to withdraw into my shell and elude the challenge of daily living.

But there is good news. Perspectives, attitudes, and the whole of life can be refreshed when "moistened" with renewed purpose and a reinvigorated prayer life. When I've found myself spiritually asleep, I know that I can ask God's Holy Spirit to awaken me from my slumber. He's always willing to revitalize my spirit.

God of life, touch my being with Your renewing, revitalizing power. Refresh me in the joy of Your salvation. Through Christ I pray. Amen.

Craving the Light?

The city does not need the sun or the moon to shine on it, for the glory of God gives it light, and the Lamb is its lamp (Revelation 21:23).

Scripture: **Revelation 21:22-27**
Song: **"O Holy City, Seen of John"**

Our friend struggles with Seasonal Affective Disorder (SAD), a regular depression that is seasonally recurrent. Most cases reoccur in winter rather than in summer, peaking in January and February when the days are gray. The most obvious treatment is something patients are naturally drawn to: light.

In fact, people with SAD crave light. They want to be close to a window; they want the shades open. Even those of us who are not affected by Seasonal Affective Disorder look forward to next month's lengthening days and increased sunshine.

Maybe this is the reason we resonate with John's vivid description of God's reign in the holy city. All else pales in comparison to the New Jerusalem. Here there is no need for a temple, for God's glory is everywhere. There is no night, no need of sun or moon. The city is its own light. The gates are flung open, and all who enter dwell in perfect safety. Our craving for light will finally be satisfied.

God of goodness and light, shine in my life. Come into those places where I feel trapped in darkness and help me see new possibilities. Fill this day and my future with the hope of Your glory and the peace of Your presence. In Christ I ask this. Amen.

Sharing the Best of Life

May the God of hope fill you with all joy and peace as you trust in him, so that you may overflow with hope by the power of the Holy Spirit (Romans 15:13).

Scripture: **Romans 15:7-13**
Song: **"More About Jesus Would I Know"**

Years ago, I sold organs in a music store. I learned that I couldn't sell these instruments unless I truly believed in them. So, in slow times, I practiced on the display models until I was quite proficient. I learned what sound each stop would produce when I pushed it. The more I practiced and learned, the more I believed in what I was trying to sell.

When a customer arrived, I could tell her honestly that I believed this was the finest product for her home. This gave me confidence, not smugness.

In much the same way, I believe that the best kind of life—a life filled with joy, peace, hope, and salvation—comes from learning to know Jesus in an ever-deepening relationship. That is my heritage; that is what I sincerely believe. So when I share the good news about Jesus with others, it needn't come out wrapped in smugness or pride. Rather, I share with joy because I believe, and have experienced, His way as the very best.

*Help me, **O Father,** to learn more about You and Your Son Jesus Christ that I might confidently share Your joy, peace, hope, and salvation with others. As I trust in You, may others see the power of the Holy Spirit shining through my life. In Christ I pray. Amen.*

A Face in the Crowd

Great crowds came to him, bringing the lame, the blind, the crippled, the mute and many others, and laid them at his feet; and he healed them (Matthew 15:30).

Scripture: **Matthew 15:21-31**
Song: **"Open the Eyes of My Heart"**

Jesus drew crowds wherever He went. Even when He wanted to be alone with the Father, the crowds found Him. He attracted throngs of people who brought their lame, blind, and mute, believing He'd bring healing.

He also drew multitudes that simply wanted to hear Him teach. He told them stories that related to their everyday lives, and taught them the truths of God. He began His ministry by reading Scripture, and then He told the crowd: "Today this scripture is fulfilled in your hearing" (Luke 4:21). The crowd wanted to throw Him off a high cliff!

And then there was the crowd on Palm Sunday— sometimes they cheered Him; sometimes they jeered Him. Some were glad He came; others wished He would go away. Some were enthusiastic; some were apathetic.

Truth is, I am one of the faces in Jesus' crowd. I want to be more than a mere spectator, though. I want to follow wherever He goes and be a part of His mission in the world. How is it with you?

God, I confess I'm sometimes little more than a bystander, sometimes a face in the crowd wondering what You can do for me. In those times, turn my attention back to how I can help Your cause. In Jesus' name, amen.

Listen Up!

My sheep listen to my voice; I know them, and they follow me (John 10:27).

Scripture: **John 10:22-30**
Song: **"The Shepherd of Love"**

Our little flock of black-faced sheep always came running when we called. Whether we were standing at the fence with a treat or calling them in for the night, when they heard us, they came. They knew us, and we knew them. We knew Rosie, with her beautiful eyes; Dinger, with his warning bell; Old Mamie, with her bony back. They were a flock, but they were individuals too.

It is no accident that Jesus calls us His sheep. Sheep may throw their heads around and act tough and independent, but without someone caring for them—providing for their basic needs, keeping them safe from danger—they will not survive long. Their dependency, however, is part of what makes them so lovable. One word from the shepherd, and they know that all is well.

Do you know the sound of Jesus' voice? Does it seem distant and hard to hear? Or is it near and familiar? A sheep's job is simple: listen to the shepherd. What is the Shepherd saying to you today?

Lord, sometimes I don't listen very well. My mind wanders as a sheep wanders, nibbling here and there. Teach me to listen, to recognize Your voice above all others. In Your precious name I pray. Amen.

February 8–14. **Sarah Overturf** lives with her husband and three children in Longmont, Colorado, where she is a writer and a school librarian.

What Time Is It?

"The time has come," he said. "The kingdom of God is near. Repent and believe the good news!" (Mark 1:15).

Scripture: **Mark 1:9-15**
Song: **"'Tis Almost Time for the Lord to Come"**

I once went for about a year without a watch. Mine had broken, and for one reason or another, I never got around to getting a new one. I found, surprisingly enough, that I got along just fine. After all, I have a clock by my bed, on the stove, in my car, and even on my thermostat. And there are clocks at work, in stores, on buildings. During that year, I could probably count on one hand the number of times I had to ask someone for the time.

When we ask another person for the time, we get a straight forward answer. And when we ask God what time it is, we also get a direct, albeit very different, answer. The first message Jesus preached was, "The time has come." The kingdom of God, He said, is near, and the people needed to be ready for it.

God's kingdom is still near. The two thousand years that have gone by are nothing when held up to eternity. And we still need to be ready. We can get along just fine without a watch on our wrist, but we still need to know what time it is. It's always the best time to repent and believe the good news.

Lord, this day is filled with so many things I need to do. When I look at a clock, remind me of Your time. Help me to remember that Your kingdom is very near. In Christ's name I pray. Amen.

Leftovers

They all ate and were satisfied, and the disciples picked up twelve basketfuls of broken pieces of bread and fish (Mark 6:42, 43).

Scripture: **Mark 6:34-44**
Song: **"Break Thou the Bread of Life"**

Not everyone cares for leftovers, but I do. Given the choice between a fresh sandwich and leftovers for lunch, I'll choose the leftovers every time.

I don't know how the disciples felt about leftovers, but they each got a basketful they would never forget. In the space of a few short minutes, they went from questioning Jesus to distributing His abundant blessing. Jesus didn't feed the crowd a snack: He gave them a feast. A feast so big, there were leftovers.

Those baskets of leftovers told the disciples that it wasn't their job to feed the crowd. It was their job to trust the one who could. Instead of questioning and crunching numbers, all they needed to do was look at the crowd and say, "I don't know how," and then look at Jesus and say, "but I know You do."

When we don't know what to do, let us look to the one who does. Sometimes all we have to do is reach into the basket to find more than enough. And sometimes, we even get to pick up the leftovers.

Lord, *You always do more than I can imagine. Instead of questioning You, help me to look to You in total trust, ready to be part of Your blessing. In the name of the Father, the Son, and the Holy Spirit, I pray. Amen.*

I Doubt It

Immediately the boy's father exclaimed, "I do believe; help me overcome my unbelief!" (Mark 9:24).

Scripture: **Mark 9:14-27**
Song: **"Believe Ye That I Am Able?"**

In the movie *The Sound of Music*, the abbess, in speaking of Maria's fitness for the abbey, tells the other nuns, "I always try to keep faith in my doubts." It's a compelling line that made me pause as I enjoyed the movie again with my family.

Doubt is often viewed as a weakness. But I've come to see that doubt is often the most honest expression of faith we humans can have.

The boy's father obviously had a great deal of faith, or he would not have brought his son to the disciples in the first place. When he encountered Jesus, he knew his belief came up short. He knew, just as we always know when we meet Jesus, that there was so much more that he didn't begin to grasp. Yet he instantly came to the right place: I do believe, but I know I don't believe as well as I should. So help me. Help me overcome this unbelief that lurks in me.

Doubt gives faith room to grow and flourish. A sincere doubt that seeks earnestly for the truth can lead us to growth. It's when we feel we have all the answers that faith is stifled.

God, when doubts press in, enlarge my faith. Like the boy's father, I do believe; I need Your help to believe more completely. In Jesus' name, amen.

Moving Mountains

I tell you the truth, if anyone says to this mountain, "Go, throw yourself into the sea," and does not doubt in his heart but believes that what he says will happen, it will be done for him (Mark 11:23).

Scripture: **Mark 11:20-25**
Song: **"Faith Grasps the Blessing"**

I once saw a bumper sticker that said, "I'm not lost; I'm exploring." I had to laugh, because I related so well. Call it what you will, the truth is that I get lost very easily. Thankfully, I live within view of the Rocky Mountains. Just knowing they loom to the west is often enough for me to get my sense of direction squared away.

Some days, however, when a storm moves in, I can't see the mountains. The view in any direction looks the same. I'm without my compass.

When Jesus taught His disciples about prayer, He told them they could move mountains. Frankly, those words frighten me. I need my mountains. How else will I know where I am?

The answer, of course, is that I will be right where God wants me to be. I will be more dependent on Him, more trusting of His guidance, more reliant on Him for the next step. I wonder sometimes why we fail to pray for the mountains in our lives to move. Is it because they give us a sense of security, and we're afraid to let go?

Lord, *You know the mountains looming in my life right now. Help me look only to You for guidance as I climb. In Jesus' name, amen.*

Are We There Yet?

Seeing what was ahead, he spoke of the resurrection of the Christ, that he was not abandoned to the grave, nor did his body see decay (Acts 2:31).

Scripture: **Acts 2:29-36**
Song: **"Rise, Glorious Conqueror"**

I love taking trips with my family. I love how the excitement builds as we pull out maps and pore over the glossy travel guides. We plan and research and plan some more, all the while counting down until it's time to leave. And then, once we're on the road, we hear the ongoing chorus: "How much farther? . . . Are we there yet?"

The patriarchs and prophets of the Old Testament lived constantly with "Are we there yet?" King David knew God's promise that a messiah was coming. But he didn't know when. And so he waited.

We too have a promise from God, and like David, we are waiting. We know that Jesus will come again. But we don't know when. And so we wait.

We don't wait passively, however. We've been given God's Word to study as a map, and we have our own travel guide, the Holy Spirit, to prepare not just ourselves, but those around us as well. We're in for the journey—not just of a lifetime, but of eternity. And we'll be there soon. Very soon.

Lord, *thank You for the promise that You are coming again. Build in me the expectancy that says today could be the day. In the name of the Father, the Son, and the Holy Spirit, I pray. Amen.*

Getting Personal

"But what about you?" he asked. **"Who do you say I am?"**
(Matthew 16:15).

Scripture: **Matthew 16:13-27**
Song: **"I'll Tell the World That I'm a Christian"**

Ask a random sampling of people who Jesus is, and
you'll get a wide variety of answers. A good man, a
prophet, a teacher, a radical revolutionary. Opinions are as
varied as the people holding them. When Jesus asked His
disciples who people said He was, they likewise offered
several points of view. But Jesus wasn't interested in a
public opinion poll; He looked for a heartfelt, personal
response.

Peter's answer has become the foundation of the
Christian faith. "You are the Christ, the Son of the living
God" (v. 16) is what sets Christianity apart from all other
religions. For the Christian, Jesus was not merely a good
man or a wise teacher. He is the risen Savior.

The next time you hear a discussion of religious fig-
ures, take the opportunity to declare your faith the way
Peter did. Ask the pointed question that Jesus asked.
Opinions can be discussed endlessly, but sooner or later
each person needs to answer the question of who Jesus is.
And that may put us on the spot. Yet, as writer Wendell
Phillips once said, "Christianity is a battle, not a dream."

*Lord, I believe that You are the Christ, the Son of the living God. Help me
to be bold in sharing that truth today, for this is how the kingdom battle
unfolds. In Your precious name, I pray. Amen.*

Eyewitness Account

We did not follow cleverly invented stories when we told you about the power and coming of our Lord Jesus Christ, but we were eyewitnesses of his majesty (2 Peter 1:16).

Scripture: **2 Peter 1:16-21**
Song: **"Tell Me the Story of Jesus"**

I witnessed it, watching in horror as a pick-up truck veered out of its lane and smashed into a friend's car. Thankfully, no one was seriously injured. The truck's driver tried to deny his responsibility, but the police were quite interested in my firsthand, eyewitness account.

The apostles were eyewitnesses too. How wonderful to walk with Jesus, to dine with Him, to hear Him teach. They witnessed His miracles; they heard the voice of the Father affirming Jesus as His Son. They even saw Jesus raised to life, and then ascending to Heaven.

We encounter difficult days when our faith may be tested. We may begin to doubt in the darkness what seemed so sure in the light. It's then that we can return to the beginning point of faith—to the clear, firsthand accounts of those who were with Jesus. After all, you just can't argue with an eyewitness. Let Christ shine in your heart, no matter how dark your days may seem.

Father, thank You for the faithful witness of those who were with Jesus. May their testimony be a constant source of strength and faith for me. In the name of Jesus, my Savior, I pray. Amen.

February 15–21. **Dan Nicksich** is the senior minister of First Christian Church in Somerset, Pennsylvania.

Witnesses to the Light

[John] came as a witness to testify concerning that light, so that through him all men might believe. He himself was not the light; he came only as a witness to the light (John 1:7, 8).

Scripture: **John 1:6-13**
Song: **"Shine Forth, O Sun of Boundless Love"**

According to legend, it was the year 490 BC when a Greek soldier named Pheidippides ran about 25 miles from Marathon to Athens to deliver news of a battle against the Persians. "Victory" was all he could manage to say before he collapsed and died.

It would seem there's a certain inherent danger in being a messenger. We state it this way: "Don't shoot me, I'm only the messenger."

Prophets, as messengers, were frequently persecuted for their messages. John the Baptist could not know the fate that was in store for him. But John understood his role, that of being a witness to the light, Jesus the Christ.

Messengers of the light must realize they are not the one that matters. The spotlight is not theirs to seek. Messengers of the light realize that it's not about them; it's all about the anointed one of God.

What an incredible responsibility! What a privilege! Whether to friend or family, to the neighbor next door or to someone across the seas, be a witness to the light.

*Thank You, **Lord,** for the great opportunity of sharing a message of hope and life with a lost and dying world. Give me a sense of gratitude each day of my life. In Jesus' name I pray. Amen.*

Accusations Abound

But when the Pharisees heard this, they said, "It is only by Beelzebub, the prince of demons, that this fellow drives out demons" (Matthew 12:24).

Scripture: **Matthew 12:22-28**
Song: **"Ten Thousand Angels"**

Ronald Taylor served 12 years in prison for a crime he didn't commit. Then, in 2007, DNA testing proved that the 47-year-old Taylor was innocent despite his 1995 conviction. It's too bad there's not a similar test that would end the rumors and accusations so often directed towards God's people. Consider some biblical examples . . .

Though Moses was God's handpicked choice, his leadership was constantly challenged. Joseph was sold into slavery by his brothers and falsely imprisoned in a foreign land. Jealousy led Cain to kill his righteous brother Abel. The prophet Jeremiah was thrown into a muddy cistern by an enraged king, and the apostles Peter and Paul both suffered imprisonment because of their faith.

Of course, Jesus, the man who sought only to do His Father's will, was accused of the greatest evil. His power to heal the demon-possessed was called satanic. His desire to do good was branded as evil.

Some may not understand the things you say or do in God's service. Some may even falsely accuse you—you and Jesus, that is.

Dear Father, may I never shrink back from those times when people revile me, simply because I am faithfully serving You. In Jesus' name, amen.

God Is So Good!

Jesus had compassion on them and touched their eyes. Immediately they received their sight and followed him (Matthew 20:34).

Scripture: **Matthew 20:29-34**
Song: **"Now Thank We All Our God"**

I recall a wonderful hospital visit with a young mother who just couldn't stop praising God. "Why are we so blessed?" she said. "Now we have a beautiful baby boy to go along with our little girl. Both are healthy, and our family feels complete. God is so good!"

On the other hand, many fail to appreciate God's blessings. I'm thinking of that day when Jesus healed 10 men of leprosy. Only one returned to give thanks.

A rich young man walked away from Jesus when he judged the price of eternal life to be too costly. And a large number of disciples turned away from Jesus, refusing to follow Him any further—and this on a day after 5,000 had been miraculously fed!

Two blind men were different. In faith, they cried out for mercy. In faith, they asked to see. In faith, they followed Jesus after receiving their sight.

As for me, I marvel at the prayers God has answered over the years, with my best in mind. My devotional journal bears ample testimony to His goodness. All the more reason to follow Jesus!

God, today I come with no requests; my thankful heart must be expressed. Lord, we don't say it often enough: "Thank You." In Jesus' name, amen.

The President Is Coming!

When Jesus entered Jerusalem, the whole city was stirred and asked, "Who is this?" (Matthew 21:10).

Scripture: **Matthew 21:1-11**
Song: **"Let Jesus Come into Your Heart"**

President Bush was coming to our town! It was the 5th anniversary of the September 11th terrorist attacks (we live about 10 minutes from the crash site of Flight 93), and I was asked to drive some of the dignitaries to the memorial site. They came in by helicopter, with the presidential party flying on Marine One. Others followed in three or four smaller copters.

I witnessed the intense preparations, bomb-sniffing dogs, and sharpshooters spreading out in the woods around us. I can relate to the Scripture that notes, "The whole city was astir."

There wasn't such advance notice when Jesus arrived in Jerusalem. But news of this itinerant prophet had spread. His good works preceded Him, and soon a jubilant crowd welcomed Him with waving palms and shouts of praise.

President Bush's visit ended within an hour. The helicopters, Secret Service, police, and all the dignitaries departed soon after. The excitement was over. What a contrast to those who welcome Jesus into their lives and rest in His comforting, abiding presence.

Dear Father, how excited we get when some celebrity is close to us. Help me carry a sense of excitement each day—because the Lord of all creation dwells within me! In Jesus' name, amen.

Honest or Dishonest?

Why do you stare at us as if by our own power or godliness we had made this man walk? (Acts 3:12).

Scripture: **Acts 3:11-16**
Song: **"Here I Am to Worship"**

It was the bank teller's error; she had given the man 20 dollars too many. "Excuse me, ma'am," said the man. "But I think there's been a mistake."

The teller instantly became indignant. "Sir, I counted your money twice. I'm sure I didn't short you."

"Well, I don't mean to be any trouble, but I think these two $20s stuck together, so you actually gave me too much money."

The teller's attitude instantly changed. "Oh, I'm so sorry for what I was thinking of you. You certainly are an honest man."

The man hesitated, a pained look on his face. "Actually I'm not, but Jesus died for me, so I try to be honest for Him."

I love the way he deflected the praise and directed it to Jesus. Did you notice how Peter and John were able to do the same? Did you notice how quickly they used God's healing power to proclaim the gospel?

What does God get credit for in your life? It's more than shouting "Praise Jesus" now and then. It's telling others that Jesus has changed you in a positive way.

Lord, I truly want others to see Jesus in me. I truly want others to know that Jesus has changed me. In His precious name, amen.

Transformed to Serve

There he was transfigured before them. His face shone like the sun, and his clothes became as white as the light (Matthew 17:2).

Scripture: **Matthew 17:1-13**
Song: **"I'll Go Where You Want Me to Go"**

You can't help but notice George's bulging biceps as he carries a pot of soup from the kitchen. He rarely speaks of his former career as a professional wrestler. "Too many obsessive fans," he says. Besides, he's no longer the same man. He's a regular at preparing soup in an inner-city relief center. No longer in the limelight, he dines with drug addicts, the poor, the homeless.

Transfigured—a complete, total change. It's not confined to an incident in the life of Jesus. It's actually God's intent for every believer. So, a celebrity athlete is transformed into a servant. Fishermen were changed into apostles. Jesus was transfigured into divine glory as three men watched in wonder. It's all a part of God's plan.

Like Peter, we're inspired to build our shrines, to worship. But God wants to be sure we don't de-emphasize obedience. "This is my Son, whom I love . . . Listen to him!" It's in obedience, balanced with sincere worship, that we allow God to continue His work of transformation within us. Better than a life of celebrity, seek out a transformed life of service.

God, help me find contentment in service. And, by Your Spirit within, keep transforming me into Your likeness, day by day. In Jesus' name, amen.

Openhanded: A Command

I command you to be openhanded toward your brothers and toward the poor and needy in your land (Deuteronomy 15:11).

Scripture: **Deuteronomy 15:7-11**
Song: **"Just a Little Talk with Jesus"**

I drove down the sunny freeway, feeling cloudy inside. Suddenly, I realized I was about to pass the best exit to grab lunch. Too late, I thought, glancing at the exit ramp. A homeless person stood there with a cardboard sign. "Send someone to share a meal, Lord," I prayed, before trying to retrieve my interrupted thoughts.

But God nudged my heart. He *had* sent someone—me. I didn't want to turn around, though. I wanted to hurry home, escape the worried mood that chased me. Yet God had shown me love in so many ways over the years—including feeding my children when we received no child support for six months. . . . I put on my blinker.

After buying food at a fast food restaurant, I hurried over to the woman. "I felt God urging me to bring you lunch," I said, feeling awkward.

Her brown eyes lit up. "Thank you. God bless you."

As I hustled back to my car, I felt happy and peaceful. I'd fumbled the ball, but He'd won the game of grace anyway.

Generous Lord, *help me see the poor and give whatever You urge me to give, whether I think it is a convenient time or not. In Jesus' name, amen.*

February 22–28. **Tanya T. Warrington** is a freelance writer, residing with her family in the beautiful Rocky Mountains of Colorado.

No Time Wasted Here

They all joined together constantly in prayer, along with the women and Mary the mother of Jesus, and with his brothers (Acts 1:14).

Scripture: **Acts 1:12-14**
Song: **"Wait on the Lord"**

"Has God given you any discernment yet?" I asked a fellow Christian.

"No, not yet," she answered with a sigh.

"Then we'll keep on waiting and praying," I said.

But, oh, how hard those times of waiting on the Lord! My friend is waiting for guidance about a potential job transfer. Should she move to a branch 65 miles away? She's waiting and asking other Christians to wait in prayer with her.

God has a plan. And sometimes a period of waiting and praying is crucial to that plan.

Another friend of mine once commented: "God sure seems to like to keep us waiting. He never seems to deliver a train ticket until it's boarding time." I knew what she meant—and no doubt the early disciples knew the difficulty of the long wait. However, then and now, God sometimes makes us wait far past our comfort zones. While we wait, though, He grows us. He helps us learn to walk in faithful obedience, Christian fellowship, and tenacious trust. The time is not wasted.

God, help me to wait patiently upon You today. I know You're at work, even when nothing seems to be happening. In Jesus' name, amen.

God's Gift

But Saul began to destroy the church. Going from house to house, he dragged off men and women and put them in prison (Acts 8:3).

Scripture: **Acts 8:1-3; 9:1, 2**
Song: **"Whosoever Will"**

If Saul had been my neighbor, it would have been so easy to judge him. He surely seemed headed for Hell. Not only would he not accept Jesus as the Messiah, but also he was out to destroy all those who did trust Jesus Christ.

However, salvation is never our earned reward for good behavior. Just ask Paul or the crucified criminal who died next to Jesus. The criminal who chose repentance gained eternity with Jesus in Paradise, even though he didn't have a single day to prove himself with changed behavior.

Sometimes when another hurts me deeply, it is hard to remember that God loves that person and wants to save him or her. In my pain, I see only their sins. Likewise, when I am the one who has hurt another, I struggle to believe that God could still love me.

Thankfully, God is love. He loved Paul, He loved the thief on the cross, and He loves you and me. No matter how much we have sinned in our past, we are eligible (*because* we're sinners) for God's grace.

*Thank You, **Heavenly Father,** for providing salvation as a gift. I never could have earned it. Thank You for rescuing me. Help me to avoid judging others, but instead to pray for their salvation. In Jesus' name, amen.*

God's Work

Those who had been scattered preached the word wherever they went (Acts 8:4).

Scripture: **Acts 8:4-13**
Song: **"If Jesus Goes with Me"**

I remember sitting in a Bible study when I was a young Christian, wondering what I would do if God sent me to Africa. I feared that if I fully surrendered to God, He would have me eating crickets or dying of malaria. After wrestling with such ideas for a while, I gave God my whole self. If He sent me to Africa, so be it.

Well, God hasn't sent me to Africa yet. He has molded me, however, into a different woman—one who hopes to serve as a missionary in Africa one day! (If He doesn't do that, it's all right.)

What has changed me? God's faithfulness.

Repeatedly, God proves He can do His work right where I am. He is able to use me as a witness to those who are nearby. His hope flows through me, regardless of whether I am confident or frightened, enjoying life or struggling through trials, focused on sharing with others or totally distracted.

My surrendered heart is all that He desires. It doesn't matter where I am—physically or emotionally—God is there fulfilling His purposes.

*I give You my heart anew, **Dear Lord.** Wherever I am, I want to walk with You and shine for You. Please use me however and wherever You want. In the holy name of Jesus, my Lord and Savior, I pray. Amen.*

They're Watching!

Some of the Jews were persuaded and joined Paul and Silas, as did a large number of God-fearing Greeks and not a few prominent women (Acts 17:4).

Scripture: **Acts 17:1-4**
Song: **"Shine, Jesus, Shine"**

Good news travels fast. When I returned home from a camping trip with a water bottle full of blackberries, I phoned a neighbor. I invited her and her husband over for hot pie in 40 minutes. She called back. She had bumped into another neighbor . . . and wondered if that couple could join us.

"Sure," I said, sliding the pies into the oven. I showered and then sorted our laundry. On the way back from the laundry room, I could smell the delightful aromas.

My next-door neighbor poked his head out of his door. "Smells good," he said.

"Want to join us for some pie?"

It's the same with the good news about Jesus Christ. Paul intentionally shared with Jewish men in the synagogue—but the good news spread rapidly to others.

We never know who might be listening. I've had people approach me saying, "You're a Christian aren't you?" I had not intentionally invited them to hear my hope in Christ . . . but they had watched and listened.

Dear Lord, *please shine through me. Help me to abide in You all day long, so that I will bless others through You. Use me to spread the good news about You, Your Father, and Your kingdom. In Jesus' name, amen.*

A Heart Matter

One of those listening was a woman named Lydia . . . The Lord opened her heart to respond to Paul's message (Acts 16:14).

Scripture: **Acts 16:11-15**
Song: **"O Happy Day"**

My husband led our family around the reservoir. Due to repair work on the dam, the water was gone. The ground that had been soft and gooey a few months before was now dry and hard. It looked somewhat like an alligator's skin. The land's moisture had evaporated away, and the sun's heat had baked the soil. Once land reaches such a state, rain will fall on it but not readily soak in.

Have you ever let a houseplant get excessively dry and then tried to water it? Your first container of water will pass straight through the soil and pour out the hole in the bottom of the pot, making a mess. The soil has become so hard that at first it cannot soak in any water.

Before we believe in Jesus, I wonder if our hearts look like hardened soil from God's perspective. He has to open our hearts, softening our receptiveness to living water, so that we can absorb the truth of the gospel. Without the Father's help with our hearts, none of us would understand or receive His Son Jesus.

Lord, please keep my heart open to Your Spirit. Thank You for saving me from a life controlled by sin. Thank You for bringing me into an eternal relationship with You. Help me to pray for others whose hearts are hardened. In the name of the Father, the Son, and the Holy Spirit, I pray. Amen.

Love's Extravagance

Why are you giving this woman a hard time? She has just done something wonderfully significant for me (Matthew 26:10, *The Message*).

Scripture: **Matthew 26:3-16**
Song: **"More Precious Than Silver"**

Newly engaged women find people grabbing their left hands to admire their new diamonds. That sparkling testament says to others, "Here is a beloved woman." Nine years later, women still grab my hand occasionally to admire my ring.

I didn't pick out this beautiful ring—it was a marvelous, extravagant gift. It celebrates life-changing love. It prepared my heart for a new life, free from the abuse that had characterized my previous experience.

But it distresses me if a woman misses the point—looks at her own ring and offers a quick explanation about why it may be smaller. I certainly didn't marry a wealthy man, and the ring wasn't meant as a status symbol.

Jesus must have known a similar frustration when His disciples missed the heart-message of the woman's extravagant gift of anointing oil. Her love touched tender spots in Jesus' soul. It celebrated love with wonderful abundance. And it surely helped prepare Him for His fast-approaching trial on the cross.

Dear Lord, *You are so precious to me. You are worthy of the most extravagant gifts and sacrifices. You bless me so abundantly; please teach me how I can bless You. In Jesus' name, amen.*

My Prayer Notes

_____

_____

_____

_____

_____

_____

_____

_____

_____

_____

_____

_____

_____

_____

_____

_____

_____

_____

_____

_____

My Prayer Notes

_____

_____

_____

_____

_____

_____

_____

_____

_____

_____

_____

_____

_____

_____

_____

_____

_____

_____

My Prayer Notes

DEVOTIONS®

Gary Allen, Editor

***B*lessed are those who have not seen and yet have believed.**

—John 20:29

MARCH

Photo © Michael Smith
Dreamstime.com

Yes, Me

"I will not," he answered, but later he changed his mind and went (Matthew 21:29).

Scripture: **Matthew 21:28-32**
Song: **"Here I Am, Lord"**

She'd served a term as a summer missionary. She had a family missions background, and her husband felt called to missions. Nevertheless, Linda Egbert remained unconvinced that missions was God's plan for her. She was perfectly content as a minister's wife and mother.

However, she kept encountering the challenge to "leave your comfort zone." And through a gradual process of saying "Yes, Lord," she too discovered her call.

The Egberts were drawn to the Guaymi of Costa Rica, a fairly isolated mountain people who had received little Christian outreach. But now with Luciano, a Guaymi Christian who had been praying for help, these folks are being reached and discipled in the faith.

When the Lord calls us to any new form of service, we need discerning hearts that listen closely to the whisperings of His Spirit. Sometimes what we hear is clear and direct. At other times, we must proceed by crooks and turns until "not me" becomes "Yes, me."

Father, I pray for a clear understanding of Your direction this day and a desire to follow wherever You lead. May I always say, "Yes, Lord," with my feet as well as with my words. In Jesus' name, amen.

March 1–7. **Diana C. Derringer,** a former family services clinician and adjunct professor, teaches youth Sunday school and enjoys missions outreach.

His Wonder Displayed

The day is yours, and yours also the night; you established the sun and moon (Psalm 74:16).

Scripture: **Psalm 74**
Song: **"God of Wonders"**

The summer months in our community, with its beautiful lake, can present a true conflict of interests between farmers and vacationers. Weekends pose particular difficulties when the weather has been especially hot and dry. A frequent Sunday morning joke is: We don't know whether to pray for rain . . . or sunshine. I am quite confident that if we were in control of the weather—or any aspect of creation—chaos would quickly ensue.

Often when I'm tempted to complain about weather conditions, I realize how little I appreciate the wonder and majesty of every day and night. The birds singing at dawn, the breathtaking colors at sunset—they are miracles of beauty. Sometimes I take a moment to enjoy the reflection of sunlight in a rain drop or just soak in the calmness as dusk becomes dark. When I stop and really look around me, such things become awe inspiring. So, why is it so hard to take the time, to open my eyes and see the myriad ways nature displays God's love?

*Thank You for loving us, **Lord,** and demonstrating Your love daily. Thank You for the beauty of both the ordinary and the unexpected. Forgive me for failing so often to recognize Your hand at work as I travel through Your wondrous world. In the name of the Father, the Son, and the Holy Spirit, I pray. Amen.*

Are We Listening?

The LORD came and stood there, calling as at the other times, "Samuel! Samuel!" Then Samuel said, "Speak, for your servant is listening" (1 Samuel 3:10).

Scripture: **1 Samuel 3:10-21**
Song: **"I'll Be Listening"**

Have you ever noticed the uncanny abilities of certain animals? There are dogs that can tell not only when their owner calls them verbally; they also recognize the family car when it's still a great distance from the house. As young puppies, they don't display this proficiency. However, over time, they grow in their abilities. They come to know their master and develop a deep trust in that person. They respond when called or when the owner is drawing near.

Perhaps we need to watch and learn. As young Christians we may not discern God's call as clearly as someone more mature, someone who has had years to sharpen those inner listening skills. Yet even the seasoned believer often misses our Master's message. It is not that we cannot hear; we simply allow the other noises of life to drown Him out. Hence we may not recognize His voice or His movement in our lives.

Whatever the time or place, may we always heed the call of His voice. Yes, may we respond with Samuel's readiness, "Speak, for your servant is listening."

Heavenly Father, keep me attuned to Your voice so I will hear when You call, no matter the noise around me. In Christ's name I pray. Amen.

O, For Humility!

Now Moses was a very humble man, more humble than anyone else on the face of the earth (Numbers 12:3).

Scripture: **Numbers 12:3-9**
Song: **"In Christ Alone"**

"So why did *Jesus* have to die on the cross? I myself would have been willing to die for the world." Those words confused and astounded me as a college sophomore sharing my faith with a young man who was obviously troubled. He had earlier expressed a desire for prayer from Christian friends. Yet, when hearing the Bible's invitation to salvation, he seemed only to want relief from the heavy burden in his soul. His sins? He saw them merely as "enjoyable activities." He didn't want to change his way of life.

Only later did I understand that, for him, dying would have been easier than living. At that moment, maintaining his image seemed more valuable than a promise of eternal salvation.

Oh, to be like Moses, saturated with humility! All too many of us seek a difference in our lives but try to achieve it on our own terms. God desires a humble heart, one that is open to His truth, trusting His plans for our present and future.

Father, open my ears and my heart to Your Word today. Help me turn from my pride in order to fully embrace Your purpose and plan. You offer the best; may I never settle for less. I pray this prayer in the name of Jesus, my merciful Savior and Lord. Amen.

Just a Little Bit?

If anyone does not listen to my words that the prophet speaks in my name, I myself will call him to account (Deuteronomy 18:19).

Scripture: **Deuteronomy 18:15-22**
Song: **"I Surrender All"**

"Just a little bit surely won't hurt." Thus I convinced myself after receiving a gorgeous floral arrangement, a total surprise from out-of-state friends. Interspersed throughout the breathtaking collection of flowers were tiny sprigs of cedar and pine. Naturally, I wanted the gift displayed where we could see and enjoy it.

But here's the problem. I pushed from my mind a little fact: Cedar is one of my worst allergens.

I chose to focus on the beauty of the moment. However, that sick, worn-down feeling of an impending allergy attack came on strong two days later. I realized the cedar had to go, small amount though it was. (Quite literally, it was taking my breath away!)

"Just a little bit" can seem so minor in our own eyes and to society as a whole. And we may convince ourselves that no one will be hurt. Yet if it involves refusing to listen to the Lord of all, we will have to give account. As the title of a famous sermon by the great preacher R. G. Lee reminds us: "Payday, Someday!"

Lord, reveal any "little" sins I am currently ignoring and help me to eliminate them completely. May I remember that, whether good or bad, the little things in life do make a difference. Through Christ, amen.

Never Failing Love

In my distress I called to the LORD, and he answered me. From the depths of the grave I called for help, and you listened to my cry (Jonah 2:2).

Scripture: **Jonah 2:1-9**
Song: **"God Will Take Care of You"**

When my nephew's wife (and unborn child) went into severe respiratory distress, the prognosis became bleak. Many prayers ascended on their behalf.

An emergency Caesarean section followed, along with the separation of the mother and her seven-weeks premature baby to critical care units in different cities. Seemingly endless days of uncertainly lay ahead.

The agony of the situation was written on my nephew's face. Their situation touched everyone who knew them. But coupled with my nephew's heart cry was an unwavering faith in God's love and care.

We delight each day that the outcome was nothing short of miraculous. Yet we are also confident that God provides for our needs regardless of the circumstances, even when the results are not as we desire. His promises never fail, and His presence shines through in special ways—especially when our own resources dry up, and our only hope rests in Him.

*I thank You, **Lord,** for these precious lives and for the witness they have been to others. Thank You too for the growth they have known through this tremendous struggle. Draw each of us closer to You through every event we face, whether from the mountaintop or the depths. In Christ's name, amen.*

Another Chance

Then the word of the LORD came to Jonah a second time (Jonah 3:1).

Scripture: **Jonah 1:1-3, 3:1-9**
Song: **"We Are Called to Be God's People"**

Working as a juvenile counselor, I often attended court appearances with first-time youth offenders. I observed a common approach by judges for minor offenses: a good, stiff lecture with restitution, probation, and community service required. This was often followed by a warning: "You've been given a second chance; I never want to see you back here again." For such young people, it's definitely time to seek a different, more purposeful direction in life.

Jonah's reaction to God's call was to run in the wrong direction. Yet God, our eternal judge, did not give up on him. This young man suffered painful consequences for the unwise choice he made, although his punishment could have been far worse.

Realizing the error of his ways, when God issued His second summons, Jonah was ready to head in the right direction. That decision proved most beneficial for himself—and for those who would receive the gracious message of divine deliverance.

Dear Lord, *I am so grateful that You do forgive and provide second chances when we make poor decisions. Thank You also for the consequences we suffer that teach us a better way to live, painful though they are at the time. In the name of Jesus I pray. Amen.*

Power of a Clean Conscience

O Lord, hear my voice. Let your ears be attentive to my cry for mercy. If you, O LORD, kept a record of sins, O Lord, who could stand? But with you there is forgiveness; therefore you are feared (Psalm 130:2-4).

Scripture: **Psalm 130**
Song: **"Create in Me a Clean Heart"**

Shortly after becoming a Christian, I began feeling a guilty conscience for something I had once done. Although God had forgiven me for stealing a few supplies from my workplace, I knew that He wanted me to go back to my former employers and ask for forgiveness—and offer to make restitution.

I didn't want to go. With butterflies in my stomach, sweating palms, and a rapid heartbeat, I mustered up the courage to face my former boss. Fighting back tears, I told him what I had done. He responded with grace and forgiveness.

The experience helped me to more fully understand both the fear of the Lord and also His mercy. You see, I knew that if I ignored God's dealings with me through my conscience, my heart would harden to His future promptings. By being obedient, though, I felt a huge burden lift from my shoulders. What mercy!

Lord, thank You for the Holy Spirit who speaks to me through my conscience. Help me obey His gentle promptings today. In Jesus' name, amen.

March 8–14. **Judy Gyde**, of Toledo, Ohio, has been published in more than 40 publications. She and her husband, Bruce, have three grown children.

The Dark: It Keeps Calling

We look for light, but all is darkness; for brightness, but we walk in deep shadows. Like the blind we grope along the wall, feeling our way like men without eyes. At midday we stumble as if it were twilight (Isaiah 59:9, 10).

Scripture: **Isaiah 59:9-15**
Song: **"Fear Not"**

A popular movie, *Psycho*, debuted while I was in high school. My friends spoke in glowing terms about how creepy and exciting it was. Mom refused to let me see it.

Months later, I saw an advertisement for this movie—it was to be televised in the middle of the night. Ignoring Mom's warning and careful not to wake my parents, I snuck downstairs and took the portable TV to my room. Sure enough, it was the scariest thing I ever saw.

I didn't realize what a great price I'd pay. Although Mom never knew what I'd seen, I suffered the consequences. Whenever I babysat for others, I'd become quite frightened by the normal creeks and groans that homes make at night. Although I'd flip on all of the lights, I'd still feel afraid. Not until years later did I overcome my fears.

Why do we go after things we know aren't good for us? If we choose God's way, we'll walk more fully in the light. But the darkness seems always to keep calling. Help, Lord!

Thank You, **Heavenly Father,** *for leading me on Your path. Help me to make the right choices each day rather than being swayed by destructive influences. In the name of Your Son, my Savior, I pray. Amen.*

Hooray for Modern Technology!

Sing for joy, O heavens, for the LORD has done this; shout aloud, O earth beneath. Burst into song, you mountains, you forests and all your trees, for the LORD has redeemed Jacob, he displays his glory in Israel (Isaiah 44:23).

Scripture: **Isaiah 44:21-28**
Song: **"Shout to the Lord"**

We know people misuse the Internet—looking at the wrong things, talking to the wrong people. But it's great to use our computers for good things, isn't it? Many of us conduct business from our homes through the Internet. Research is simplified. We can buy and sell. And e-mail helps us stay in close touch with loved ones.

It's exciting, as well, to use computers to enjoy the magnificent things God is doing. Some churches and radio programs broadcast their services live, shows that can also be accessed later through video archives.

I love using the Internet to see what God is doing in churches all over the world. Using Google, I access God-tube and You-tube to see church worship teams playing a variety of music. I sing and worship with them. Mime and drama teams perform gospel truths right on my screen.

As with most everything God has created or allowed, it can be used for the good or the not-so-good. Computers are no exception. Let us use them for the glory of God.

*Thank You, **Lord,** for the wonderful opportunities the Internet provides. May I use it only for good purposes, promoting the values of Your kingdom and growing in knowledge of Your will. Through Christ, amen.*

God's Word Lights Our Path

I am the LORD your God, who teaches you what is best for you, who directs you in the way you should go. If only you had paid attention to my commands, your peace would have been like a river (Isaiah 48:17, 18).

Scripture: **Isaiah 48:17-22**
Song: **"Thy Word Is a Lamp"**

As a young Christian, I searched for Scriptures to help me walk close to the Lord. I discovered that God's Word could keep me from stumbling—if I'd only listen to Him.

Proverbs 3:5 became one of my favorite verses, and it complements our Scripture reading for today: "Trust in the Lord with all your heart and lean not on your own understanding."

I wish I could say that I always walk perfectly with the Lord, relying on His daily guidance. When I skip prayer time and reading the Bible, my fellowship with God suffers, and trust levels seem to decrease. I may make decisions without giving them prayerful consideration. Then I wonder why things don't go well.

Lately I've become convinced of something important: As we seek Him, follow His guidance, and give Him the credit for the good things in our lives, we'll find greater blessing and peace.

Almighty and ever-living God, *help me keep Your Word in my heart today. In every situation I face, may I sense Your assurance, guidance, and peace. Thank You for all Your goodness to me, down through the years. I pray this prayer in the name of Jesus, my Savior and Lord. Amen.*

The Best Is Yet to Come

He made known to us the mystery of his will according to his good pleasure, which he purposed in Christ, to be put into effect when the times will have reached their fulfillment—to bring all things in heaven and on earth together under one head, even Christ (Ephesians 1:9, 10).

Scripture: **Ephesians 1:3-12**
Song: **"Our God Reigns"**

It's alarming to watch the news these days: wars, hurricanes, and earthquakes fill the world scene. Skyrocketing prices, moral disintegration, and the increase of criminal activity make us wonder what this world is coming to. Yet while we live in perilous times, what we see reveals only part of the picture.

According to the apostle Paul, the unsettling things that plague us in this present age will one day come to an end. As time passes, the pieces of God's divine plan are falling into place. After all, evil never takes God by surprise. He is in control. Very soon, Jesus will return for His bride, and the times will have reached their fulfillment. We'll see perfect order come when Jesus reigns. What a glorious time that will be!

As each of us draws closer to the Lord today, we'll understand His plan more clearly. Then we'll fulfill the purposes He has for us.

Dear Father, deliver me from worry about the future, and fill me with Your perfect peace. Let Your kingdom come and Your will be done, on earth as it is in Heaven. Through the precious name of Jesus, amen.

Power of a Transformed Life

I have appeared to you to appoint you as a servant and as a witness of what you have seen of me and what I will show you. . . . I am sending you to them to open their eyes and turn them from darkness to light (Acts 26:16-18).

Scripture: **Acts 26:12-18**
Song: **"Onward Christian Soldiers"**

As witnesses, we can give a firsthand account of the work God has done in our lives. But what are the opportunities? They abound whenever we help someone walk through life's difficulties.

I recently visited with my neighbor Heather, who was struggling with marital problems. Though I didn't know exactly what to say, God helped me to simply befriend her. When I needed to speak, the words came naturally. When I suggested that prayer could help her and offered to pray for her, she opened her life to Christ.

Simply sharing with others how God transforms our lives is a powerful way to reach out. And every Christian's testimony is important. But let us remember that a large part of our witness comes through in how we live our lives before our neighbors. As Benjamin Franklin once said: "None preaches better than the ant, and she says nothing."

Dear Lord, help us to go to others and offer the hope of the gospel. Thank You, for working in my heart and in others' hearts, moving us all to receive Your truth. In all I say and do, may Your name be lifted up on high! Amen.

Appreciate Today's Blessings

Jonah was very happy about the vine. But at dawn the next day God provided a worm, which chewed the vine so that it withered. When the sun rose, God provided a scorching east wind, and the sun blazed on Jonah's head so that he grew faint. He wanted to die (Jonah 4:6-8).

Scripture: **Jonah 3:10–4:11**
Song: **"The Simple, Earnest Prayer"**

When Carol's home burned to the ground, she fell to her knees in shock. Friends from our church rallied around her, providing resources and reassuring her: "Everything's going to be all right." Many difficult days followed, but the Lord helped her through them.

Although Carol missed her lovely family heirlooms, almost everything else was replaceable. "It's amazing how much we take our blessings for granted," she says, "until suddenly they're gone." Her perspective has changed; material things just aren't as important to her as they once were.

We know that God allows bad things to happen to good people. And we won't always understand His purposes. Can't you imagine that Jonah, Job, Joseph—and countless others whom God has loved and used, down to this day—had some questions of their own regarding their sufferings? Yet God was with them all, and remains with us, in the darkest hours.

Dear Father, help me in the times when my faith is being tested, that I might stand and continue to praise You. Through Christ, amen.

Number One

Now Thomas . . . was not with the disciples when Jesus came (John 20:24).

Scripture: **John 20:24-29**
Song: **"Just As I Am"**

We gathered in the local nursing home, some of the folks in wheelchairs and in the last stages of earthly life. Elderly people have seen a lot, and many scoffed at religion. I was asked to speak to them, and gave each person a folded piece of paper. "Don't open it now! Inside is a number, and that number is God's number for you."

Clarice, 92, but with an active mind, couldn't wait. "I'm Number 1!" she cried. The others fumbled to open theirs. "I'm Number 1, as well!" "So am I." "So am I!"

We are all Number 1 to God. If I were the only person who had ever sinned, Jesus would have gone to the cross . . . just for me. I do believe that, and I explained that God wants a thoroughly personal response from each of us. When I stand before Him, He will look straight at me! For God deals with us on a one-to-one basis, never as an anonymous face in the crowd.

Thomas saw it that day. One of the twelve? Oh, he was much more than that. Thomas was loved for himself. Jesus wanted his personal response.

Father, You give me Your full attention. I give You mine, and I worship You from my heart this day. In the name of Jesus I pray. Amen.

March 15–21. **Marion Turnbull** entered the world, married, and raised a family in Middlesbrough, England, before doing mission work in Cameroon and Malawi.

Really: What Is Mine?

David replied, "No, my brothers, you must not do that with what the LORD has given us" (1 Samuel 30:23).

Scripture: **1 Samuel 30:21-31**
Song: **"Great Is Thy Faithfulness"**

Some Christians were taken hostage in Africa, and one had to share his toothbrush among six people. Sounds horrible, but consider: If all we have is from God, is anything mine to keep? Well then, perhaps we can cheerfully possess a toothbrush—or a house, or a car, or anything we need—in an open, not grasping hand.

David was a good politician, a wonderful leader of men. His wisdom flowed from his faith in God and his belief that God alone was his provider. He, like Jesus, set no store on earthly goods. Thus he was free to give up what he had in his hand, so that it might be used for God's purposes.

If I come into a sudden "windfall," can I let it go, or must I hold on to it all? David's eyes were on God; his men's eyes were on the booty.

When our children were setting out on their own, we advised them to start with a modest lifestyle, so as to be free to take on the real challenges of life. When big decisions have to be made, money should take a back seat. Yes, it should always be the servant and not the master.

*Thank You, **Father,** for all You give. May I make use of what is in my hand, to be used for the advance of Your kingdom wherever You take me this day. In the name of Jesus, Lord and Savior of all, I pray. Amen.*

Open to the Blessing!

The man with two tunics should share with him who has none, and the one who has food should do the same (Luke 3:11).

Scripture: **Luke 3:10-14**
Song: **"When I Survey the Wondrous Cross"**

My husband and I visited Christians in Mozambique during their civil war. A local family owned a house in a "safe" town, and we lodged with them there. The parents gave us their own bed and fed us evening meals. After some days we realized that the food on the table was all they could find, and the family ate whatever we left! They also cooked maize for several refugee families, people who were sleeping on the floor of their garage because their homes and crops were burned.

During a night raid, soldiers took all our luggage and cash. The local Christians heard about this and gathered a collection for us. They were hungry and had nothing, but many gave in order to help us. What a humbling and blessed experience!

I am asked to share what God has given me. But, of course, sometimes I am tempted to hang on to what I have. Can you relate? After all, I've earned it, and I'm entitled to have it. But obedience enriches me. It opens the door to ever more blessing, on and on and on.

O God, give me the wisdom and the grace to help others with the things You have placed into my hands. It is hard to let go, Lord. But help me to remember how completely You gave everything for me, through Your precious Son, my Savior. In His holy name I pray. Amen.

Can You Let Go?

As long as the son of Jesse lives on this earth, neither you nor your kingdom will be established. Now send and bring him to me, for he must die! (1 Samuel 20:31).

Scripture: **1 Samuel 20:30-42**
Song: **"Seek the Lord Who Now Is Present"**

Is it wrong to have ambition, to set a goal and work towards it? Maybe. For example, suppose that ambition is for your children. Recently an Asian girl here in England was killed by her family because she refused to enter into an arranged marriage. The parents had made their plans, but the daughter had been exposed to a different way of life and could not agree. They lost a daughter, and their lives were devastated.

Saul had ambition for Jonathan, to see him become the next king. But Saul's ambition was thwarted. He knew that God had chosen David, but he refused God's choice and actually fought against the Lord.

When I allow my ambitions to cloud my judgment, I run into fear and hatred. I'll irrationally oppose anyone or anything that stands in the way. That's when I must ask myself: Why do I want that person to just go away? Is it because he stands in the way of my ambitions? Surely, it's better if I recognize that my ambition has clashed with God's plan. (Suggestion: Let go and see Him work things out for good.)

Lord, I will trust You to work in all my circumstances for good. Through You, I can love even those who seem to oppose me. In Jesus' name, amen.

Six Big Policemen

Do not destroy the work of God for the sake of food. All food is clean, but it is wrong for a man to eat anything that causes someone else to stumble (Romans 14:20).

Scripture: **Romans 14:13-21**
Song: **"I'm Accepted, I'm Forgiven"**

One night while on duty at the hospital, my husband, Alan, received a call that the police were bringing in a violent psychiatric patient. "Be ready!" they said. Alan stood at the hospital doors as the police van approached. It backed up and opened to reveal a struggling man on the floor, heavily restrained by six big policemen.

Alan looked into the patient's face and recognized an old patient. "Hello, Bill," he said, taking him by the hand. To the amazement of the policemen, Alan led him gently into the hospital.

"What was all that about, Bill?"

"Well, think about it. What would *you* do if you had six big policemen all trying to sit on you?" The man simply needed to be understood.

It makes me wonder: Do I sometimes make the gospel too difficult? That is, do I try to push people into becoming what I think is a proper Christian? Sometimes all that's needed is a gentle hand to lead them into friendship—with me and with my Savior.

Dear God, teach me to examine my life and remove anything that may be a stumbling block to those who are seeking You. Today, show me when to speak and when not to speak. Thank You, in Jesus' name. Amen.

My Friend

I no longer call you servants . . . Instead, I have called you friends, for everything that I learned from my Father I have made known to you (John 15:15).

Scripture: **John 15:9-17**
Song: **"How Sweet the Name of Jesus Sounds"**

The office worker looks up as the friend of his boss arrives. The friend taps on the chief's door and goes in, receiving a warm welcome and full attention. The worker is annoyed. "Just watch," he says to the man at the next desk. "He'll sit at the chief's table while the staff waits on them both. It's not fair!"

Not fair? But Mr. Worker, you receive a good salary for your efforts. (Does the boss's friend expect anything? No, not really.) You have your working hours; the rest of your time is your own. You have your own personal life, and you don't expect your boss to intrude there. (But the boss's friend's life is bound up together with his.)

It is wonderfully rewarding to be a *servant* of God, but I am called to be His *friend*. A new believer is eager to work for God. Great! But more mature believers can be trusted to represent their Lord in every situation. That's because, by the Spirit of God, they have learned His ways and know Him deeply.

My gracious Lord and Master, *I can hardly believe You are pleased with me and want my friendship. I open my heart to hear Your voice and to be involved with You in Your plans for the world. In the name of the Father, the Son, and the Holy Spirit, I pray. Amen.*

Like a Limpet

Then Orpah kissed her mother-in-law good-by, but Ruth clung to her (Ruth 1:14).

Scripture: **Ruth 1:1-9, 14b-16**
Song: **"The Rock That Is Higher than I"**

We children used to play at low tide where the sea washed over rocks. Some of the rocks were covered with little pointed shells of limpets, and we once tried to dislodge one to see underneath. The more we tried, the more it stuck. It clung on—like limpets do.

Ruth clung to Naomi, sticking fast like a limpet. Orpah, the "sensible" one, saw her situation and chose the secure future she could see. Ruth clung to the only rock she knew, her mother-in-law, her people, and her God. She didn't understand much, but stuck with the hope.

When so many people were leaving Him, Jesus asked His disciples whether they would also go away. "Where can we go?" asked Peter. "You have the words of eternal life." They stuck with Jesus.

Sometimes the people around me will try to shake my trust in God. "Be sensible," they say. "Build a life for yourself." It takes faith and determination to cling to our Rock and the promises in His Word. But if we choose to live for this world only, we kiss God good-bye.

*I will cling to You, **Father,** even though this world calls me to go another way. May I remember Your ever-loving presence with me wherever I am. In this way, help me to make every decision in the light of Your perfect will for me. In the holy name of Jesus, my Lord and Savior, I pray. Amen.*

The Perfect Teacher

Be devoted to one another in brotherly love. Honor one another above yourselves (Romans 12:10).

Scripture: **Romans 12:9-18**
Song: **"Open My Eyes, That I May See"**

Joyce was my partner in our vegetarian cooking class. To my dismay, I soon realized that Joyce was a perfectionist. Before long, I labeled her as "rigid, slow, and authoritarian." I prided myself on being easy-going—and being able to get a lot done in the shortest possible time.

My agitation grew as Joyce kept measuring each ingredient with precise deliberation. By the time our classmates proudly displayed their finished dishes, our casseroles weren't even in the oven. Several times I came close to screaming, "Stop being so compulsive!"

Finally, I talked to the Lord about Joyce. And a Bible verse came to mind: "In humility consider others better than yourselves" (Philippians 2:3). I finally realized that God meant for me to honor Joyce, and to accept her in love, just the way she was.

God has made us all different. I knew I wasn't perfect, either, and Joyce probably didn't appreciate my relaxed approach to cooking. I needed to learn sisterly kindness and patience. Joyce would be the perfect teacher.

Dear Father, please help me to love others unconditionally—the way You love them and the way You love me. In Jesus' precious name, amen.

March 22–28. **Ingrid Shelton** is a retired teacher/librarian and a freelance writer. She enjoys walking, gardening, reading, and playing hand bells at church.

Encourage Each Other

I long to see you so that I may impart to you some spiritual gift to make you strong—that is, that you and I may be mutually encouraged by each other's faith (Romans 1:11, 12).

Scripture: **Romans 1:8-15**
Song: **"Blest Be the Tie That Binds"**

When a friend shared her heart-breaking trial with me, I was amazed at her strong faith. "Don't you ever get discouraged?" I asked.

"Of course," she replied. "That's why I need to keep in close contact with my Savior through prayer and reading the Bible. I also stay connected to my church, which lifts my spirit. And I thank God for the gift of my Christian friends. Their faith gives me strength, as well."

She then pointed to the apostle Paul, who was a spiritual father to numerous individuals and church groups throughout Asia. He had such a positive faith and was a constant encourager to others, even though he, like all of us, was subject to discouragement at times. That's why he longed to visit the believers everywhere. It's what nourished his faith and brought him joy.

"We all deal with problems too heavy to bear alone," my friend added. "If Paul needed to constantly talk to God and seek the company and encouragement of other Christians to bolster his faith . . . how much more do I?"

O Lord my God, thank You for the gift of Your presence, Your Word, and Your people—all of which nourish my faith. May I always praise You, even in trying circumstances. In Christ's name, I pray. Amen.

This Neighbor Too

If you really keep the royal law found in Scripture, "Love your neighbor as yourself," you are doing right (James 2:8).

Scripture: **James 2:8-13**
Song: **"Make Me a Blessing"**

Helen, a former neighbor in my condo building, seemed distant and proud. Whenever I met her in the hallway or garage and wished her a good day, she offered a brusque, standard reply: "Maybe for you, but not for me." Then she'd brush past me. *I won't try to be friendly anymore,* I thought.

But one day I noticed a tear in Helen's eye. Did she have problems too heavy to bear? How could I show God's love to her when she seemed to ignore me?

Send her a card, came the sudden thought.

A few days later I met Helen again and asked how she was doing. Surprised, she thanked me for the encouraging card and spoke of a recent loss: Her daughter had succumbed to cancer. And her son rarely came to visit. She felt no one cared, not realizing that Christ loved her and could be with her in all her grief.

Again the Lord reminded me that loving others doesn't depend on shared interests or personality. Caring about my neighbor is simply this: a command straight from the royal king of glory.

Lord of Heaven, please help me to love my neighbors as I love myself today. May I be sensitive to their needs and reach out with the peace You give me. In the name of Jesus, my Savior, I pray. Amen.

Be a Peacemaker

The wisdom that comes from heaven is first of all pure; then peace-loving, considerate, submissive, full of mercy and good fruit, impartial and sincere. Peacemakers who sow in peace raise a harvest of righteousness (James 3:17, 18).

Scripture: **James 3:13-18**
Song: **"Like a River Glorious"**

My husband was a peacemaker, at home, in the classroom, and among his fellow teachers. When a strike loomed in our school district, most staff members seemed to be in favor. Realizing the dangers that would come with a strike, my husband pointed to the potential pain. His insight and relaxed manner quieted the turbulent spirit of the staff. Their change of mind helped avert the strike. And it turned out to be the right decision.

As I look around my world, I realize that many volatile situations could be diffused. Divorces could be averted. Arguments could be avoided in the home, among neighbors, and in the workplace. How? By a peaceful spirit. Jesus had taught it to His disciples on the mountain side: "Blessed are the peacemakers" (Matthew 5:9).

How I wish to become a person who radiates peace! Only Jesus can help me here. So I ask Him to fill me with His peace. And may that gift, direct from His heart, shine forth in my own sphere of influence.

Prince of Peace, I'm so thankful to know that You are the source of a peace that surpasses my understanding. Please help me to carry a peaceful spirit into every circumstance I'll face this day. In Your name, I pray. Amen.

Jesus Loves Us All

The Sovereign Lord declares—he who gathers the exiles of Israel: "I will gather still others to them besides those already gathered" (Isaiah 56:8).

Scripture: **Isaiah 56:3-8**
Song: **"In Christ There Is No East or West"**

When the Israelites returned to Jerusalem after their 70-year exile, there were Gentile converts and eunuchs among them who were denied certain religious privileges. God himself reassured those folks, though. If they worshiped Him only, He would give them comfort, help, and full acceptance within His temple.

In the New Testament, we find the apostle Peter initially thinking that God's kingdom was for Jews only. After all, Gentiles were apparent idol-worshipers, and it was against Jewish law to associate with them. Through a vision, God taught Peter a much better way to approach those who would soon become his brethren in Christ (see Acts 10:28).

Today, God still invites all people into His fold. In my own town, I find various cultures and religions. Some are searching for God outside the traditional church, and they aren't sure whether He will accept them. God, who knows their hearts, is able to bring them to himself and begin transforming those same hearts.

My Lord God, thank You for accepting all who are willing to trust You alone for salvation. Help me to love and pray for my neighbors, regardless of background or culture. In Jesus' precious name, amen.

From Buddha to Jesus

Now in Christ Jesus you who once were far away have been brought near through the blood of Christ (Ephesians 2:13).

Scripture: **Ephesians 2:11-20**
Song: **"Nothing but the Blood"**

Ten-year-old Carol lived in Seoul, Korea, with her Buddhist family. One day she followed the sound of ringing bells into a Christian chapel. There she learned that the blood of Christ, shed on the cross, would cleanse her of all sins. Soon she joyfully entered the waters of baptism.

However, her Buddhist mother became angry at Carol's decision to follow Jesus. She forbade her to attend the Christian church, so Carol could go only occasionally.

As Carol matured in her faith, she began to pray for her mother, who became a Christian several years later. Then, both of them prayed for the rest of the family. In time, Carol's father, along with five of her brothers and sisters, left their Buddhist lifestyle and bowed to Christ. At last they understood that only Jesus could give them the peace they'd sought from the Buddha.

I too have precious family and friends who seem to walk far from God. Like Carol and her mother, I pray that God might draw them closer, ever nearer to the saving grace of Christ.

Gracious Father, *thank You for those who are proclaiming, by word and deed, that You are the one true God. May I be faithful in witness to Your goodness, by all I do and by all I say. In the name of Jesus, Lord and Savior of all, I pray. Amen.*

Trusting Jesus

May the LORD repay you for what you have done. May you be richly rewarded by the LORD, the God of Israel, under whose wings you have come to take refuge (Ruth 2:12).

Scripture: **Ruth 2:5-12; Ruth 3:9-11**
Song: **"Trust and Obey"**

Sam was Jewish, but as a young man he was baptized into Christ through the witness of a friend. Because of his family's hostility toward his new faith, Sam had to move from home and forfeit his inheritance, leaving him almost penniless. But Sam trusted Jesus. He labored as a janitor, and his church friends became his new family.

Sam reminds me of Ruth, a Moabite widow. Ruth courageously left country and family for the sake of Naomi, her Jewish mother-in-law. She went with her to Israel, turning her back on the gods of Moab to worship the living God. And God provided for them through the kind actions of Naomi's kinsman, Boaz. The greatest blessing came when Boaz married Ruth, and she became the great-grandmother of King David—and, thus, an ancestor of Christ (see Matthew 1:5).

As for Ruth, so for Sam. God met all of Sam's daily needs and blessed him with a godly wife. Together they have created a Christ-centered home. Ruth and Sam trusted God, living with courage and faith, and God rewarded their actions. Would you have done the same? Would I?

Father in Heaven, *may I always seek and follow Your guidance through prayer, Your Word, and godly friends. In Jesus' name I pray. Amen.*

Bow Gratefully

But I, by your great mercy, will come into your house; in reverence will I bow down toward your holy temple (Psalm 5:7).

Scripture: **Psalm 5**
Song: **"Holy, Holy, Holy!"**

I observed an 18-year-old, who had just graduated from high school, go to the end of a 400 foot pier. He sat down with his long legs dangling over the edge and for 25 minutes watched the sun set. Transfixed by what God was doing, he didn't move a muscle. Upon returning to his backyard, he saw me on my next-door deck and hollered out across the way, "God did good, didn't He?" He had just watched a miracle, knew who was responsible for it, and was bowing down in his heart.

The psalmist begins with God's mercy toward him . . . and soon moves to his reverence for God. That reverence puts him in a holy place of worship, on his knees. He bows before the God of his blessings. Aware of who God is and what God does—he humbles himself. He is deferential because he is grateful. God's grace conditioned his heart for reverence and awe.

Here's the key to it all: The shortest distance to reverence is gratitude. May I walk that path today.

Dear Father, *thank You for being so good to me. Everything I have comes from You. I see the blessings and know the giver. Everywhere I go, You get me there. Praise to You, in Jesus' name. Amen.*

March 29–31. **Philip Barnhart,** who has retired to Florida, ministered to eight churches over a period of 45 years. He has written several books and numerous articles.

Tell Your God-Story

I will give you words and wisdom that none of your adversaries will be able to resist or contradict (Luke 21:15).

Scripture: Luke 21:12-19
Song: "I Love to Tell the Story"

We come to Jesus and know His great love for us. Our hearts are warm with the knowledge of God's grace and goodness. We have a bold impression of God's touch, deep in our souls, and we want to share it with others.

Then comes a crisis of confidence. Who are we to speak of such things? What could we possibly say? We get lost in the gripping web of Moses' self doubt and Gideon's low self-esteem. Down the slippery slope of Amos's disclaimer we go. The dithering tone of Jeremiah's excuse becomes our own.

We may need a spiritual gift to be an evangelist, but not to be a witness. What we need to be a witness is a love for God and a passion for God's people. Wanderers across the wilderness of life know about the oasis and tell their fellow travelers where it is.

So, witnessing can be summed up in four words: tell your God-story. In other words, everyone who knows God has a God-story.

Almighty and everlasting God, I saw You shine on another's face, heard You sing in another's heart, and listened to words about You from another's mouth. Someone showed me to You. Someone told me about You. Someone led me to You. May I go forth now to do the same. In the name of the Father, the Son, and the Holy Spirit, I pray. Amen.

Be What You Are

You are the light of the world. A city on a hill cannot be hidden (Matthew 5:14).

Scripture: **Matthew 5:11-16**
Song: **"Let the Lower Lights Be Burning"**

I remember the excitement in our country when John Glenn piloted a space capsule around the earth. As the astronaut looked down upon Earth on the dark night of February 20, 1962, he saw an unusual glow from a particular spot below him. He was told that the people of Perth, Australia, had turned on all their lights in his honor. Immediately he asked to send a message to those citizens: "Thank you for lighting the way!"

Jesus says we are the light of the world. This is not something we aspire to, or hope for, but something we *are*. To be a Christian is to be a bringer of light.

Darkness cannot drive out darkness. Only light does that. Nothing dispels darkness like light. In fact, the more light that shines, the less darkness there is.

People can find joy in the darkest times, if somebody turns the light on. When Christians are at their best, people who walk in darkness see a great light. And that light is none other than the Savior shining out from within them.

Dear Lord, You are the light of the world, and thus so am I. It is only when I am touched and transformed by You that I shine. When I lose contact with You, my light goes out, for I can only be a reflection of Your eternal glory. In Your precious name I pray. Amen.

DEVOTIONS®

Gary Allen, Editor

*B*ut I . . . will
come into your
house; in
reverence will
I bow down
toward your
holy temple.

—Psalm 5:7

APRIL

Photo © Lastdays 1
Dreamstime.com

DEVOTIONS® is published quarterly by Standard Publishing, Cincinnati, Ohio, www.standardpub.com.
© 2009 by Standard Publishing. All rights reserved. Topics based on the Home Daily Bible Readings,
International Sunday School Lessons. © 2006 by the Committee on the Uniform Series. Printed in the
U.S.A. All Scripture quotations, unless otherwise indicated, are taken from the HOLY BIBLE, NEW
INTERNATIONAL VERSION®. NIV®. Copyright © 1973, 1978, 1984 by International Bible Society.
Used by permission of Zondervan. All rights reserved. Where noted, Scripture quotations are from the
following: *King James Version* (KJV), public domain.

April 1

Talk, in Order to Hear

Answer me, O LORD, out of the goodness of your love; in your great mercy turn to me (Psalm 69:16).

Scripture: **Psalm 69:16-20, 29-33**
Song: **"Great God, with Love You Heard My Voice"**

David *talks* to God because he wants to *hear* from God. He appeals to God's love and mercy, believing these divine attributes will turn God toward him. David is convinced that when he confidently talks to God, he will certainly hear from God.

Hearing from God depends on talking to God. Talking to God is prayer. So if you can talk, you can pray.

Think about how easy it is to talk on your cell phone. Prayer is your cell phone to God. It instantly puts you in God's presence, where you can talk with God about whatever is important to you at the moment.

In recent years, a certain company has captured attention with its phone ads. Those ads depict people in every imaginable place on earth asking the question, "Can you hear me now?" When we pray, God hears and answers us now. No one gets a busy signal on God's prayer line, whether He answers with a yes, no, or wait.

Dear God, to whom I can talk anytime and anywhere, thank You for never putting me on hold. I can always count on Your open line. You answer, listen, and speak to me. You breathe Your will into my heart. Nothing blesses me more than that. Thank You, through Christ my Lord. Amen.

April 1–4. **Philip Barnhart,** who has retired to Florida, ministered to eight churches over a period of 45 years. He has written several books and numerous articles.

Best Side? Inside!

Leaning back against Jesus, he asked him, "Lord, who is it?" (John 13:25).

Scripture: **John 13:21-30**
Song: **"Is There Ambition in My Heart?"**

Jesus had forecast a betrayer in their circle, and one of the disciples wanted to know who it was. According to another account, the question was individual and personal, "They were very sad and began to say to him one after the other, 'Surely not I, Lord?'" (Matthew 26:22).

Each (except Judas) must have expected a negative answer, for they didn't perceive themselves as defectors. They had looked inside themselves and found no betrayal there. No matter what was on the outside, the truth was on the inside.

When God's people built the tabernacle in the wilderness, there was nothing rich in its outside appearance. The costly things were all within, its covering of rough badger skin giving no hint.

Similarly, the best side of us is the inside of us. We are made in God's image, and that likeness is inside ourselves. That is, we too are *personal*, having intellect, emotions, and will. The eternal is internal. The goodness we desire to show on the outside exists on the inside. May we let it shine through.

Lord God Almighty, *who looks on my inside and knows what is there, keep the internal of me aligned to the eternal of You. Be strong in my heart and work from the inside out. Through Christ I pray. Amen.*

Hear Your Name!

Jesus said to her, "Mary" (John 20:16).

Scripture: **John 20:11-18**
Song: **"In the Garden"**

On that inaugural resurrection morning, Jesus turned to one whose eyes flooded with tears, her heart crumbling to pieces. He said to her, "Mary." Before that, He had stopped a parade in His honor to look up to the top of a sycamore tree. There a tax collector perched with his expensive robes pulled up around his knees. He said to him, "Zacchaeus."

Long after that meeting with Mary on resurrection morning, Jesus would confront a religious fanatic on the way to Damascus, one intent on eliminating the new Way. Jesus would say to him, "Saul." He knew and called each by name.

One time a man came to the church where I was the minister and asked me a tough question. The answer I gave subsequently defined my theology and my life. He asked, "What is the greatest theological thought you ever had?" I mulled it over and then answered: "The fact that Jesus knows my name." You see, "He calls his own sheep by name and leads them out" (John 10:3).

Dear God, I stand amazed that You know who I am. There is no uncertainty in Your heart and no ambiguity in Your spirit about that. Nothing about me is vague to You. You know my sitting down and my rising up and all that transpires in between. Thank You for loving me, just the same. In the precious name of Jesus I pray. Amen.

Perfect Attendance

In a little while you will see me no more, and then after a little while you will see me (John 16:16).

Scripture: **John 16:16-20**
Song: **"He Lives"**

On a hot day in Rio de Janeiro, a tour group stopped to look up at the huge statue of Christ on a mountaintop. The Lord of All stands there with His arms outstretched as though blessing those below.

In the group was a mother and her small child. As they stood there looking, clouds suddenly moved in and obscured the statue. Seeing this, the child exclaimed, "Look, Mommy! He was there, but then the clouds came. Will He be there when they go away?"

The little one's mother took a small hand in hers and said, "Of course, dear, God is always with us, even on the cloudy days." When Jesus ascended to Heaven, He promised to come back. So, in "a little while" we will definitely see Him.

In the meantime, we are promised the presence of the Lord in our hearts. God started by walking with His human creatures in a garden; now He lives inside us. We can't go anywhere apart from His presence, so we are never truly alone. We might say that God "keeps us company" on a daily basis and is closer to us than we are to ourselves.

Lord, when there is no cloud in the day, no flame at night, You are with me. In my life You have perfect attendance. Thanks, in Jesus' name. Amen.

Witness with Washing

A new command I give you: Love one another. As I have loved you, so you must love one another. By this all men will know that you are my disciples (John 13:34, 35).

Scripture: **John 13:31-35**
Song: **"Angry Words"**

It's easy to love the lovable, but what about the ones who are hard to love? I find it quite difficult to love those who are hurting me, for example. But that's exactly what Jesus says we must do. We must do it, that is, if we are to let the world know we're His genuine disciples.

That witness often starts with how we speak to each other. Thus we must choose our words carefully, stop and think about what we truly want to reveal—His love. Becoming defensive doesn't allow us to reflect love. But speaking softly and gently, showing we care, does indeed convey concern for our neighbor, even when we're in serious conflict.

With our words we can actually serve one another. As Jesus served by washing the feet of His disciples, so we can serve by "washing with words." Tell a little girl that she is pretty, or offer an encouraging "high five" to the teen standing at the corner. What a witness it is to wash one another this way!

O Lord, help me to convey Your love throughout this day. And let it start with the very first words out of my mouth. In Jesus' name, amen.

April 5–10. **Barbara Robinson** is an author, educator, and student in the Christian Writers Guild. She lives with her husband and pets in St. Cloud, Florida.

Where the Heart Is

Store up for yourselves treasures in heaven . . . For where your treasure is, there your heart will be also (Matthew 6:20, 21).

Scripture: **Matthew 6:19-24**
Song: **"We'll Never Say Goodbye"**

When I was 4 years old, I lived in a rented apartment house. I felt rich living in my make-believe world of fairy tales, in sunshine and fresh air, swinging on my board-and-rope swing under a giant pecan tree. My world was happy and content. But all that changed when I lost my daddy on Christmas Day.

Lost and alone without a husband, Mom raised me on Bible verses and told me that Daddy was waiting for me in Heaven. I grew up poor, but rich in faith. Yet, over the years, the losses continued. I've lost my husband, my mother, and my baby sister.

Yet I've found that, though life is no fairy tale, neither is God's Word. I've been comforted, knowing God plans to reunite all believers. He calls us all home when He is ready, and the loved ones who have gone before us wait for us there, very personal treasures above.

We only live in our temporary earthly home a short while. Let us look forward to our eternal heavenly home with Jesus, our true treasure.

Lord God Almighty, I no longer live and grieve without hope, all because of the wonderful promises in Your Word. Thank You so much for the rewards of obedience while I await the day when I will see You, face to face. In the name of the Father, the Son, and the Holy Spirit, amen.

Do No Harm!

Love does no harm to its neighbor. Therefore love is the fulfill-ment of the law (Romans 13:10).

Scripture: **Romans 13:8-10**
Song: **"Walk in the Light"**

Over many years in the classroom, I've taught some kids who weren't too easy to love. In fact, some of them seemed determined to resist any kindness. Many lacked the superficial "lovable appearance," social skills, or man-ners of others who appeared more lovable on the surface. When I scratched that surface and penetrated it—no mat-ter the child's appearance—I was able to give and receive genuine love.

According to the apostle Paul, the practice of love is like the practice of medicine. The first rule in both is: Do no harm.

What will that mean for you today, in practical terms? For me, it means remembering that no matter how much love I give, I can never give enough; an outstanding debt of love is always owed to others. For I myself have been grasped, first, by an unconditional love from the Lord himself. As French author François de La Rochefoucauld once said: "There is only one sort of love, but there are a thousand copies."

Dear Heavenly Father, guide me to walk in Your footsteps today, that I may love even the unlovable. Show me how I can be a better neighbor and make a difference in the lives of others. Most of all, Lord, allow me to share Your good news with sincere love. I pray in Jesus' holy name. Amen.

Your Next Neighbor?

A Samaritan, as he traveled, came where the man was; and when he saw him, he took pity on him. He went to him and bandaged his wounds, pouring on oil and wine. Then he put the man on his own donkey, took him to an inn and took care of him (Luke 10:33, 34).

Scripture: **Luke 10:29-37**
Song: **"Who Is Thy Neighbor?"**

Distracted by the fine, delicate leaves of a dogwood tree, I stepped off the pavement and fell flat on my face. God spared my teeth, but I was afraid to stand. In pain and uncertain if I had broken bones, I felt the hands of someone lifting me as others rushed by without pause. I looked into the kind face of an elderly man; he helped me to my feet. I could see the concern and pity in his eyes.

I had scratches and "sidewalk burn" on my face, and my mouth was bleeding. But I had a loving Samaritan, a complete stranger, to help me find medical attention. Thanks be to him and to God!

Today's Scripture reminds me of the many "neighbors" I've encountered in passing over the years—seemingly chance acquaintances who've had mercy on me nonetheless. I'm also reminded that Jesus said to do "likewise." Can I? Will I? In fact, is that a potential neighbor walking toward me this very moment?

Heavenly Father, *You have told me to have mercy and take pity on others. Give me eyes to see the hurt all around me. And give me the wisdom to know how to respond in Your name. Through Christ, amen.*

Be Merciful to Enemies

I tell you who hear me: Love your enemies, do good to those who hate you, bless those who curse you, pray for those who mistreat you (Luke 6:27, 28).

Scripture: **Luke 6:27-36**
Song: **"Lord, While Afar Our Brothers Fight"**

My little friend's swing set sat untouched in her yard. No loving father took time to push her. She said her daddy was busy making a living—that her daddy had a much more important job than my daddy did.

Maybe she wasn't a friend after all! She'd tease me and brag about how she'd always have so many nice things. But all I'd ever have was what Daddy could put together for me with a board and some rope. I ran crying to Mom.

I suppose I didn't realize that the girl was hurting deep inside. She truly missed her father as she watched my dad push me on a board-and-rope swing.

When people strike out, they're hurting. That is when we are called to pray for them, to do good to them, to bless them in every way we can. Taking this biblical approach we'll actually grow in faith and endurance. As Edwin Chapin put it: "Never does the human soul appear so strong as when it foregoes revenge and dares to forgive an injury."

Dear God, give me the strength and self-control I need to turn my enemies into friends. Some would love to see me fail, but teach me to forgive, forget, and let go of past wrongs. And please send Your Comforter to those who harbor deep hurts within them. Thank You, in Jesus' name. Amen.

He Lives—the Spirit of Truth!

I will pray the Father, and he shall give you another Comforter, that he may abide with you for ever; even the Spirit of truth; . . . but ye know him; for he dwelleth with you, and shall be in you (John 14:16, 17, *King James Version*).

Scripture: **John 14:15-17**
Song: **"Be Still and Know"**

My heavenly Father sent me a Comforter; I thank God He was with me when I lost my sister. I went to my knees beside my bed when I received the news of her death. His gentle touch was like a dove descending upon my shoulder. As I prayed for her, I felt comfort and peace. I knew she was with God because He had prepared a place for her, and then called her home.

Yes, I know this Spirit of truth. He lives within me, and I've been blessed and comforted by Him. He is there when I need Him, like a hand on my shoulder, reassuring me of God's presence and love.

Historian Edward Gibbon once said, "I was never less alone than when by myself." At first that sounds a bit strange, doesn't it? But consider: When we who know the Lord pull away from the crowd and find a place of solitude, we're responding to a heavenly calling: "Be still and know that I am God" (Psalm 46:10). In those quiet moments we can experience the touch of the Comforter, the one who lets us know that we never walk alone.

Dear Father, *thank You for sending Your Holy Spirit to dwell within in me as a down payment on Heaven. Praise to You, through Christ. Amen.*

A Love That Shines Bright

Whoever loves his brother lives in the light (1 John 2:10).

Scripture: **1 John 2:9-11, 15-17**
Song: **"Shine Jesus Shine"**

My friend Kathy knows two families who each lost a son under tragic circumstances. Her cousin lost a 7-year-old son when an older boy gave him a push and he fell into a rushing creek and drowned. Even though the accident took place over 30 years ago, Kathy rarely has a conversation with her cousin when her son's name is not mentioned. She is bitter because the boy who pushed him is now a grown man with a wife and children. The dark cloud of grief so overshadows her that it has damaged her relationships with family and friends.

The other couple lost a son in a car accident caused by a drunk driver. With God's help they worked through their grief and forgave the man who killed him. They became active in Mothers Against Drunk Drivers. They are available to comfort other parents who have lost a child to a drunk driver. Instead of gloom their lives shine with love for others who are hurting.

Hating another person, no matter how justified the emotion may seem, is never good fo us. It will cause us to stumble through life in a dark fog of bitterness. But allowing God to take away our hatred and replace it with His love will enable us to be a light shining in the darkness for others to see.

Father, remove all hatred from my heart. Help me to forgive others as You have forgiven me, so that I can walk in the light of Jesus. Amen.

April 11. **Cheryl J. Frey** is the owner of an editorial services in Rochester, NY. She loves to spend time with her family.

He Loves You, Warts and All

We also rejoice in God through our Lord Jesus Christ, through whom we have now received reconciliation (Romans 5:11).

Scripture: **Roman 5:1-11**
Song: "Our Cities Cry to You, O God"

Grace is hard to understand because we live in a world where a great deal of what we get is what we have earned. A salesperson sells more? Her salary increases. A batter improves his average? His next contract reflects it. A pass receiver starts dropping the football? He is dropped from the team.

But then into the game of life steps a coach called God, and we are now members of a very special team. He sets before us His rules, His divine hopes that we will live better and be better. Then when we believers falter, fall, and fail, He points to the cross and says, "Don't worry, I won't drop you. I love you anyway. Nothing you do will make me stop loving you and forgiving you. Others may give up on you, but I'm your loving Father, and that isn't the way I work."

The cross! Consider it. Look at Jesus hanging there and remember: He did not die there because He was a sinner. Rather, He gave His life because we are.

Father, help me never forget that grace isn't just what I do but who You are. And may I begin each day with Your wonderful promise of reconciliation echoing in my ear. Through Your precious Son, Jesus. Amen.

April 12–18. **Neil Wyrick** is an ordained minister, religious dramatist, and evangelist who has authored nine books. He lives in Miami, Florida.

Do You Believe?

You refuse to come to me to have life. . . . If you believed Moses, you would believe me, for he wrote about me (John 5:40, 46).

Scripture: **John 5:39-47**
Song: **"Believe and Obey"**

It happened over 2,000 years ago. It happens still, this refusal to come to Jesus despite all the evidence that He is who He says He is: the Son of God. Without these words, without this divine essence stirring our souls, we are nothing. And if you do not truly believe this, your faith becomes little more than a hobby, as you pick up a bit of a religious tidbit here and a little religious tidbit there, but no substance.

I believe—and it is an explanation of who I have decided to be, as well as who I have decided to follow.

I believe—and behind these words is my Christian conversion already accomplished (or perhaps your own Christian conversion still just over the horizon).

Believe that no man can serve two masters, though many try. Believe, and therefore the Lord is your shepherd. Believe, and therefore in the Lord put all your trust, in full surrender.

It is one thing to see through a glass darkly. It is something else to be totally, terribly blind. Believe, and therefore make a joyful noise unto the Lord.

Almighty God, help me "Shout for joy to the Lord" (Psalm 100:1) and refuse to allow the weakness of a diminished faith to set in. In the name of Jesus, I pray. Amen.

Which Law?

I tell you that unless your righteousness surpasses that of the Pharisees and the teachers of the law, you will certainly not enter the kingdom of heaven (Matthew 5:20).

Scripture: **Matthew 5:17-20**
Song: **"There Is a Redeemer"**

Jesus was firmly into both law and love. He offered salvation by grace while at the same time setting up impossible goals. Was He then a contradiction, or was He instead the Son of God, telling it like it is? That with God nothing is impossible, even total forgiveness for ongoing sins? How else can we enter Heaven? Certainly we cannot earn our way into Heaven. If there were a magic number that guaranteed our admission, for instance 795, would we find ourselves permanently behind the eight ball if we ended up with a total of only 794?

Yet, saved by grace, do we not still owe God our best? This is not a contradiction. It is a study in compassion: the law of law and the law of love. He loves us, and He commands us to love Him and each other in a way that is greater than the law.

"I have been crucified with Christ and I no longer live, but Christ lives in me" (Galatians 2:20). It is that simple. It is that profound.

Lord, help me to both feel and better understand, the magnificence of the law of love, the forgiveness on the cross, and the challenge to bring my best before You, my Master and my King. May all I say and do this day bring praise and glory to Your name. Through Christ I pray. Amen.

Hypocrisy Isn't Hip

Woe to you Pharisees, because you give God a tenth of your mint, rue and all other kinds of garden herbs, but you neglect justice and the love of God. You should have practiced the latter without leaving the former undone (Luke 11:42).

Scripture: **Luke 11:42-44**
Song: **"Christ, You Call Us All to Service"**

Jesus underlines the dangers of hypocrisy, naming some of the many ways it can come to call. And He warns—lest our hypocrisies stay around as permanent house guests in our lives.

The Pharisees certainly weren't pikers when it came to making the art of living difficult. Six hundred exacting rules for proper living can hardly be called a lesson in restraint! Indeed, it could be said that without an exceedingly good memory, a person was absolutely sure to disobey one—and more than one—of their laws on a regular basis.

Pure and simple, it is easier to memorize the Ten Commandments and have perfect church attendance than to simply be . . . kind. In fact, it is possible even to memorize Matthew, Mark, Luke, and John and still be a miserable human being. Hypocrisy comes in many forms, none of them good.

O Lord, save me from hypocrisy. How subtle it is! So keep me from living in front of a distorted mirror that allows me to think what is twisted is not twisted at all. Help me to see where I am being hypocritical, and give me the fortitude to change. In Jesus' name, amen.

Ownership? By What or Whom?

He who belongs to God hears what God says. The reason you do not hear is that you do not belong to God (John 8:47).

Scripture: Luke 8:39-47
Song: "How Firm a Foundation"

None of us have become who we are in a moment. Little by little we have chosen paths that lead to becoming a mature servant of God. Yet we all know that it is easier to take a nap than it is to take on life's challenges with courage. According to Jesus, listening is a part of the challenge. We must learn to hear God. But, of course, we must actually belong to Him first, placing ourselves on the road to ever more change and growth through His Spirit.

I've noticed that I am willing to change . . . when I can be in control of the process. But the change God calls me to is the transformation that will occur as I learn to walk with Him, moment by moment. It's easy for me to make a resolution and try to follow it. It's harder to give myself to God's will, long before I know exactly what He will ask me to do. In other words, it's not just resolutions but a relationship. That is what it is all about.

"O come, let us worship and bow down, let us kneel before the Lord our maker!" (Psalm 95:6, 7, *King James Version*). Here lies the beginning of knowledge of our Lord and His ownership of us.

Most merciful God, improve my hearing. Help me move the ear of my soul closer to Your eternal voice. Then it will be harder to ignore Your commandments. Through Christ my Lord, amen.

Love: A Way of Living

I pray that you, being rooted and established in love, may have power, together with all the saints, to grasp how wide and long and high and deep is the love of Christ (Ephesians 3:17, 18).

Scripture: **Ephesians 3:14-19**
Song: **"God's Love Made Visible"**

"Wide and long and high and deep is the love of Christ." What a vision! It describes the eternal compassion of our Lord, and its boundless measure fills me with awe. God, your God and mine, is a celestial chef offering an unbelievable feast of love and forgiveness. Therefore, sit at the throne of grace and enjoy every morsel of this eternal meal—this eternal love.

And why argue with the biblical menu? It is all there, written down. And we placed our order when we affirmed our faith at baptism. So, now: eat, drink, enjoy and be merry with your forgiven, God-saved life.

I accept this gift of boundless, ever-expanding love with the simple faith of a child of God. In His awesome presence, I am humbled, driven to my knees to simply say: "Jesus loves me, this I know, for the Bible tells me so" (Anna B. Warner).

Dear Heavenly Father, help me to survive with joy the challenges of life today. Remind me that I carry with me a backpack filled with Your love and constant concern. In the name of Your Son, my Savior, I pray. Amen.

Brother's Keeper?

Love your neighbor as yourself (Matthew 22:39).

Scripture: **Matthew 22:34-40**
Song: **"Just a Closer Walk with Thee"**

If we could somehow love our neighbor as much as we love ourselves, would we would love them *twice as much* as we do now? Not that we do not want to follow this commandment. It's just that loving ourselves comes so much more naturally, right?

If you're like me, you tend to fall back on the ancient words of Cain: "Am I my brother's keeper?" And the answer to this, if we listen closely to Jesus, is clear: Yes!

Love is the great unifier. And to practice the kind of love our Lord is speaking of, we'll likely need a personality change—more patience, more kindness, more forbearance.

Here's the toughest part for me: We're not talking about a few additional good deeds or a few extra Christian courtesies. Instead, it's no more overinflated ego trips; it's making my mouth smaller, so I'll have trouble fitting my foot in it.

Perhaps one of the secrets to practicing the kind of love our Lord teaches is this: Concentrate on how much we are alike—in our needs, in our dreams, and in our essential sinnerhood. As someone has said, "The ground is level at the cross."

Lord, teach me that true loneliness comes when I have forgotten how to love. Let me be the first to reach out today. In Jesus' name, amen.

April 19

Who Wants to Know?

Praise awaits you, O God, in Zion . . . Where morning dawns and evening fades you call forth songs of joy (Psalm 65:1, 8).

Scripture: **Psalm 65:1-8**
Song: **"I Will Search"**

A busload of teens sing as they head to a Friday night football game: "Everywhere we go, people want to know: who we are, so we tell them. We are the Knights, the mighty, mighty Knights!" They shout in high expectation. But should their team lose, the return bus ride home will be hushed and silent.

The psalmist tells us that our God, who hears and answers our prayers, will not fall silent. In fact, He calls forth joyful songs. And His mighty acts of creation and redemption are certainly worthy of constant, noisy praise. Let such songs ring out through the universe, without ceasing!

Since my God is so great, I wonder if He couldn't use me as a witness to His goodness today? In other words, could this be said of me: "Everywhere I *go*, people want to *know*: who I am, so I tell them. I am a child of the king, the mighty, mighty king!"

O Lord, who hears all prayers, You hear me. You forgive me. Your love and care toward me are gracious, relentless, and merciful. I worship You with all my heart, and I come before You to be transformed into Your image. In the holy name of Jesus, my Lord and Savior, I pray. Amen.

April 19–25. **SanDee Hardwig,** writer, tutor, prison minister, lives in Brown Deer, Wisconsin, with her two cats, Angel and Odie.

Rescued, Grateful!

Great is Your love toward me; you have delivered me from the depths of the grave (Psalm 86:13).

Scripture: **Psalm 86:8-13**
Song: **"Jesus Paid It All"**

I doubled over and slipped under the water once more. It happened fast, there was no time to holler "Help!" But someone dragged me, coughing and sputtering, onto the beach. I couldn't thank Eddie enough. "Just glad I was there," he said. Later, I shouted at the stars, "I'm *alive!*"

Jesus took all our sins upon himself before He died on the cross for us. We can hardly express our gratitude, and we certainly can't repay Him. But we can praise Him from the depths of our being, just as the psalmist did. And we can share with others what He has done for us.

Henry Ward Beecher once said: "Gratitude is the fairest blossom which springs from the soul." I know it's true. I've been rescued physically, emotionally, and spiritually through the years, and I am so grateful to God.

I imagine you've had some close calls too? Life on earth is fragile and, as the apostle Paul said, we die daily. Nevertheless, our great God gives us victory over every deadly peril we face—even, in the end, triumphing over the grave itself.

*How can I thank You, **Lord?** Nothing I can say or do seems enough. I can only bow before You in grateful praise and ask You to help me reach out to others with Your salvation. Give me the courage to do it—and the wisdom to do it in ways that would please You. In Jesus' name, amen.*

Prison Walk

He will teach us his ways, so that we may walk in his paths (Isaiah 2:3).

Scripture: **Isaiah 2:1-4**
Song: **"Show Me Your Way"**

Otis lives in a high-security prison. I always look forward to visiting him. He encourages me, never complaining of his circumstances. There's a peace about him that's hard to explain; his face shines with it.

Thank God for the changes I've seen in Otis over the years. He's a living example of Isaiah's words: The Lord will teach us. As any of us learn from God, we will naturally begin "walking" in the paths He sets before us. That's what I see taking place in Otis, one who could have chosen, instead, to let bitterness shrivel his soul.

What awesome promises the prophet declared! In the last days, countless hearts will be moved to worship the Lord. Not just a few here and there, not just a lonely prisoner or a long-forgotten widow or a struggling teenager—but "many peoples" and "all nations" will finally stream to the house of God in worship.

I long for that day, don't you? Until then, let us discover our spiritual gifts and use them in the Lord's service. And may we enjoy the blessed fellowship of those who already sincerely worship Him, no matter where they live.

My Lord God, thank You for Your patience with me. Keep teaching me Your ways, so I may walk in Your paths, one day at a time. In the precious name of Jesus I lift up my heart in praise. Amen.

Let Us Stand, and Sing

Standing beside the sea . . . They held harps given them by God and sang . . . the song of the Lamb (Revelation 15:2, 3).

Scripture: **Revelation 15:2b-4**
Song: **"Glory to the Lamb"**

How I long to go back to Benidorm, Spain, on the Mediterranean Sea! I squinted in that glorious light, even with sunglasses, walking on sparkling sand. Deep blue waves, with white surrounding cliffs, glittered brightly. Even now, when I close my eyes and envision that beach (28 years later), a peace washes over me.

Last week at church our worship team sang, "Glory to the Lamb. For He is glorious and worthy to be praised, the Lamb upon the throne; and unto Him we lift our voice in praise." Their voices and instruments poured celestial-like sounds throughout the sanctuary. There was a moment when everyone seemed to sense God's presence. When the last notes ended, a quiet peace spread through the congregation.

These two memories are like a prelude to Heaven for me. Maybe one day you and I will stand by the sea of glass and sing eternal praises together. If it is such a wonderful thing to do on earth, how great will it be on that other shore?

Lord God Almighty, *I lift my voice to praise Your holy name! May Your will be done on earth as it is in Heaven. Help me find the words to glorify You, not only on Sunday, but all week long. I do want to be among those who reign victorious through Your power, O Lord. In Jesus' name, amen.*

There He Is

When did we see you sick or in prison and go to visit you?
(Matthew 25:39).

Scripture: **Matthew 25:31-40**
Song: **"Spirit, Touch Your Church"**

Otis misses his daughter, Kylira. He hadn't seen her for seven years; she's 9 years old now. His love for her motivates him to move forward in rehabilitation, while he sends letters and even crochets gifts for her.

Then one day, when I brought Kylira to visit her dad in prison, she was shy at first. They played cards, shared riddles, took turns reading, and had photos taken. Kylira hugged her father tightly when we left. What a blessing to see them together!

Jesus said, "I was sick and you looked after me, I was in prison and you came to visit me" (v. 36). The people wondered how that could be. But Jesus explained, "Whatever you did for one of the least of these brothers of mine, you did for me" (v. 40).

Imagine ministering to Jesus through acts of kindness to others. Do we try to make it more difficult? More complicated? Perhaps our longing for closeness with Jesus really is just that simple: to watch for a person in need. And then to step forward with help, seeing the face of the Lord himself, right there before us.

*Thank You, **Jesus,** for Your wonderful parables and for the call to serve You through serving others. Help me recognize the many opportunities that will surely come my way today! I pray in Your holy name. Amen.*

Payment Is Coming

When you give a banquet, invite the poor, the crippled, the lame, the blind, and you will be blessed. Although they cannot repay you, you will be repaid at the resurrection of the righteous (Luke 14:13, 14).

Scripture: **Luke 14:7-14**
Song: **"Satisfy My Soul"**

Here's a recent e-mail prayer request that came to Doug, a friend of mine (with names changed).

> Pray for spiritual encouragement, healing, and provision for John and Mary. They willingly work every odd job they can find. Side by side, they dig ditches, tear out walls, hang drywall, paint, sell belongings and blood plasma, so they can move to a place with more job opportunities. This couple will be homeless in two weeks, if no one takes them in. Do you know of any organizations that help released inmates and families? Please send contact information.

After prayerful consideration and no expectation of repayment from complete strangers, Doug responded, "How much do you need for a deposit and first month's rent?"

Almighty and gracious Father, guide me to those You would have me bless. Give me wisdom, discernment, and a pure heart—expecting no earthly reward in return. Help me keep my eyes on Your Son's own self-giving service, and make me a better servant of Him! In the name of the Father, the Son, and the Holy Spirit, I pray. Amen.

Just Say Yes!

The servant came back and reported this to his master. Then the owner of the house became angry and ordered his servant, "Go out quickly into the streets and alleys of the town and bring in the poor, the crippled, the blind and the lame" (Luke 14:21).

Scripture: **Luke 14:15-24**
Song: **"Better Is One Day"**

Janet, DeAnna, and Kitty serve at a homeless shelter. They asked volunteers to invite some residents to lunch so they could tour beautiful Holy Hill, a nearby monastery, after church. The guys eagerly accepted the invitation. One even brought his teenage daughter who lived with her grandparents. Who could have imagined how blessed both guests and hosts would be that day!

When Jesus spoke of a banquet, His hearers associated the future kingdom of Heaven with a great feast. Everyone would be invited, of course. But only those with open hearts would actually end up in attendance.

That is the key to knowing and fellowshiping with God forever: responding with an open heart to His open invitation. It really doesn't matter whether we have a beautiful home of our own or we are "between homes." The Lord calls each of us to dwell with Him. Our job is simply to say, "Yes!"

*Thank You for the invitation to follow You, **Lord.** I accept, but I mess up a lot. Forgive me! And keep reminding me that I am nothing without You. Through Christ I pray. Amen.*

A Future with Hope

You will seek me and find me when you seek me with all your heart (Jeremiah 29:13).

Scripture: **Jeremiah 29:10-14**
Song: **"Ask for the Showers of Blessing"**

Due to alcoholism in my family, from my late teens and most of my twenties my life was in constant upheaval. I married at age 18. But by 24, I'd had three children and a marriage that ended bitterly. I'd attended church sporadically, at my husband's family's urging. All of my children had been baptized, and I took them to Sunday school.

Most often I did not stay for worship. You see, my prayers were bitter, overflowing with this one, big question: *"Why me?"*

One day my minister came for a visit, and I told him about my feelings and my prayers. In a gentle, quiet voice he asked, "Have you sincerely prayed for help?"

That question changed my life.

I began by asking for help and attending both Sunday school and worship. Soon, I was eagerly looking forward not only to Sundays but Wednesday's prayer and Bible study. Not only had I found the Lord; He had first found me—and carried me through the most difficult times.

O God, thank You for carrying me when I could hardly take another step in my life. You are the greatest! In Jesus' name I pray. Amen.

April 26–30. **Judy Verberkmoes** writes from her home in Moultrie, Georgia, where she enjoys reading good books and studying the Bible in depth.

Faithful Servant

To one he gave five talents of money, to another two talents, and to another one talent, each according to his ability. Then he went on his journey (Matthew 25:15).

Scripture: **Matthew 25:14-21**
Song: **"Jerusalem, My Happy Home"**

The Lord blesses us believers with various spiritual gifts. It's up to us to discover what our gifts are, and then to put them to good use in mutual ministry. Clearly, we are not to "cover up" these gifts or ignore them.

For many years I wondered what my spiritual gift was. Then one day, while I was at work, a family member came up to me and quietly said: "Your gift of taking care of terminally ill persons is a true blessing. And you are blessing not just to the patients, but to their families, as well."

I had become a nursing assistant and gradually became a private-duty sitter to terminally ill patients. Working with these courageous folks—sometimes for only a few days and sometimes for a year or longer—I truly did not realize my concern and caring was a gift from God. I just knew that deep down inside, it felt right for me to give whatever comfort I could.

Do you know what your gift is? If so, I hope you have found a way to use it in the kingdom. Then the Lord will multiply your efforts in ways you never could have imagined.

O God, thank You for my gift. I pray You continue to bless each suffering family and help them know Your loving presence. In Jesus' name, amen.

Faithful in Very Little

Whoever can be trusted with very little can also be trusted with much, and whoever is dishonest with very little will also be dishonest with much (Luke 16:10).

Scripture: Luke 16:10-12
Song: "Faith in Jesus"

A while ago I read an interesting article from a New York City newspaper: four young friends, ages 9 through 12, felt sorry for a group of homeless people living in old buildings, boxes, and underpasses near the low-income housing area where these friends lived. On Friday, Saturday, and Sunday nights, each boy made two peanut butter and jelly sandwiches, wrapped up a few cookies, and made two separate lunches.

Then, with two parents acting as chaperones, they walked to a street near one of the underpasses and distributed the lunches. This sack-lunch foray quickly grew into actual meals, given regularly. Soon clothing and blankets were also donated by others who had heard of the young peoples' caring outreach.

This happened many years ago, and these children today are wonderful adult leaders in their own communities. They had begun by giving what little they could—and how quickly it grew!

O Jesus, remind me often that, as I share my gifts, You will entrust me with even more opportunity and responsibility. Please guide me in how best to use those gifts for Your glory. And keep me ever willing to take up self-sacrifice as You willing took up the cross for me. In Your name, amen.

Trustworthy Stewards

I care very little if I am judged by you or by any human court; indeed, I do not even judge myself. My conscience is clear, but that does not make me innocent. It is the Lord who judges me (1 Corinthians 4:3, 4).

Scripture: **1 Corinthians 4:1-5**
Song: **"Trusting Jesus, Wonderful Guide"**

Today is our 26th wedding anniversary. The past seven years have been wonderful, but the early years of the marriage weren't as great. You see, we both had a lot to learn about trust, and I'd always found it hard to rely on anyone at all. Finally, after many days and nights of prayer, I was at least able to trust in . . . God! (And, in time, I became willing to trust others.)

On my journey to trusting, I also realized that I should judge no one, but leave that up to God. And one reason for this, no doubt, is that our judgments of others is always a bit skewed in our own direction. As poet Henry Longfellow once put it: "We judge ourselves by what we feel capable of doing; while others judge us by what we have done."

The apostle Paul had clearly come to see something of the same. So, what a relief to know that I don't need to concern myself with others' perceptions of me—except to pray for them and give comfort where and when I can.

Dear Lord, *show me what to do today. Put words of comfort in my mouth and comfort in my hands. In all I do and say, keep me far from the dangers of judgmentalism. In the name of Jesus, my Savior, I pray. Amen.*

Pass On This Knowledge

Since the day we heard about you, we have not stopped praying for you and asking God to fill you with the knowledge of his will through all spiritual wisdom and understanding (Colossians 1:9).

Scripture: **Colossians 1:15-23**
Song: **"I Need Thee Every Hour"**

I know I'm speaking in analogies here—and of great mysteries—but sometimes I like to consider the Father-Son relationship in the Trinity. I wonder if it gave the Father a good feeling to, in a sense, "pass on" to his Son Jesus all His powers, just as any proud parent, eager to pass on good family values, business practices, or cooking recipes. The list of the things we want to pass on is endless. (Yes, I know, the analogy breaks down so quickly!)

We know that, in human history, the Lord had tried various ways to get us to change our ways, but we wouldn't listen. Then the Father sent the Son, who traveled over land and sea, teaching us how to live. Some listened, many did not. Jesus was betrayed, sentenced to death, and crucified. He died not for His sins, but for mine and yours. On the third day, keeping His promise, He rose again, was here a little while, and then ascended to Heaven.

These are the great truths of the gospel for us to pass on to our children. When we are filled with this knowledge, heavenly wisdom will follow.

Father, thank You for sending Your son to save me from my sin and teaching me Your statutes daily. In the name of the Holy Trinity, I pray. Amen.

My Prayer Notes

_____

_____

_____

_____

_____

_____

_____

_____

_____

_____

_____

_____

_____

_____

_____

_____

_____

_____

_____

_____

DEVOTIONS®

Gary Allen, Editor

You will seek me and find me when you seek me with all your heart.

—Jeremiah 29:13

MAY

Photo © Jake Fellbach
Dreamstime.com

DEVOTIONS® is published quarterly by Standard Publishing, Cincinnati, Ohio, www.standardpub.com. © 2009 by Standard Publishing. All rights reserved. Topics based on the Home Daily Bible Readings, International Sunday School Lessons. © 2006 by the Committee on the Uniform Series. Printed in the U.S.A. All Scripture quotations, unless otherwise indicated, are taken from the HOLY BIBLE, NEW INTERNATIONAL VERSION®. NIV®. Copyright © 1973, 1978, 1984 by International Bible Society. Used by permission of Zondervan. All rights reserved.Where noted, Scripture quotations are from the following, used with permission of the copyright holders, all rights reserved: *King James Version* (KJV), public domain. *New American Standard Bible* (NASB), © The Lockman Foundation, 1960, 1962, 1963, 1968, 1971, 1972, 1973, 1975, 1977, 1995.

Could You Admonish Me?

We proclaim him, admonishing and teaching everyone with all wisdom, so that we may present everyone perfect in Christ (Colossians 1:28).

Scripture: **Colossians 1:24-29**
Song: **"Preach the Gospel"**

The apostles certainly had a tremendous responsibility—teaching everyone! I wonder if the adults, when being taught, paid any more attention than do some of the teenagers in today's classrooms. But that's another story. I myself, a full-grown adult, don't like to hear certain things.

For example, I'd rather not be told to stop doing what pleases me. To be told that something is wrong and that we must not partake of it again just doesn't strike a pleasant chord with most of us. But isn't that what "admonishing" means? And the Scripture calls us to provide this blessed service for one another: "teach and admonish one another with all wisdom" (Colossians 3:16).

Today I pray that how I live my life will help others move forward toward maturity in Christ, the "perfection" Paul speaks of here. And if I become a hindrance to that blessed goal, I also pray (fearfully) that some loving sister in Christ will admonish me and call me to a better way.

Dear Lord, *grant me the courage to change my sinful ways and the strength to return again to You when I fail. In Jesus' name, amen.*

May 1, 2. **Judy Verberkmoes** writes from her home in Moultrie, Georgia, where she enjoys reading good books and studying the Bible in depth.

Extend That Peace

To the holy and faithful brothers in Christ at Colosse: Grace and peace to you from God our Father (Colossians 1:2).

Scripture: **Colossians 1:1-14**
Song; "I've Got Peace like a River"

What a glorious greeting Paul gave the Greeks waiting for him and Timothy. Grace, goodwill, peace, no worries or unrest. All this from God, *our* Father too, who still gives us all this and so very much more.

In churches like mine, we have a peace-sharing rite during worship before the offertory. We turn to those around us and say: "The peace of the Lord be with you." Echoes of the apostle, so long ago!

Ever wonder what you could do to extend peace to your neighbor—during the week,—in practical ways? Perhaps they are a young family and would appreciate grandparent-like involvement from someone (like me) who could read to their children on a busy afternoon. Or maybe a recently returned military vet might enjoy going to a ball game with a potential new mentor.

In so many ways we can extend grace and peace. Often such caring concern can lead to significant conversations about life and faith. But the thing is, we'll no doubt have to step out of our comfort zone to attempt such things. But when we do and see the results—what peace and joy for us, as well!

Dear Father, *make me aware of my neighbors' needs and guide me in my efforts to lead them to You. Through Christ my Savior, amen.*

It Works

It pleased God by the foolishness of preaching to save them that believe (1 Corinthians 1:21, *King James Version*).

Scripture: **1 Corinthians 1:20-25**
Song: **"Rescue the Perishing"**

The minister sensed my interest in becoming a minister myself. So he asked me to share a short, 15-minute message for the vesper hour. Vespers were held an hour before the regular evening service and were normally attended by only a handful of people. Since I had never preached before, my mentor showed much wisdom in scheduling this inexperienced teenager for the early service.

For my text I chose Proverbs 30:26, a verse about conies being "a feeble folk." Having no idea what conies were, I substituted squirrels. It was a monumental mistake. Half way into my message, a man raised his hand and blurted out that conies were rabbit-looking woodchucks that lived in high rocky crags, *not* pine trees.

I could feel my preaching career coming to an abrupt end. Flustered, I stumbled through the rest of my message and ended with a lengthy prayer—giving people ample time to leave the sanctuary. Instead, they lined up to thank me. And I discovered an interesting thing about the foolishness of preaching that day—it works.

Lord, help me to prepare well when I have to speak. But do make up the difference between my foolishness and Your wisdom. In Jesus' name, amen.

May 3–9. **Charles E. Harrel** ministered for more than 30 years before stepping aside to pursue a writing ministry. He enjoys digital photography and teaching.

Hey, Preacher!

We do not preach ourselves, but Jesus Christ as Lord, and ourselves as your servants for Jesus' sake (2 Corinthians 4:5).

Scripture: **2 Corinthians 4:1-6**
Song: **"Make Me a Servant"**

"Hey preacher, I thought you only worked on Sundays." I nodded my head and smiled back, wishing he knew the half of it. Gene ran the lumberyard in town. I'd come in that morning to purchase materials for a benevolent outreach project: a widow needed repairs on her leaking roof. Not getting an answer from me, Gene teasingly pressed the issue. "So, why are you here on your week off?"

After whispering a short prayer for direction, I told Gene about today's itinerary. "After I fix a neighbor's roof, I will sort food at the food bank, then visit shut-ins at the retirement center. If there's time, I'll work on Sunday's sermon." Jim didn't say much after that.

The following week, I made another trip to the lumberyard. Gene met me at the door: "Hey preacher, who are you helping today? Let me know if you need an extra hand."

When we preach Christ by serving others, the world will take notice. Often, the best sermon is the example we set by our deeds.

Dear God, not everyone attends my church or listens when I preach Your Word. Many stand on the sidelines, watching, judging my actions. And this I welcome—for if they see me as Your servant, they might respond by opening their hearts to the Master. In the name of Jesus, amen.

Prophets Still Needed

It was [Christ] who gave some to be apostles, some to be prophets, some to be evangelists, and some to be pastors and teachers, to prepare God's people for works of service (Ephesians 4:11, 12).

Scripture: **Ephesians 4:11-16**
Song: **"Chosen and Sent by the Father"**

I grew accustomed to reading the witty sayings on a church sign over on Division Street. Sometimes they posted upcoming services or community news. One Friday, while driving home from work, I glanced over my shoulder to read the message for that day. Instead of a catchy quote, I found this announcement: "Prophet from Scotland preaching tonight—7 PM. Come hear God's Word."

I usually expect to hear ministers, teachers, and evangelists speaking from the pulpit. So when someone mentions prophet or apostle, I become a little skeptical. In retrospect, I can see that my perspective isn't supported by today's verse.

Old Testament believers needed prophets, and, according to Paul, we still need them today. The Holy Spirit engifted prophets to convey spiritual wisdom, point out iniquity, and edify the body of Christ with their words. Prophetic ministry helped the first-century church grow and become an effective witness to a lost world.

Lord, since the laborers are few and the harvest great, please raise up people for the ministry, regardless of titles we give them. In Christ I pray. Amen.

All Pieces Necessary

Just as each of us has one body with many members, and these members do not all have the same function, so in Christ we who are many form one body, and each member belongs to all the others (Romans 12:4, 5).

Scripture: **Romans 12:3-8**
Song: **"Bind Us Together"**

Long before video games, high-definition television, cell-phone text messaging, and surfing the World Wide Web, people entertained themselves with less technical pursuits. One of them was putting jigsaw puzzles together. My sister and I loved working on them: the more pieces, the better. If Mom and Dad joined in, then we each took a corner and worked toward the middle. Sometimes it took weeks to complete one—all the more fun.

Occasionally, pieces disappeared, no doubt chewed up by Whiskers, our dog. What a disappointment to work for weeks on a picture and not finish it because of missing pieces! It didn't matter which ones were gone; without all of them, the picture was incomplete, fragmented.

The same holds for the church. We need everyone and every ministry if Christ's body is to be whole and healthy. Each jagged-edged member fits perfectly together when Christ becomes the focus of the picture. All members have their own specialty, each one complementing the other.

O Lord, I realize my contributions to the body of Christ are valuable. When I am absent from the body, an essential piece of the ministry is missing. Being needed feels good! Thank You, in the name of Jesus. Amen.

Looking Ahead

So then, dear friends, since you are looking forward to this, make every effort to be found spotless, blameless and at peace with him (2 Peter 3:14).

Scripture: **2 Peter 3:14-18**
Song: **"When the Roll Is Called Up Yonder"**

I met Smeedy at the Carpenter Shop, a teen outreach ministry in Reedley, California. He rarely missed a service or function. Smeedy was the first to arrive and the last to leave. He always carried a paperback *Good News for Modern Man*, which he folded in half and tucked into the right back pocket of his jeans. When not reading this Bible, he was praying. Sometimes you had to interrupt him if you wanted to speak with him.

A few kids thought Smeedy's behavior strange. And yes, he was a unique personality. But to me, he seemed like the real deal—the kind of Christian mentioned in the book of Acts. I respected his dedication and faith in God.

Smeedy believed Jesus could return at any time. So he'd often ask people whether they were ready to stand before God and give an account of their lives. The approach didn't endear him with everyone. But we know that the disciples shared the same concern. In today's verse, Peter looks forward to a future day in eternity called the Day of the Lord. Since this day of reckoning is approaching, Peter exhorts us to conduct our lives accordingly.

Lord, help me live in expectation of what lies ahead in eternity. Until then, may my conduct be acceptable in Your sight. In Jesus' name, amen.

Canceling the Code

Having canceled the written code, with its regulations, that was against us and that stood opposed to us; [God] took it away, nailing it to the cross (Colossians 2:14).

Scripture: **Colossians 2:11-19**
Song: **"At the Cross"**

"Well, how do you plead?" asked the judge at traffic court. "As guilty as the serpent in the Garden of Eden," replied the minister. Bewildered, the judge asked Dale to explain his answer.

Dale told him that in the garden, Adam blamed Eve, Eve blamed the serpent, but the serpent had no one to blame. "And neither do I, so I'm guilty as charged."

The judge laughed at the minister's reply. "That's the most sincere plea I've heard in years, and it's refreshing too." Amused with his honesty, the judge dismissed the case and forgave Dale's speeding ticket.

Seldom are offences forgiven, especially when we truly are guilty. But that is exactly what happened on the cross. With His atoning death, Jesus paid the penalty for sin and canceled the written code against us. Although the Old Testament was a good tutor, we no longer need to keep its numerous laws and regulations. Now, only one code is expedient: that we put our faith and trust in Jesus Christ.

Dear Father, *Your Son's sacrifice removed the barriers that separated me from You. Your new covenant gives me hope for the future and the freedom to serve You daily. Thank You. In Christ's name I pray. Amen.*

Depend on Christ

See to it that no one takes you captive through hollow and deceptive philosophy, which depends on human tradition and the basic principles of this world rather than on Christ (Colossians 2:8).

Scripture: **Colossians 2:1-10**
Song: **"Do Not Worry"**

Philosophy comes from the Greek word *philosophia*, which means the "love of wisdom." Therefore, philosophers were those who studied and debated the finer aspects of wisdom as they searched for the meaning of life. In his first letter to the Corinthians, Paul noted that the Jews sought after signs while Greeks looked for wisdom. No wonder Greece gave birth to three of the greatest philosophers: Socrates, Plato, and Aristotle.

There's nothing wrong with searching for wisdom; even the Bible tells us to ask for it when we lack understanding. But philosophy based on purely human ideals, apart from divine revelation, can lead us astray. Such philosophy can leave us empty and hollow, like a hole dug for no purpose.

So let us pursue Christ today—His wisdom, His righteousness, and the theology of the cross that the apostle Paul so masterfully proclaimed. This school of thought always leads to eternal life.

Father, You gave me the greatest textbook in the world. My Bible has everything I need: wisdom, hope, and the words of truth. By reading it daily, I feel prepared for every situation. Thank You, in Jesus' name. Amen.

I Wanna Hold Your Hand

Do not fear, for I am with you; do not be dismayed, for I am your God. I will strengthen you and help you; I will uphold you with my righteous right hand (Isaiah 41:10).

Scripture: **Isaiah 41:4-10**
Song: **"Under His Wings"**

Baby Alana's huge blue eyes sparkled as she took her first step. Three more and she reached her daddy's waiting arms. Tiny steps, but big enough to open a whole new world of exploration and choices.

For weeks she had tried to walk but became distracted, lost her balance, and tumbled to the floor. Tonight, however, she kept her eyes on the goal. Nothing was more important than reaching her father's arms. She trusted him to be there for her, and he was.

In Matthew 14:28-32, Peter walked on water, focusing intently on Jesus. But when he looked away at the stormy situation, he began to sink, crying "Lord, save me!" Like Alana, Peter fell when he became distracted and lost his focus.

As we walk through life, let's remember to focus on God. We can trust His promise to uphold us with His righteous right hand.

Almighty and everlasting God, *amidst confusion and fear, help me focus on You rather than the trying situation. I know You can walk me through it! In the holy name of Jesus, my Lord and Savior, I pray. Amen.*

May 10–16. Author **Barbara E. Haley** has worked as an elementary school teacher and piano instructor. She lives in San Antonio, Texas.

Reflections of God

"You are My witnesses" declares the LORD, **"that I am God"** (Isaiah 43:10-13).

Scripture: **Isaiah 43:10-13**
Song: **"I Would Be Like Jesus"**

Scottish evangelical writer and lecturer Henry Drummond once said, "You can take nothing greater to the [unbelieving] world than . . . the reflection of the love of God upon your character. That is the universal language." Thus Isaiah told the people of Israel: remember God's love and power, soak it in and *witness* to it.

In so many ways, witnessing means reflecting what has first shined upon us. In Acts 4, when the religious leaders of the day saw the courageous works of Peter and John—and then discovered how uneducated these disciples were—they were astonished. They "took note" that the men had been with Jesus. He was reflected in them.

But a mirror can only reflect what it faces. In the same way, as we spend time with God, face to face in prayer, we begin to reflect His character and love to others. Later, when admonished for telling others about Jesus, Peter and John said, "We cannot help speaking about what we have seen and heard" (Acts 4:20). Spending time with Jesus had radically changed them. And what a life goal for you and me: that others might see Jesus reflected in us.

Father, guard my tongue and straighten my ways that I might spread Your love. As I spend time with You, may my life genuinely reflect Your character—and may others truly see Christ in me. In His name, amen.

A Little Bit: Just Enough

If you have faith as small as a mustard seed, you can say to this mulberry tree, "Be uprooted and planted in the sea," and it will obey you (Luke 17:6).

Scripture: **Luke 17:1-6**
Song: **"'Tis So Sweet"**

Smiling politely, I hurried out the door. For a solid week I had faithfully made good choices. But I'd still only lost two-tenths of a pound. I wanted to quit.

Forcing myself to continue, however, I returned the following week and stepped on the scale. Thank goodness— another pound and a half! My spirits soared as I watched the attendant total the weight I'd lost in five months.

"You're almost there," she said. "Only two-tenths of a pound from your goal." What I wouldn't have given for that same two-tenths I had despised just the week before. It wasn't enough then, but now it was all I needed. How quickly its value had increased!

Two little words, *have* and *need*, made all the difference. When it's small, what we have can lead to anxiety and despair. However, when that same amount is *all we need*, it suddenly produces relief and hope.

Christ says we only need faith the size of a mustard seed. Let's take Him at His Word. May we walk in faith as He guides our lives to fulfill His purposes this day.

Dear Lord, *teach me to look to You, beyond any discouraging circumstances around me. Remind me that the faith You have planted in my heart is always enough to accomplish Your will. In Jesus' name, amen.*

Still Producing Fruit!

The fruit of the Spirit is love, joy, peace, patience, kindness, goodness, faithfulness, gentleness and self-control. Against such things there is no law (Galatians 5:22, 23).

Scripture: **Galatians 5:22-26**
Song: **"Holy Spirit, God of Love"**

In a small town near London, England, a grapevine, about 1000 years old and kept under glass, produces several tons of grapes a year. The vine's single root is at least two feet thick, and though the smaller branches stretch 200 feet from the main stem, they bear much fruit. Distance makes no difference; those branches are connected to the vine, and the life of the vine flows through them.

We are not responsible to grow the spiritual fruit in our lives. Only the Holy Spirit can do this. But we can certainly strive to remove any deterrents to growth—the disease of an unforgiving spirit, the entanglement of worldly concerns, and the deprivation of trying to live apart from the vine.

Planting a healthy vine in bad soil will not produce fruit. Neither will planting a dead vine in fertile soil. Growth requires a healthy vine and fertile soil. Christ is the vine, and we are the branches. When we abide in Christ, we will bear much fruit. When we remain apart from Him, we can do nothing (see John 15:5).

*Thank You, **Lord**, for Your life in me. Though I know it usually hurts, I invite You to continue to prune my life—my thoughts, my words, and my deeds. Produce good fruit through me, in Jesus' name. Amen.*

Christ: The Perfect Pitch Fork

Here [in our new life hidden with Christ in God] there is no Greek or Jew, circumcised or uncircumcised, barbarian, Scythian, slave or free, but Christ is all, and is in all (Colossians 3:11).

Scripture: Colossians 3:1-11
Song: "Brethren, We Have Met to Worship"

In *The Pursuit of God*, A. W. Tozer points out that "one hundred pianos all tuned to the same fork are automatically tuned to each other. They are of one accord by being tuned, not to each other, but to another standard to which each one must individually bow." He goes on to make the point that, when we gather for worship, we should each look intently to Christ. That's when we experience true Christian unity—more so than if we turn from Him and merely strive for closer fellowship.

When I cut out fabric for a quilt or for curtains, I use such a standard. I make a pattern for what I want and cut the pieces according to that pattern. I learned the reason for this method the hard way—after measuring each new piece from the last piece I'd cut. At first, the pieces were only marginally different, but by the time I finished, the difference was remarkable.

So let us focus on Christ in all things. We will become more like Him, and we will live in unity with each brother and sister who also grows into His likeness.

O God, I can only imagine the beauty of thousands upon thousands worshiping You in the unity of the Spirit. Praise You, through Christ. Amen.

Taking the High Road

Whatever you do, work at it with all your heart, as working for the Lord, not for men (Colossians 3:23).

Scripture: **Colossians 3:18-25**
Song: **"Workman of God"**

Years ago, my teenage son earned money cutting the neighbor's grass. As he paced back and forth across the back lot, another neighbor on the other side of the fence stepped outside, motioning. My son switched off the mower and turned to the man.

"You've got the blade set way too low," the man said. "At that rate, you'll only need to mow once a week. Set the blade up. They'll need their lawn mowed more often, and you will make more money."

More money? Yes.

Integrity? Christian character? Absolutely not.

My "Mama pride" swelled when my son chose to take the high road and not follow the man's advice.

Martin Luther wrote, "The maid who sweeps her kitchen is doing the will of God just as much as the monk who prays—not because she may sing a Christian hymn as she sweeps but because God loves clean floors. The Christian shoemaker does his Christian duty not by putting little crosses on the shoes, but by making good shoes, because God is interested in good craftsmanship."

Dear Lord, help me sense Your call in all that I do. May I do my very best, not only when others are watching, but with sincerity of heart and reverence for You, no matter who sees. In Jesus' name I pray. Amen.

Dress for the Occasion

As God's chosen people, holy and dearly loved, clothe yourselves with compassion, kindness, humility, gentleness and patience (Colossians 3:12).

Scripture: **Colossians 3:12-17**
Song: **"Change My Heart, O God"**

When I taught first grade in public school, I used to pretend to spray the ceiling with self-control as the students entered the room. Throughout the day, as children misbehaved, I encouraged them to "pull down some self-control and put it on." They loved doing this. And in the process, their attitudes and behaviors usually improved.

Later, when I taught fourth grade in a Christian school, I told the students about this and pointed out that self-control is a fruit of the Spirit, available to everyone. We need only ask for it and choose to exercise it.

I recall Bible teacher Joyce Meyer saying that she never once walked into her closet and had clothes jump onto her body. She had to *choose* what to wear and take the time to clothe herself.

Somehow, it seems the old self has no problem re-outfitting our bodies daily. As we walk in the image of our Creator, we must be aware of this. That is, we'll need to keep removing the old stained garments and keep stepping into the garments of righteousness, cleansed by Christ's blood.

Lord, where do I need to be cleansed and re-dressed? Please continue to renew my soul as I choose to walk in Your image. In Jesus' name, amen.

Pass the Salt Shaker, Please

Let your conversation be always full of grace, seasoned with salt, so that you may know how to answer everyone (Colossians 4:6).

Scripture: **Colossians 4:2-9**
Song: **"Speak for Jesus"**

A certain men's Sunday school class had been constantly lagging in attendance. They voiced concern that soon no one would be left but the four regular leaders! What's more, those leaders didn't always show up, either, if it wasn't their turn to teach.

However, the speaker at a church leadership workshop offered a solution. "It's simple," he said. "You have to be excited about what you're doing. Talk it up. Do this every chance you get." Paul gave similar advice to the church members in Colossae, calling them to pay close attention to their speech. When they spoke of Christ, their message should have a little "spice" in it!

Can we become dull and nonchalant in our conversations about Christ? I think so. That's when a change in us can change our situation. That's when "shaking things up" can be a good thing.

Dear Father in Heaven, put some salty excitement into my witness today. I know You deserve all that I can give, whether I'm talking to You or talking to others about You. Yes, keep me in Your grip of passion! In the name of Your Son, my Savior, I pray. Amen.

May 17–23. **Jimmie Oliver Fleming** writes from Chester, Virginia. Her favorite hobby is piano playing, and her second favorite is gardening.

Plain and Simple

Whoever has my commands and obeys them, he is the one who loves me. He who loves me will be loved by my Father, and I too will love him and show myself to him (John 14:21).

Scripture: **John 14:21-24**
Song: **"Oh, How I Love Jesus"**

"Don't you just love this pudding?" I asked my friend Sarah. She responded with a sigh. "Yes, though I wish you wouldn't use that word so loosely. I mean, you don't have to *love* everything. It OK to just *like* some things."

"True," I replied. "And I like green beans. However, I love banana pudding."

"I know. But can you truthfully say you love the one who prepared it for you?"

Her question caught me off guard. "Well, I admit there was a time when I couldn't say that about her. Yet it's not true anymore, of course."

"Of course, because her delicious banana pudding won you over, right?"

"Nope. I believe Jesus himself did it. And I do try to keep His commandments, as I'm sure you do too."

"Why, sure I do. And that's the truth, plain and simple."

"Yes, plain and simple," I agreed. "And by the way, you're not off the hook. It's still your turn to take us out to lunch next Tuesday."

Loving Father, thank You for the effect of Your Word upon my life. I would be lost without Your loving commands. In Jesus' name I pray. Amen.

Prove It!

When they had finished eating, Jesus said to Simon Peter, "Simon son of John, do you truly love me more than these?" (John 21:15).

Scripture: **John 21:15-19**
Song: **"My Jesus, I Love Thee"**

A tough question for Peter! He'd already denied Jesus three times. Now the Lord asked him three times: "Do you love me?"

Because of his past denials, it might have seemed that Peter really didn't love Jesus. However, this impulsive disciple would be graced with second (and third) chances. And during Peter's reinstatement, Jesus gave Peter a great calling: he must feed Christ's sheep.

And thus the Lord treats you and me. First, despite all our failures, weaknesses, and denials, Christ picks us up and forgives us as we come to Him in repentance. And, as He did with Peter, He gives us a sacred calling. We must use our spiritual gifts to build up the church, to feed one another through a mutual ministry of love and care.

The Lord still asks us daily: "Do you love me?" And when we respond in the affirmative, He responds in the way He did to Peter (if I may paraphrase): "OK . . . prove it!"

Dear Lord and Redeemer, give me a sincere heart when it comes to loving You. Thanks for restoring me when I fail. I want to be obedient to all of Your commands, but I need Your courage and power to follow through. Thanks again for being with me always. In Your precious name, amen.

All Things Working Together?

We know that in all things God works for the good of those who love him, who have been called according to his purpose (Romans 8:28).

Scripture: **Romans 8:28-39**
Song: **"Now I Belong to Jesus"**

God always works for my good? Sometimes it's hard to believe. At other times I've found this belief to be a life saver. Here's a simple example: Just as I entered the church for a funeral one afternoon, my cell phone rang. Although it was a "wrong" number, I still considered it a "good" call. Without it, I wouldn't have remembered to turn my cell phone off for the service.

I recall another time when I had to stop and pick up someone's trash from my driveway before leaving for work. Apparently, the plastic bag had fallen off the garbage truck, and picking up the strewn contents put me 15 minutes behind my schedule. How did this work for my good? If I'd been on time, I might have been involved in the accident at an intersection I cross every morning.

I know bad things happen to God's people, for He has allowed human will much freedom until Christ returns. But I also know that, as I seek God's guidance, He oversees my world, moment by moment. I will continue to thank Him for the blessings, small and great, sprinkled into my days.

*Thank You, **Dear God,** for being who You are, working on my behalf in little things as well as in big things. In Christ's name I pray. Amen.*

A Refreshed Heart

Your love has given me great joy and encouragement, because you, brother, have refreshed the hearts of the saints (Philemon 7).

Scripture: **Philemon 1-7**
Song: **"For You I Am Praying"**

No doubt, as Philemon received this complimentary letter from Paul, his heart was refreshed too. Words of encouragement can do this for us. Whether delivered by letter, phone, or even e-mail, they soothe the spirit.

Naturally, prayers are also important. Paul mentions this first in his letter to his friend and fellow believer. "I always thank my God as I remember you in my prayers" (v. 4).

Like Paul, I regularly lift up the needs of certain people in my prayers. "I'm praying for you," I tell them, and I mean it. "Even when you don't hear from me, just know that I'm thinking about you and praying for you."

"I know," folks will often say, "because I can feel it."

I have also "felt" the prayers of others, so I know how important it is to keep extending this form of silent affirmation from afar. It's not that my thoughts or words are in any way magical or working some power on their own. No, it's the Lord himself who chooses to bless those for whom we desire His blessing. (I think this brings Him "great joy" too!)

O God, may I encourage others with my words to them. And may I lift them up for Your blessing as I pray for them. In Jesus' name, amen.

Out of Love, Do More

Confident of your obedience, I write to you, knowing that you will do even more than I ask (Philemon 21).

Scripture: **Philemon 19-25**
Song: **"Father, I Adore You"**

Did Philemon readily grasp Paul's request to do more? If it were me, I would have a question for Paul: "How *much* more?"

Maybe you can relate? Because doing more—or doing one's best—is no small feat. For example, when a widow gave two pennies as her offering, Jesus deemed this to be her best. "'I tell you the truth,' he said, 'this poor widow has put in more than all the others'" (Luke 21:3). She did it out of love, the "more" that comes from the heart.

But it's risky to do more, to love when we could play it safe instead. If you are facing such a choice these days, then cherish with me these word from Alfred Lord Tennyson:

I hold it true, whate'er befall;
    I feel it, when I sorrow most;
'Tis better to have loved and lost
    Than never to have loved at all.

Such words ring true for every relationship we enter. It will be risky to put ourselves forward in love. But think of the greater risk when we allow fear to harden our hearts.

Father, build into me the willingness to go the extra mile for souls who need to be loved. Love them through me! In Jesus' name, amen.

An Appeal of Love

Although in Christ I could be bold and order you to do what you ought to do, yet I appeal to you on the basis of love (Philemon 8, 9).

Scripture: **Philemon 8-18**
Song: **"Freely, Freely"**

Love is a powerful four-letter word. And it's influence far surpasses that of the three-letter word, *law*. For example, the law, in Deuteronomy 23:15, 16, states, "If a slave has taken refuge with you, do not hand him over to his master. Let him live among you wherever he likes and in whatever town he chooses. Do not oppress him."

But what would love do? Not only would love free a slave; it would do much more. It would send a *former* slave back into the church as a full-fledged Christian brother. It would ask all the believers to treat him with full and equal respect. This is the law of love, a law of the heart. No form of legalism can match it!

Paul sent slave Onesimus back to his master, Philemon, and offered to repay Philemon any debt his slave may have owed. But the law of love must prevail in the master's heart. As Paul said: "If you consider me a partner, welcome him as you would welcome me" (v. 17). Where such love surges forward, mere law will be left in the dust.

*Thank You, **Lord and Friend,** for giving me the appropriate words to say to You. Though sometimes at a loss for words, there's much I need and want to say to You. Your love holds me captive. Yet I know that You have set me free. Through Christ my Lord, amen.*

Sound Words in Red

If anyone advocates a different doctrine and does not agree with sound words, those of our Lord Jesus Christ, and with the doctrine conforming to godliness, he is conceited and understands nothing (1 Timothy 6:3, 4, *New American Standard Bible*).

Scripture: **1 Timothy 6:3-10**
Song: **"My God Said It"**

WWJD: What Would Jesus Do? You see it on shirts, bracelets, books, and bumper stickers. But today I would suggest another acronym—*WWJS:* What Would Jesus Say? What would He say about godly living or sound doctrine? Thankfully, in some Bibles we can still find the words of Jesus in red. What He says ought to stand out.

How blessed we are to have the anointed words of our Lord! Christian doctrine flows from truth Jesus taught. To benefit from His sound words, though, we must read and meditate on them. We can hug them to ourselves and allow them to guide each day.

"I am the way and the truth and the life"(John 14:6)—wonderful words from Jesus. We can trust words in red like that. Through them we have life, abundant life, now and forever.

Dear God, thank You for giving me the Bible, which records the acts and words of Jesus. Help me to cherish these words as they draw me closer to Father, Son, and Holy Spirit. I pray this prayer in the name of Jesus, my Savior and Lord. Amen.

May 24–30. **Phyllis Qualls Freeman** has published hundreds of articles and devotionals. Retired, she lives with her husband, Bill, in Hixson, Tennessee.

He Draws Them

All the tax collectors and the sinners were coming near Him to listen to Him (Luke 15:1, *New American Standard Bible*).

Scripture: Luke 15:1-7
Song: "Jesus Calls Us"

When my grandson William was younger, he experimented with a magnet and little silver-colored metal pieces. He was amazed by the magnet's power. He used it with paper clips, straight pins, and small nails. All of these were instantly drawn by an invisible force.

What was it about Jesus that caused the unrighteous to be drawn to Him? Why did Jesus appeal to publicans? Was it His charismatic personality that got their attention? Or was it that, as He spoke the truth, their souls were laid bare and needful? Surely, at that point, resistance was futile.

I've talked with several potential "prodigals" who've tried hard to pull away from their faith. They've told me: "I just couldn't be happy until I responded to the tug on my heart, the call to renew my relationship with Christ."

Jesus said, "If I am lifted up from the earth, [I] will draw all men to Myself" (John 12:32, *NASB*). One of the greatest callings on our life is to lift up the name and character of Christ. But remember this: He himself will do the drawing.

Powerful God, *thank You for drawing me to yourself through Christ. Help me to exemplify the virtues of Christ and continually lift Him up to others so they will experience the heart-tug of Your Spirit. In the name of the Father, the Son, and the Holy Spirit, I pray. Amen.*

Sharing the Joy

When she has found it, she calls together her friends and neighbors, saying, "Rejoice with me!" (Luke 15:9, *New American Standard Bible*).

Scripture: **Luke 15:8-10**
Song: **"Again I Say Rejoice"**

American prisoners of war (POWs) captured during the Vietnam War were tortured and imprisoned. Many endured deplorable conditions for years. Then, suddenly, the war was over.

And on my television screen, I saw returning prisoners. I shed tears of joy as former POWs emerged from airplanes onto U.S. soil. My heart swelled with pride in their courage and loyalty. They probably didn't feel like heroes, but in my mind they were. And each soldier was someone's lost loved one—now found.

My brother was already safely home from that war, and I was grateful for that. But I could also rejoice along with others on those wonderful family-reunion days.

We can always choose to say "praise the Lord" when others are blessed. To rejoice with others in their good fortune grows us into better human beings. In effect, we are simply demonstrating the great words of a long-gone poet: "No man is an island."

It's true. Your blessing is mine, as well.

My Lord God, help me to share the burdens of my neighbors and friends. Then, when they receive answers to their prayers, enable me to participate in their happiness as well. In Jesus' name I pray. Amen.

Need to Run to the Father?

When he had spent everything, a severe famine occurred in that country, and he began to be impoverished (Luke 15:14, *New American Standard Bible*).

Scripture: **Luke 15:11-24**
Song: **"Lord, I'm Coming Home"**

October 27, 1929, called "Black Thursday," saw the crash of the stock market in the United States. Some senior citizens today still remember the rationing of certain grocery products. They saw the increasing numbers of the unemployed and skyrocketing suicides. Hopelessness struck many families as they wondered: When will things get better?

When the young runaway experienced his own "Black Thursday," he quickly determined to return home. In his time of need, he wanted to reunite with his family.

We may meet someone today who is impoverished financially, spiritually, or emotionally. Someone may sit in the pew next to you who is reaching the point of desperation. Yet their intense anxiety may be the very thing that causes them to return to family and faith.

Are we ready to assist in their return? If they are ready to hear the truth and run into the Father's arms, will we applaud their choice with joy?

Father, thank You for keeping me through devastating circumstances. Help me to be alert to others enduring hard times. When I see them running back to You, help me to run alongside and guide them into Your loving arms. This I pray in the name of my Savior, Jesus. Amen.

Grumbling or Grateful?

These men are grumblers and faultfinders; they follow their own evil desires; they boast about themselves and flatter others for their own advantage (Jude 16).

Scripture: **Jude 8-16**
Song: **"Give Thanks to God, for He Is Good"**

When my brother's little girls visited in our home, one of them grumbled about something that didn't go right. "OK," said my brother. "You know what you need to do." So Stacy began, "I'm thankful for my mom and dad, and I'm thankful for us coming to visit Aunt Phyl, and I'm thankful for . . . ."

Whenever one of them complained about something, Thomas would ask them to tell him five things for which they were thankful. It sure seemed to keep their conversations more positive.

I can learn from this! Next time I'm primed to find fault, maybe I'll remember to do a little thanking first. After all, grumbling is just a habit, and it can surely be broken with a little practice.

And here's a dirty little secret about constant faultfinding: it reveals the faults of our own souls. Poet and theologian François de Salignac Fénelon put it this way: "Had we not faults of our own, we should take less pleasure in complaining of others."

Awesome God, help me to speak positive and uplifting words. Keep me from grumbling and faultfinding. Bring honor to Your name through my grateful praise. In the name of Christ I pray. Amen.

Building Up Your Spirit

You, beloved, building yourselves up on your most holy faith, praying in the Holy Spirit (Jude 20, *New American Standard Bible*).

Scripture: **Jude 17-25**
Song: **"Be Strong in God"**

My husband and I have a treadmill. It isn't doing us any good, though, because we don't use it. I guess we just lack the commitment. However, our son, daughter-in-law, and grandson work out regularly. They use the treadmill, and the guys lift weights. When they're done, their joints ache, but they've gained strength and muscle tone. So it must be true: "No pain, no gain."

We have what we need to grow strong in spiritual life. We've got Christ, the apostles, the church, the Bible, the creeds, all the saints and martyrs, along with all the theology and witness that has unfolded in two vast millennia.

But do we "use" this holy faith handed down to us?

Just one small example: I've done it before and maybe you have too—praying, and then realizing that my mind is far from thoughts of God. When I take time to focus only on God, I feel the inspiration of the Spirit. Then I can intercede in prayer as well as come into communion with the Lord. This builds up my faith and my commitment.

Gracious God, I want to grow and be strong in the holy faith. Help me consistently meditate on You in my quiet time. Let my prayers be anointed by the Holy Spirit, praying for Your will to be done in every request. In the name of Jesus I pray. Amen.

Passing It Along

Beloved, while I was making every effort to write you about our common salvation, I felt the necessity to write to you appealing that you contend earnestly for the faith which was once for all handed down to the saints (Jude 3, *New American Standard Bible*).

Scripture: **Jude 3-7**
Song: **"Find Us Faithful"**

In the 1930s my maternal grandmother put Scripture tracts under her daughter's head when she (my mom) was sick. Grandmother believed—in a quite literal sense!—that God's Word could help restore health to her daughter. When Mom had her own family, she prayed unceasingly for our health and welfare.

And me? Every morning is my own prayer time. My grown children remember that my Bible study books were always spread out on the kitchen table in the early hours of the day. And one of my sons told his fiancé that I was "a woman of prayer." (Now *that* warmed my heart!)

I'm simply thanking God that I can pass on the faith that was "handed down" to me. In fact, it doesn't stop with me. My children know Jesus as their own Savior and have passed the truth of the gospel on to a fifth generation, my grandchildren. But remember: Even if you have not seen the faith of Christ mirrored in your own family, the "passing it along" can begin with you.

Father, I desire to live Christlike before my children and others of the next generation, so they will know the reality of Your love. Help me to pass along the goodness of the faith in all I do and say. In Jesus' name, amen.

Don't Trifle with God

These men have set up idols in their hearts . . . I will do this to recapture the hearts of the people of Israel, who have all deserted me for their idols (Ezekiel 14:3a, 5).

Scripture: **Ezekiel 14:1-8**
Song: **"Cleanse Me"**

A certain teenager rebelled. *Those old fogies don't understand. I've got to be my own person, do my on thing.*

His parents didn't know their son secretly experimented with many things they had forbidden.

Police raided a party and arrested the young man.

"Mom, Dad! Please come get me. Tell me what to do. They think I sold drugs."

"We did tests," the police told the parents. "Your son has drugs in his system and there's evidence he sold drugs."

In grief the parents told their son, "You've chosen to disregard us and got yourself into this mess. We can't get you off the hook."

The elders in today's Scripture also had self-will on the throne of their hearts. They had no intention of submitting to God's message.

Whenever we refuse to submit to God's will, we commit idolatry. If we love our idols (including ourselves) more than we love God, there is no reason to ask Him for anything.

*Forgive me, **Lord,** for the times I've wanted my own way instead of yours. Cleanse me from all idolatry. I submit to you in Jesus name. Amen.*

May 31. **Judith Vander Wege** is a freelance writer who lives in Orange City, Iowa with her husband Paul.

DEVOTIONS®

You ought
to live holy and
godly lives.

—2 Peter 3:11

JUNE

Photo © *Jake Hellbach* |
Dreamstime.com

Gary Allen, Editor

DEVOTIONS® is published quarterly by Standard Publishing, Cincinnati, Ohio, www.standardpub.com.
© 2009 by Standard Publishing. All rights reserved. Topics based on the Home Daily Bible Readings,
International Sunday School Lessons. © 2006 by the Committee on the Uniform Series. Printed in the
U.S.A. All Scripture quotations, unless otherwise indicated, are taken from the HOLY BIBLE, NEW
INTERNATIONAL VERSION®. NIV®. Copyright © 1973, 1978, 1984 by International Bible Society.
Used by permission of Zondervan. All rights reserved. *The Living Bible* (TLB), © 1971 by Tyndale House
Publishers, Wheaton, IL. *Holy Bible, New Living Translation* (NLT), © 1996. Tyndale House Publishers.
The Revised Standard Version of the Bible (RSV), copyrighted 1946, 1952, © 1971, 1973.

Grace Transforms

God wants us to turn from godless living and sinful pleasures and to live good, God-fearing lives (Titus 2:12, *The Living Bible*).

Scripture: **Titus 2:11-15**
Song: **"I Believe in Miracles"**

Nicky Cruz, coleader of the dreaded Mau-Mau's, a violent teenage gang, met David Wilkerson in New York City in 1958. David had heartfelt compassion for these gang members and told them of God's love for them. Yet Nicky was filled with hate. "You come near me, preacher," he said, "and I'll kill you."

Wilkerson's response? "You could do that. You could cut me in a thousand pieces, and lay them out in the street, and every piece would love you."

That kind of love could not be resisted. In the course of time, Nicky opened his heart to Christ. And he changed dramatically. He threw away his drugs, began hugging and smiling, and let go of his hatred. Instead of nurturing the hardness that once froze his soul, he became open and joyous. In fact, Nicky eventually attended Bible college, became an evangelist, and has lived a God-fearing life of peace and love ever since.

*Thank You, **Lord,** for the miracle of grace that transforms lives, including mine. Along each step of my way today, help me to turn to You for the wisdom and guidance I need. In Jesus' name, amen.*

June 1–6. **Judith VanderWege** is a freelance writer in Orange City, Iowa. She and her husband, Paul, have a music ministry in the area.

Why Struggle in the Snare?

Happy is the man who does not sin by doing what he knows is right (Romans 14:22, *The Living Bible*).

Scripture: **Romans 14:22, 23**
Song: **"Yield Not to Temptation"**

There's this little matter of "self-indulgence." Is it a problem for you, too? I know I'm supposed to take good care of the body God has given me. And I know it would be best for me to lose at least 10 pounds. Therefore, it would be helpful to eat smaller meals and fewer desserts. But then I see something that would be soooo delicious.

Good-bye resolve. Hello indulgence.

I know Jesus can give me the strength to resist my temptations. But I often forget He's in charge and fail to ask for His strength and peace. I impulsively trash my planned diet and put myself on the throne of my life— right where Christ should reign each moment.

What is the solution? Confess my sin and receive forgiveness. Pray for constant alertness to His guidance and the strength to follow it.

That is surely the way to happiness—simply doing right in the first place, avoiding the sticky problems of sin. As the great medieval poet John Dryden once put it: "Better shun the bait than struggle in the snare."

Father, forgive me for frequent self-indulgence. Thank You for Your grace that makes it possible for me to do Your will. I know that, without You, I can do nothing. But with You, all things are possible. Please help me conquer my problem of overeating. Through Christ, amen.

Jesus Did It

So, whether you eat or drink, or whatever you do, do all to the glory of God (1 Corinthians 10:31, *Revised Standard Version*).

Scripture: **1 Corinthians 10:23–11:1**
Song: **"Glory to His Name"**

How can a human being bring glory to God? Yes, praising and thanking Him certainly glorifies Him. But are our words and prayers enough?

In the classic book by Charles Sheldon, *In His Steps*, a minister, Henry Maxwell, struggles with these questions: "What does following Jesus mean? What would Jesus do?" He challenges members of his congregation to pledge that they won't do anything—for a solid year—without asking themselves first, "What would Jesus do?"

Jesus stressed over and over again that we should love . . . love God above all else, and love one another as He loves us. If we sincerely want to follow Him, then in every situation we must ask, "What is the loving thing to do?"

Today's Scripture calls us to do all to the glory of God. That involves action—*doing* the loving thing in every situation we face. We may have a "right" to do something other than that. And it may not be immoral or wrong to do otherwise, strictly speaking. But if our action causes another person pain, it is usually best to give up our rights. So often, Jesus did just that.

O Father in Heaven, please give me the power and wisdom to do the loving thing, as Your Son, Jesus, would do, in every situation. I pray this prayer in His precious name, my merciful Savior and Lord. Amen.

Money or Mercy?

Continue to love each other with true brotherly love (Hebrews 13:1, *The Living Bible*).

Scripture: **Hebrews 13:1-7**
Song: **"Mercy Is Boundless and Free"**

When we do the loving thing, sometimes it hurts us financially. My dad used to run a dry-cleaning business, and Mom wondered why they weren't making much money at it. One day she discovered that Dad had charged only 25 cents to dry-clean a dress. "Frank, how can you pick up this dress, take time to mark down who it belongs to, clean it, press it, deliver it—and then charge only 25 cents? Do you really expect to make any profit that way?"

"But she can't afford any more," he replied. In that situation, the money wasn't the important thing to him. He did the loving and kind thing.

Another way to be kind and loving, according to today's text, is to remember those in prison. We are to "suffer with them." Many Christians in the world today languish in prisons for their faith; some are tortured and killed. They need our prayers, and the ministries that help them need our support. Using our money this way, rather than "loving it," is one way to do what Jesus would do.

Heavenly Father, bless those who are persecuted so severely simply for being true to You. Thank You for ministries that help the persecuted as much as they can. Show me what I can do to help. In the name of Your Son, my Savior, I pray. Amen.

Follow His Example

I have given you an example to follow: do as I have done to you (John 13:15 *The Living Bible*).

Scripture: **John 13:3-15**
Song: **"Saved to Serve"**

It is clear in today's Scripture, as well as in Charles Sheldon's book, *In His Steps,* that following Jesus' example may be humbling and embarrassing. One of Sheldon's characters is a bishop who oversees wealthy congregations; he resigns his position to work in the slums. Another is a college president who feels led to get involved in difficult politics so he can make a difference in his town. These were tough decisions. But each person wanted to honor Jesus as Lord and pursue a joy greater than they'd ever known. Yet, by their service, they also shared in Christ's sufferings.

Peter considered it beneath Jesus to wash His disciples' feet. And he must have recoiled when Jesus said that every disciple must also have a servant's heart. But after Jesus' resurrection, Peter and most of the other disciples obeyed Him without question.

True servants of the Lord will want what the Master wants. Our greatest joy, then, is simply to fit into His plans, for He alone gives purpose to our lives.

*Thank You, **Lord Jesus,** for leaving Your position in glory in order to serve us. Help me now to follow Your example, that I might be a blessing to those around me. Yes, show me how to fit into Your plans for my life today! In Your most holy name I pray. Amen.*

Joyful Imitators

You became imitators of us and of the Lord; in spite of severe suffering, you welcomed the message with the joy given by the Holy Spirit (1 Thessalonians 1:6).

Scripture: **1 Thessalonians 1**
Song: **"Joy and Light"**

Our minister tells of a missionary in Japan who was asked, "Do you take only beautiful girls in your school?"

"Oh no," was the answer. "Everyone is welcome at our school."

"Then why are the girls all so beautiful?" the Buddhist lady asked.

"We teach them to love the Lord God with all their heart, soul, mind, and strength," replied the teacher. "That is what makes them beautiful . . . from the inside out."

"I don't want my girl to become a Christian," said the Buddhist, "but I want her in school to get the beauty."

Many who convert from Buddhism, Islam, and other faiths do "get the beauty" but also suffer severely for their new faith. In the exciting book *Jesus Freaks,* the Christian pop-rock band dc Talk tells of thousands of martyrs who joyfully stood strong for Christ in spite of suffering.

We can live like Jesus with joy, because it is the Holy Spirit within us who produces that joy. Our task is simply to respond to Him with all we've got, even when it means suffering.

Lord, *thank You for this abundant life in relationship with You—for the joy that reigns even amidst unhappy circumstances. In Jesus' name, amen.*

Back to the Basics

Evidently some people are throwing you into confusion and are trying to pervert the gospel of Christ (Galatians 1:7).

Scripture: **Galatians 1:1-10**
Song: **"The True Shepherd"**

When talking about spiritual things today, some use Christian terms like Holy Spirit, peace, and prayer. If we listen long enough, we'll also hear some of these folks making disturbing statements: "I am God." "Jesus was just a man." "There are many ways to Heaven."

While those who hold to New Age teachings say they are thinking "outside the box" of organized religion, they're actually perverting God's Word and causing confusion. After all, if I'm God and you're God, then why do we need a Savior? And why should I follow the narrow way of Jesus when so many religious options will get me to the same eternal destination?

Perversion of truth had a different face two thousand years ago. A heretical group had wormed its way among the Galatians and emphasized law over grace. Paul hit the problem head-on in his letter, guiding the Galatians back to the basics of salvation they so readily forgot. Even today, with New Age ideas saturating the media, this is a great time to brush up on the basics of our faith.

Lord, *You know our day as You knew Paul's day. You haven't changed, so keep biblical truth alive in my heart. In Christ's name, amen.*

June 7–13. **Sherri Langton** is an editor and freelance writer living in Denver, Colorado. She plays drums and percussion at her church.

Checking the Facts

Now the Bereans . . . received the message with great eagerness and examined the Scriptures every day to see if what Paul said was true (Acts 17:11).

Scripture: **Acts 17:10-14**
Song: **"Thy Mercy and Thy Truth, O Lord"**

Another urban legend, I inwardly sighed as I read the e-mail. This one claimed that, according to Johns Hopkins University, plastic containers heated in the microwave produce cancer-causing dioxins that are released into food and body cells.

Oh, really? I checked an urban legend Web site and read the details of the myth—and why it wasn't true. Still not satisfied, I pulled up Johns Hopkins' Web site and found the study on plastics. Sure enough, the hospital's facts debunked the cancer scare.

In Paul's day, some would have attached the term "urban legend" to Jesus. As news about Him spread beyond Jerusalem, so did questions: God in the flesh? Raised from the dead? The Bereans decided to find out for themselves by checking Paul's preaching against the Scriptures. No hoax here, they discovered. The good news really was good.

Web sites come and go, but the Scriptures remain. May I search them before anything else in matters of faith.

Father, thanks for the Word that has stood the test of time. May I always use the Scriptures as the source of truth—the written Word revealing the eternal living Word, Jesus Christ the Lord. In His name I pray. Amen.

Letting Go

Without faith it is impossible to please God (Hebrews 11:6).

Scripture: **Hebrews 11:4-7**
Song: **"'Tis So Sweet to Trust in Jesus"**

"Catch me, Daddy!" Fear and excitement danced in me as I sat atop the slide and gripped the sides. I wanted to fly down the slick surface into my father's waiting arms. Other kids had done it, but my 4-year-old hands just couldn't let go. It was a long way down to the bottom. If Dad missed me, I thought, I'd crash in the sand.

After many long moments and my father's persistent reassurance, I let go. Dad caught me in his arms and hugged me close. My father wouldn't have asked me to trust him and then suddenly pulled away.

Neither does my heavenly Father play such tricks. He delights in my trust. Since that playground episode five decades ago, my challenges have been a lot steeper than that slide: job stresses, a layoff, surgeries, the wayward-ness of family members. Now I face an even steeper slide: the passage into midlife and my parents' failing health.

Many days I find my fingers wrapped tightly around fearful practical concerns. But I also see my heavenly Father with His arms wide open, ready to catch me. I just need to let go.

Heavenly Father, when my burdens become too much, renew a childlike faith in me. Show me how to let go and trust You more, knowing You'd never let me fall. In the name of Jesus, who lives and reigns with You and the Holy Spirit, one God, now and forever, amen.

It's All You Need

Dear children, let us not love with words or tongue but with actions and in truth (1 John 3:18).

Scripture: **1 John 3:18-24**
Song: **"Love Divine, All Loves Excelling"**

When the Beatles sang the song "All You Need Is Love" in June 1967, they created a mantra that perfectly fit the Summer of Love. Who wouldn't embrace a message like that—to get along with your brothers and sisters on this planet?

Ironically, three years later, the Beatles split—in part because of bitter squabbling among the four members. Their message of love for humanity failed at the everyday level of interpersonal relationships.

The apostle John explains why. Love is more than words; it is action. I can't just *say* I love another; I must show it. While we automatically think of this as serving others and meeting their practical needs, active love also means turning the other cheek, forgiving an offense, surrendering our agenda for the sake of unity. And when a Christian brother or sister wrongs me, I must not spread a bad report to other believers.

This kind of active love is what Jesus modeled for us. It glues us together as the body of Christ. And that kind of love, John would say, is all you need.

My Lord God, I struggle with loving others as I should—even my fellow believers in the church. Help me live what true love is, to love as Your Word defines it, especially those who seem so unlovable at the moment. In the name of Jesus, my Savior, I pray. Amen.

Plant Food

We will never stop thanking God that when we preached his message to you, you didn't think of the words we spoke as being just our own. You accepted what we said as the very word of God—which, of course, it was. And this word continues to work in you who believe (1 Thessalonians 2:13, *New Living Translation*).

Scripture: **1 Thessalonians 2:13-16**
Song: **"Wonderful Words of Life"**

Every summer I mercifully resist the urge to buy hanging plants for my patio. Though I love their colors and scents, I always unintentionally kill them with too much water.

My neighbor is just the opposite from me. Beginning in May, her patio bulges with hanging and potted plants thick with healthy leaves and vibrant blossoms. I'm in awe of her. The trick, I understand, is plant food. A careful gardener doesn't just water plants; she works food into the soil. That way, the plant pulls up all the nutrients it needs and will thrive for many weeks.

I like to think that God sees me as a plant in His garden, and His Word keeps me alive. The Holy Spirit acts as the gardener, working that nourishment into the soil of my heart. It challenges me, comforts me, and corrects me. If I feed off the Word daily, I will become a mature, beautiful witness to His goodness and care.

Lord, feed me from Your Word. Don't let it become optional or ordinary but essential for each day, as I hunger for its truths. In Jesus' name, amen.

Pride and Joy

What gives us hope and joy, and what is our proud reward and crown? It is you! (1 Thessalonians 2:19, *New Living Translation*).

Scripture: **1 Thessalonians 2:17-20**
Song: **"The Prodigal Son"**

My younger sister, Susan, is experiencing a growth spurt. Not physically (she's nearly 50 years old) but spiritually. Chronic back pain keeps her awake at night, so she uses the time to pray. She yearns to learn more about God and to fellowship with women of like faith, so she attends a women's Bible study.

This is all the more remarkable, considering that Susan spent much of her twenties as a "prodigal daughter." One day my persistent prayers were answered, though: Susan returned from the distant land of godless living and fell into her Father's waiting embrace. Now God is her closest friend. Jesus is her Lord, Savior, companion, counselor, confidante.

I never tire of telling others what God has done in my sister's life. And so I know a little of what Paul must have felt about the Thessalonians. His investment of persevering prayer in them had paid off. And he burst his buttons over their growing faith as I do the same over Susan's. My joy is this: knowing that my sister by blood is also my sister by water and the Spirit (see John 3:5).

Dear God, thank You for the joy of a returned child. Keep me from growing weary in praying for others, like Susan, who have not yet felt the tug of home in their hearts. In Jesus' name I pray. Amen.

Who's Clapping?

We are not trying to please men but God, who tests our hearts (1 Thessalonians 2:4).

Scripture: **1 Thessalonians 2:1-12**
Song: **"Servant of God, Well Done!"**

When I decided to take up drums, my parents wisely banished me to the basement. Fine with me; I liked the long hours of practicing by myself. But when God called me into music ministry, I exchanged four blank concrete walls for a congregation of two thousand people! I was thrust from privacy to the public, overnight.

Though I loved playing, I didn't like being up front. Our worship leader emphasized that the choir and orchestra were playing to an audience of one, that we were to be invisible, so others would see Christ. But I couldn't block out all those watching eyes.

Then came the praise from people. The "atta girl's" pumped up my pride. Before long, I wasn't trying to please an audience of one but trying to gain popularity for *this* one. God knew my heart, and I am thankful that He worked to correct my focus (through a few musical mistakes). I'm still playing drums in ministry, but with a changed heart—one that strains to hear one set of hands applauding . . . from far above.

Lord God in Heaven, You alone know who I am on the inside and how others see me. Keep me centered on pleasing You rather than impressing people, on possessing a genuine faith that fuels the gifts You've given me. In the name of Your Son, my Savior, I pray. Amen.

All for One, One for All

All the believers were one in heart and mind (Acts 4:32).

Scripture: Acts 4:32-37
Song: "Love in Any Language"

The long lines at the Multiple Sclerosis Walkathon registration tables bustled with activity. Volunteers gathered information, explained routes, and took pledge envelopes. Others distributed T-shirts and water bottles.

Participants moved to the starting line, greeting their fellow walkers with hugs and handshakes. No one jockeyed for position, but rather seemed focused on camaraderie and a purpose greater than self.

Like me, most team captains had MS or had lost a loved one to the disease. Some were in wheelchairs. Although I could walk, I knew I couldn't complete the five miles. The heat and too much exertion rendered my gait wobbly and slowed my pace to a crawl. But I also trusted my team members to carry me the distance if necessary.

As I gazed at the crowd committed to helping us, I saw Jesus on their faces and in their actions. Each person present had given up something—time, energy, money—for a common good. One heart and mind, walking in the hope of wholeness. What better picture of the church?

Dear Father, I thank You that Your Spirit teaches me to love unconditionally, to give without measure, and to minister sacrificially to others. In the precious name of Jesus I pray. Amen.

June 14–20. **Brenda Blanchard** lives in Schertz, Texas, with her husband, Nelson, and one very spoiled cat, Persey. She has written for numerous publications.

Help Me Obey!

O Sovereign Lord, you have begun to show to your servant your greatness and your strong hand. For what god is there in heaven or on earth who can do the deeds and mighty works you do? (Deuteronomy 3:24).

Scripture: **Deuteronomy 3:23-29**
Song: **"How Great Thou Art"**

Standing on a volcano in Hawaii, I witnessed two awe-producing events. There was the majestic beauty of thick, orange-red lava flowing down the mountain. This was followed by the instant devastation of a tall tree in the lava's path. The sight awed and humbled me, knowing the Lord alone has such infinite power. He alone deserves praise, far beyond our appreciation for His creation.

Moses and his people knew this truth well. They stood before the Lord their God at Horeb, the foot of the mountain blazing with fire, and heard His voice. And the Lord would show them His great strength and favor by taking them out of slavery, helping them conquer other kingdoms, and giving them a land long promised. The Lord gave them laws to follow too so they could witness to all people of His holiness.

Here's the sad part: despite all the Lord showed them, they disobeyed Him. I too have seen His mighty hand, and my prayer ever rises before Him. Help me obey, Dear Lord!

O God, Creator of Heaven and earth, burn Your Word into my heart that I might obey always. In Jesus' name I pray. Amen.

A Righteous Kingdom

Say to those with fearful hearts, "Be strong, do not fear; your God will come, he will come with vengeance; with divine retribution he will come to save you" (Isaiah 35:4).

Scripture: **Isaiah 35:1-4**
Song: **"My Savior First of All"**

Can you imagine a place where our exalted Jesus in all His glory sits upon His throne, reigning as king over all the earth? Oh, what a land of beauty it will be, a kingdom where righteousness becomes the crowning jewel. This new Eden's origin and authority is heavenly in nature, with knowledge of the Lord universal, and harmonious relationships the norm. After all, Satan will have been removed from the scene. Justice prevails, physical restorations occur, joy and peace abound.

Our Lord promises all these things, and He will deliver. He does not lie. So we can trust this: As believers, we will reign with Him (see Revelation 20:1-6), because we serve a great God who wants to reward us for our love and faithfulness to Him.

Our challenge is to be strong, without fear. And it *is* a challenge, isn't it? Life's burdens can become quite heavy. But let us remember that even our trials can lead us to God's goodness. As the great thinker Francis Bacon once said: "Prosperity is not without many fears and distastes; adversity not without many comforts and hopes."

Holy God, Your Word is the Lamb's story from cover to cover. I pray salvation comes to those who do not know You. In Jesus' name, amen.

Offended?

Even Christ did not please himself but, as it is written: "The insults of those who insult you have fallen on me" (Romans 15:3).

Scripture: **Romans 15:1-6**
Song: **"Forgive Them, O My Father"**

I know a lady who dislikes thin women merely because . . . they're thin. As a child, she was teased for being fat. Like her, many people have let offenses and insults cripple their relationships.

What makes us take offense and nurse that offense? The obvious answer: pride. Sadly, pride breaks relationships through bitterness, anger, and unforgiveness. But by walking in the Spirit, we can overcome the sad effects of offensive words and actions in our day-to-day encounters.

I received the Holy Spirit at my baptism. However, there are times when I don't give myself to Him! I need soul-renewal daily if I'm to be Spirit-controlled. Yes, I need constant recollection of His sacrifice. He bore every insult on the cross for me and for you.

When we let His Spirit lead us, His grace allows us to extend grace to someone else. That is the only way we can truly and deeply love the unlovely.

Father, Your Son's shed blood gives me freedom to live a Spirit-filled life. Teach me to walk in Your love so I can forgive any insults that come my way. Because of You, I don't have to live in anger or bitterness. I can choose to let those offenses go and give them to You. In the name of Jesus, amen.

Don't Quit Now

One night the Lord spoke to Paul in a vision: "Do not be afraid; keep on speaking, do not be silent" (Acts 18:9).

Scripture: **Acts 18:1-11**
Song: **"Faith of Our Fathers"**

There are days when I want to quit writing, even while knowing the Lord has called me to this ministry. I began this pursuit believing that if I wrote what God asked of me, and if I wrote it well, then the works would be published. However, getting published involves more than I ever imagined!

Paul, too, knew he had a divine calling to proclaim the gospel. But he kept coming against opposition, even to the point of abuse. Finally, in frustration, Paul "shook out his clothes in protest and said to them, 'Your blood be on your own heads! . . . From now on I will go to the Gentiles'" (v. 6). Thankfully, he pursued another route and continued reasoning with folks about Jesus.

Like Paul, my journey as a witness for Christ has brought me to a few roadblocks, potholes, and stop signs. Yet I've also experienced green lights and wide-open highways for sharing Him on the printed page.

You see, for any of us on the road with Christ, the hazard lights sometimes flash "abandon the call." Yet because of Jesus and His love, we keep on walking, speaking, writing, loving Him back from the heart.

Father, thank You for Your Holy Spirit, who guides me to do Your will. I ask for more patience and self-control during every trial. In Christ, amen.

For the Greater Good

Paul stayed on in Corinth for some time. . . . Before he sailed, he had his hair cut off at Cenchrea because of a vow he had taken (Acts 18:18).

Scripture: **Acts 18:18-23**
Song: **"All Hail the Power of Jesus' Name"**

Paul cut off his hair because of a vow? It made me stop and ponder. A vow? A purification rite of Mosaic law? Isn't this the same Paul who preaches that we're no longer under the law but under grace through Christ Jesus?

Then I thought of the primary purpose of the law. It wasn't given as a means of salvation, but rather as a way by which Israel could be "set apart" in holy living and thus draw the nations to the one true God. Paul isn't double-minded; his goal is clear: to win all people to Christ, by word and also by action.

If my actions offend someone, then I can be sure that he or she will have trouble hearing what I say. Paul too knew this about the Jewish people with whom he would be reasoning in the synagogue. "To the Jews I became like a Jew, to win the Jews," he once said (1 Corinthians 9:20).

It's a good principle for us today. We can't compromise on moral absolutes. But when it comes to the "gray areas" of life, let's care first for our potential brothers and sisters in Christ, offering no undue offense.

Father, Your plan for Your people from the beginning of time is perfect. I thank You that Your law points us to Jesus, and that the righteousness of the law is fulfilled in us as we yield to the Spirit. In Jesus' name, amen.

A Heart for Others

We sent Timothy, who is our brother and God's fellow worker in spreading the gospel of Christ, to strengthen and encourage you in your faith (1 Thessalonians 3:2).

Scripture: **1 Thessalonians 3**
Song: **"Bring Your Burden"**

Do you have a burden for others? As I read this letter from Paul, I could feel his concern coming through the pages. He hurt for the Christian community in Thessalonica and desperately sought a credible report about their commitment to Christ. Unable to leave Athens, Paul sent Timothy.

Jewish and Roman persecutions had escalated at this time. And many of the persecutors followed Paul from city to city, threatening his life. The apostle thus feared the Thessalonians might have decided to turn from their faith amidst such tough trials. Had they stood firm?

With the Thessalonians extending their hands in fellowship to Timothy, Paul could rejoice and be encouraged, even in the midst of persecution. Paul's prayers were answered, and his burden lifted, as Timothy returned with good news: the gospel had taken root. Paul's heart overflowed with joy in knowing this body of believers remained focused on Jesus, the center and core of their faith.

O God, help me to love more like You love each day. Help me to see the needs of those around me and to offer comfort and assistance wherever I can. In the name of Jesus, Lord and Savior of all, I pray. Amen.

Gentle Words

When Priscilla and Aquila heard him, they invited him to their home and explained to him the way of God more adequately (Acts 18:26).

Scripture: **Acts 18:24-28**
Song: **"Search Me, O God"**

Something was missing when Apollos spoke. He knew the Scriptures. He knew the Lord and spoke with passion, proclaiming Jesus as the Messiah. And people listened. But he only knew and told about John's baptism, the one following repentance for sin. The baptism in Jesus' name would tell of their faith in the finished work of Christ.

As Priscilla and Aquila listened to Apollos, they wanted him to know this important revelation. They knew he needed to know more.

But did they confront him in front of the people and tell him he wasn't telling the whole truth? No, they invited him to their home. There, in private, they explained what was missing, teaching in gentleness and love. What an example for us too!

And Apollos accepted their teaching. He was then encouraged to leave Ephesus and go to Corinth. There he was able to tell about Jesus Christ as the Savior, bringing the gospel to many with his powerful speaking.

Heavenly Father, *when I find it necessary to correct or teach someone, help me speak the truth with gentleness. In Jesus' name, amen.*

June 21–27. **Elizabeth VanLiere** lives in Montrose, Colorado. She hopes her devotionals will touch the hearts of others and draw them closer to Christ.

The Path of Life

You have made known to me the path of life; you will fill me with joy in your presence, with eternal pleasures at your right hand (Psalm 16:11).

Scripture: Psalm 16:7-11
Song: "All the Way My Savior Leads Me"

Robert Frost's poem "The Road Not Taken" ends with these words:

> . . . two roads diverged in a wood, and I—
> I took the one less traveled by,
> And that has made all the difference.

I have the same choice. I can join others on the "me" road. The way they walk may seem like more fun at the moment. Choosing that way lays claim to a popular cultural mantra: "I'm worth it." However, it's a dangerous choice. As Jesus said: "Wide is the gate and broad is the road that leads to destruction" (Matthew 7:13).

Or I can choose to journey along with those who walk with the Lord, a road much less traveled. God has made this road, known to us in His Word, the path of life. If I choose this way, at the end I will find joy in God's presence. What a difference a single choice can make.

Dear Heavenly Father, *thank You for showing me the path of life through Your Word. Keep me from the temptation to turn aside, for doing so would lead me away from You. And Lord, I am so looking forward to being in Your presence. Praise to You, my Lord Christ! Amen.*

What a Mentor!

I will instruct you and teach you in the way you should go; I will counsel you and watch over you (Psalm 32:8).

Scripture: **Psalm 32:6-11**
Song: **"He Leadeth Me"**

When I first began writing, I attended several workshops. There I learned how to use words, vary the length of my sentences, and write for certain age groups. I also learned the importance of following a publisher's guidelines.

Next, I joined a writers' group. We would read our pieces to one another and critique our work. One friend pleaded, "Please tell me the good things first. It's so hard hearing the bad things about my writing." I agreed with her. I disliked cutting sentences or "killing" the ideas I considered to be my "darlings."

Just so, trying to do God's will sometimes seems difficult. Yet when I read the Bible I find that the word *obey* appears often. Thankfully, God's instruction and counsel are always stellar. He may indeed confront me with the "bad things" in my character. But He has chosen to place His Spirit within me in order to clean up my act, personally. What a great God He is! He continually watches over me, much as a mentor watches over my writing. A blessed bonus!

Dear Lord, my wonderful instructor, help me to be willing to follow Your guidelines. I know they are the best possible wisdom for my life. Teach me from Your great guidebook, the Bible, and help me take each word to heart. In the name of Jesus, my Savior, I pray. Amen.

In Full View

A man's ways are in full view of the LORD, and He examines all his paths (Proverbs 5:21).

Scripture: **Proverbs 5:21-23**
Song: **"I Cannot Hide from You"**

"Grandma, do you have eyes in the back of your head?" This is the same question my own children once asked. To their amazement, as a mother and grandmother, I always seemed to know when someone was into mischief.

Usually time-out followed the misdeed. And then I would hear a trembling, "I'm sorry. I won't do that again." I would kiss away the tears and forgive the child.

The Lord doesn't need eyes in the back of His head. I'm reminded of this whenever I fly. Depending on which direction I'm heading, I can see from the east to the west or from the north to the south. And so it is with God. He sees every path I take, whether it is good or bad.

Even knowing this doesn't mean I always take the good route. The above verses from Proverbs scare me a bit, for if I take the wrong path, I might not get back on the right way! I know God forgives me when I repent and turn back to Him. But I'd rather not grieve Him with my mischievous wanderings.

Almighty and most merciful God, knowing You see me at all times doesn't keep me from doing wrong. It is when I realize I grieve You that I feel most ashamed. Help me walk in Your way today, dear Lord. In the name of Jesus, who lives and reigns with You and the Holy Spirit, one God, now and forever, amen.

The Blessing of Obedience

See, I am setting before you today a blessing and a curse—the blessing if you obey the commands of the Lord your God that I am giving you today (Deuteronomy 11:26, 27).

Scripture: **Deuteronomy 11:26-32**
Song: **"O How Happy Are They Who the Savior Obey"**

Does God speak to us as He did long ago to the Israelites? My grandson, Sam, believes He does. Sam is married, with three young daughters who are five years old and under. He and his wife, Melodie, believed God was telling him to go to Bible college to become a minister. It meant leaving home and driving for two full days to another city, finding a place to live, and landing a part-time job.

Studying, caring for his family, and working left little free time for Sam. But God blessed him, just as He promises when we obey Him. At the close of this school year, Sam learned he had made the Dean's List.

Furthermore, he will be able to quit his part-time job this fall. You see, he and Melodie are now running a storage facility. As part of the benefits, they live in a rent-free house on the property, which nicely supplements their salary for caring for the storage units. What an example this young couple has given me as they work together to raise a family while serving the Lord.

Loving Heavenly Father, I see the joy of my grandson and his wife as they do Your will. I see the blessings You have poured out on them. Help me to be as obedient as they have been. In Jesus' name, amen.

Homeland Ambassador

Behold, I am coming soon! My reward is with me, and I will give to everyone according to what he has done (Revelation 22:12).

Scripture: **Revelation 22:8-13**
Song: **"The King's Business"**

Missionaries are my favorite people, and I'm glad our church supports several of them. One couple, though, lives in constant danger, making me wonder: Why would they commit themselves to such a scary life?

When I asked, the young man said, "God put these people in my heart. I want to reach as many of them as I can. I want to help them know God and to receive salvation through Jesus Christ."

The Lord says He will reward everyone according to what they have done. Surely our missionaries will receive great reward. But does that leave me, the one who stays at home, merely looking on? No, God hasn't called me to travel to foreign lands. But I can support those who do with prayer and donations.

And I can remember that I too am a commissioned messenger of Christ, no matter where I am. As the apostle Paul said: "God was reconciling the world to himself in Christ, not counting men's sins against them. And he has committed to us the message of reconciliation. We are therefore Christ's ambassadors" (2 Corinthians 5:19, 20).

God, I know I need not travel far to be Your witness. Help me proclaim Your goodness right here in my own neighborhood. Through Christ, amen.

A Bit Questionable?

God did not call us to be impure, but to live a holy life. Therefore, he who rejects this instruction does not reject man but God, who gives you his Holy Spirit (1 Thessalonians 4:7, 8).

Scripture: **1 Thessalonians 4:1-12**
Song: **"Help Me to Be Holy"**

Several years ago my husband and I planned to leave at about 3 AM for a winter trip to Mexico. We had already cleaned out the refrigerator, so we ate dinner in a local restaurant. I chose a salad and some pieces of chicken that appeared a bit underdone. That night, as we drove on our way, I developed a severe stomachache. The farther we drove, the worse I felt.

Arriving in Mexico, I had all the symptoms of the flu and finally went to the doctor. Because food in Mexico at that time was sometimes suspect, the first thing he asked me was, "Where have you eaten since you arrived here?"

"In our trailer," I said. "I brought food from the U.S." After a checkup he found I was infected with a certain strain of bacteria. Several antibiotics, and several days later, I was finally pronounced OK.

Impurities not only infect our bodies. They can infect our character too. And the best defense is to stay away from anything that appears the least bit questionable.

O God, as I walk with You and learn from You, give me the purity of Your own holy character. Keep working in me, I pray. Through Christ, amen.

He's the Shelter

The Lord will be a refuge for his people, a stronghold for the people of Israel (Joel 3:16).

Scripture: **Joel 3:11-16**
Song: **"A Safe Stronghold Our God Is Still"**

I grew up in an age in which "the end times" was a popular subject. Hal Lindsay's book on the end of the world, *The Late Great Planet Earth,* sold millions of copies. End-time films directed at teens seemed bent on scaring youth into the kingdom. And adult Christians debated whether Jesus would return before or after the tribulation described in Revelation.

Although it's tempting to fear the future after reading certain prophetic portions of Scripture, I don't think that was God's intention. In today's Scripture, the Lord follows up a description of destruction with the assurance that He will be a refuge for His people. This is what we should contemplate rather than various theories on His time of arrival.

We tend to be more preoccupied with tomorrow's practical worries than a theological debate. But we can confidently face an uncertain tomorrow, no matter what our circumstances. We have the rock-solid assurance that God will be our shelter in the storm.

Lord of the future, I don't always understand Your Word about end times. But I know You hold me safe in Your hands. Through Christ, amen.

June 28–30. **Bonnie Doran,** of Denver, Colorado, writes devotionals and novels. She enjoys cooking and reading works of science fiction.

In or Out?

Paul said, "John's baptism was a baptism of repentance. He told the people to believe in the one coming after him, that is, in Jesus" (Acts 19:4).

Scripture: **Acts 19:1-10**
Song: **"My Faith Has Found a Resting Place"**

I like to put people in boxes. I'll decide that Betty is strongly opposed to the gospel, or that Will is a super-Christian destined for the ministry. Then there are the people in between. They're harder for me to classify. Some are uninterested in spiritual things. Others long for more understanding but haven't learned the vocabulary. Regardless, I judge these fellow travelers and decide whether they're "in" or "out."

My attitude is contrary to the examples I find in Scripture. Jesus told a teacher of the law, "You are not far from the kingdom of God" (Mark 12:34) when he expressed an accurate understanding of God's decrees. Apollos knew only the baptism of John, yet embraced the Christian faith after Priscilla and Aquila taught him about Jesus.

In today's passage, Paul didn't condemn Apollos's disciples. Instead, he explained the gospel to them. Their eager response proved they already had one foot in the "in" box. So let's follow Paul's example and encourage folks toward the kingdom, starting right where they are.

God of all love, release me from my desire to categorize people rather than meet their spiritual needs wherever they are. Help me to see them through Your eyes and speak Your words of encouragement. In Jesus' name, amen.

Anticipation

Two women will be grinding with a hand mill; one will be taken and the other left. Therefore keep watch, because you do not know on what day your Lord will come (Matthew 24:41, 42).

Scripture: **Matthew 24:36-44**
Song: **"I Can Only Imagine"**

My friend's family members were chosen as finalists in the television program, "Extreme Makeover: Home Edition." The network's decision was kept a secret from everyone. The first time my friend and her family would learn they'd won was when the show's bus pulled up in front of their house. Needless to say, my friend made sure she wasn't getting her nails done or or doing grocery shopping on the day the bus might possibly arrive.

We await an even better event than the hope of a brand new house. Jesus himself will return to earth to right all wrongs and take us to our heavenly home.

In today's Scripture, Jesus says we don't know when He will return. I suspect He will arrive at an unlikely time, because the whole world will be caught off guard.

So He encourages us to wait eagerly for that day, to stay alert and watch for Him. I don't know what will happen to those folks who view His return as an unwelcome surprise. But I don't want to be among them.

God of the past, present, and future, help me to eagerly await Your coming and make sure I'm ready to greet You as friend and Savior. Also, may I learn to bow my heart to You now, so that I will joyfully bow my knee to You then. In Your precious name I pray. Amen.

My Prayer Notes

_____

_____

_____

_____

_____

_____

_____

_____

_____

_____

_____

_____

_____

_____

_____

_____

_____

_____

_____

_____

DEVOTIONS®

The Lord will be a refuge for his people.

—Joel 3:16

JULY

© iStock Photo

Gary Allen, Editor

DEVOTIONS® is published quarterly by Standard Publishing, Cincinnati, Ohio, www.standardpub.com.
© 2009 by Standard Publishing. All rights reserved. Topics based on the Home Daily Bible Readings,
International Sunday School Lessons. © 2006 by the Committee on the Uniform Series. Printed in the
U.S.A. All Scripture quotations, unless otherwise indicated, are taken from the HOLY BIBLE, NEW
INTERNATIONAL VERSION®. NIV®. Copyright © 1973, 1978, 1984 by International Bible Society.
Used by permission of Zondervan. All rights reserved.

Setting Boundaries

"No," they replied, "there may not be enough for both us and you" (Matthew 25:9).

Scripture: **Matthew 25:1-13**
Song: **"Help Somebody Today"**

My church assists people who stop by the office needing emergency help, such as gasoline or rent money. A minister on staff will talk with them, determine their needs, and pray with them before offering practical help. We usually give such folks "the benefit of the doubt."

Several years ago, we had to stop providing aid to a certain man when we learned he was taking advantage of our generosity. He showed up weekly in a nice car, insisted we help, and showed no gratitude when we did. We finally had to cut off assistance for the sake of others.

The wise virgins may have had a similar dilemma. The foolish ones were capable of buying their own oil and should have done so earlier. But they imposed on the generosity of their peers.

Each of us faces situations in which we must set boundaries, financially or emotionally. Let us seek God for discernment. We need to know how much we should help others—and when to help them help themselves.

God of all provision, *I recognize that I'm called to help others in need. However, sometimes their demands overwhelm me. Help me respond with both compassion and discernment. In Jesus' name I pray. Amen.*

July 1–4. **Bonnie Doran**, of Denver, Colorado, writes devotionals and novels. She enjoys reading, cooking, and science fiction.

I'll Be Seeing You

We believe that Jesus died and rose again and so we believe that God will bring with Jesus those who have fallen asleep in him (1 Thessalonians 4:14).

Scripture: **1 Thessalonians 4:13-18**
Song: **"Come, Dearest Lord"**

My brother Jim had terminal cancer. When Mom called me to say he was in the hospital, I quickly booked a flight from Denver to Los Angeles.

He looked pale and thin when I saw him, yet he was upbeat. He joked with the family and talked about his police work. When the doctor told him he was in the last stages of the disease, he turned to the police chaplain and said, "Well, I guess we need to plan a funeral." As I left, I hugged my brother and said, "I will see you again."

He died two weeks later, at home, before I could return. Yet, although I didn't see him again before he died, I won't break my promise. I will indeed see him again when Jesus returns.

Jesus promised He would die but then rise again, and He did exactly what He said. That gives me confidence that He will fulfill His promise to return—and reunite us with our loved ones.

I still miss my brother, of course. But I know he's not gone forever. I will see him again.

***Lord of the resurrection**, thank You for Your promise that we will see our loved ones again. Let me live in that hope and confidence, in spite of the tears that sometimes dim my vision. In the name of Jesus, amen.*

Bungee Cords

May God himself, the God of peace, sanctify you through and through. May your whole spirit, soul and body be kept blameless at the coming of our Lord Jesus Christ. The one who calls you is faithful and he will do it (1 Thessalonians 5:23, 24).

Scripture: **1 Thessalonians 5:12-24**
Song: **"Sanctifying Power"**

If the Christian life is a race, I've struggled to train for it. I have the right shoes and know the track. When the race begins, I start out well enough, then I begin slowing down, as if there's an invisible bungee cord attached to my waist. Eventually, the cord pulls me, and I tumble backwards in the dust. Can you relate?

I can name most of those bungee cords that keep me from being victorious in this race. Impatience is an old favorite. Then there's pride, which gets in the way every time I insist I can do God's will without His help (though I've landed in a heap often enough that I should know better). Then there's the unrelenting pull of the world, luring me back to the tyranny of the urgent—or to "good" things that aren't quite the best things.

How glorious to serve a God who can snip all those bungee cords and let me run free! Thankfully, He alone is the one in charge of sanctifying me. He is faithful, and as I yield to Him, He will do it.

Holy God of faithfulness, free me from the cords of sin and distraction so I can run free in Your strength. I pray this prayer in the name of Jesus, my Savior and Lord. Amen.

Ships of the Desert

You are all sons of the light and sons of the day. We do not belong to the night or to the darkness (1 Thessalonians 5:5).

Scripture: **1 Thessalonians 5:1-11**
Song: **"Lead, Kindly Light"**

Camels are remarkably suited for the desert. Their humps allow them to survive several weeks without food or water. Pads on their feet support them, like snowshoes, on deep, shifting sands. And their long hair keeps them warm on cold desert nights.

One amazing feature is their eyelids: They have three sets of them. The two outer lids have long, curly lashes to protect their eyes from dust and sun. The third eyelid moves from side to side and wipes sand away like a windshield wiper. Its clear membrane is thin enough that the camel can see through it. During a sandstorm, a camel will close this eyelid and still be able to navigate. In other words, this animal can find its way through a sandstorm with its eyes closed.

God has outfitted us for life in the light, just as He created camels for the desert. We can act as children of the day because God has already given us the "equipment" we need—His Word, His indwelling Spirit, and the fellowship of His people. We just need to make use of these wonderful blessings.

Dear Lord, I'm often tempted to sit in the darkness rather than venture into Your light. Give me the strength I need to live as a child of the day. In the holy name of Jesus, my Lord and Savior, I pray. Amen.

Clinging Fears?

Cast all your anxiety on him because he cares for you (1 Peter 5:7).

Scripture: **1 Peter 5:6-11**
Song: **"Leave It There"**

Too often I pray about a burden in my morning prayer time but continue to brood about the crisis during the day. A wonderful lady named Denise, the first mentor God placed in my life, passed on a practical way to cast my anxieties on God.

"Picture the specific need resting in the palm of your hand," she said. "As you pray, lift it to Heaven and imagine putting it into God's able and caring hands. Then you can turn your own hand upside down and shake it to make sure you've let go."

Or is it still clinging to my hand? If so, I repeat the prayer, and it does help me to let go.

I know that God cares about all the things—big and small, short and tall—that make you and me anxious. And surely He wants us to give them to Him, to pour our burdens into His hands. The challenge for me is this: When I pray about my cares, am I truly willing to leave them in His able hands?

Dear Father in Heaven, *I know You care, so I give You my fears to carry today. By Your Spirit, keep me from grabbing them back. In the name of Your Son, my Savior, I pray. Amen.*

July 5–11. **Kathy Dawes** is a freelance writer, Bible study leader, and antique dealer in Owasso, Oklahoma. She and her husband have two sons.

Sweet Fellowship

He went upstairs again and broke bread and ate. After talking until daylight, he left (Acts 20:11).

Scripture: **Acts 20:7-12**
Song: **"Blest Be the Tie That Binds"**

Recently my husband and I enjoyed a three-hour lunch with a couple, Gary and Marsha, whom we've known for almost 20 years. Because of job changes, each of us had moved from the state where we began our friendship.

After an overseas mission trip, Gary took early retirement, went to seminary, and now serves as a minister in a small town. So, when I accompanied my husband on a business trip close to that town, I arranged our happy lunch date.

We talked and ate and continued to share, encouraging one another in our family lives, our work challenges, and our witness for Christ. We could have visited until asked to leave the restaurant; it was so good to see our old friends and to know how we were all growing and being challenged in our Christian walk.

In our Scripture today, the apostle Paul visited with the believers at Troas before he traveled on to Jerusalem, knowing what awaited him. Their time together lasted all night and into the dawn. It would be their last visit, but it was precious, sweet fellowship.

Lord God, *thank You for giving me friends who love You. Show me how I can encourage them and make time for them when life becomes so busy. In the precious name of Jesus I pray. Amen.*

Glimpse of Heaven

I heard every creature in heaven and on earth and under the earth and on the sea, and all that is in them, singing: "To Him who sits on the throne and to the Lamb be praise and honor and glory and power, for ever and ever!" (Revelation 5:13).

Scripture: **Revelation 5:9-14**
Song: **"To Him Who Sits on the Throne"**

What a beautiful picture the apostle John paints! He describes the almighty God sitting on His throne in Heaven and the scarred Lamb of God standing by it. Tens of thousands of angels circle around the throne, worshiping the Lamb in one voice as He takes a scroll that only He is entitled to open. Then we—every created being—join in the worship.

All will one day attribute to the Father and His Son the blessing, honor, and glory due Him forever and ever. We will praise Him for eternity.

Of course, we don't have to wait for Heaven to worship our awesome God. For example, as I have become more and more concerned by the things I see on television, I often simply turn it off. Then I can play some wonderful worship music as I go about my chores. This simple choice influences my perspective, lifting my vision to the heavenly realms. (Actually, that's where we're living right now. See Ephesians 2:6.)

Dear God, I give You praise and honor today. You are worthy of all my worship. Please show me how I can glorify You in the most practical ways this day. In the name of Christ I pray. Amen.

No More Tears

The Lamb at the center of the throne will be their shepherd; he will lead them to springs of living water. And God will wipe away every tear from their eyes (Revelation 7:17).

Scripture: **Revelation 7:9-17**
Song: **"No Tears in Heaven"**

There is so much heartache in this world. The summer after my son graduated from high school, a close friend of his was in a car that suffered a direct hit from a drunken driver. At ten in the morning! The young friend died at the scene, and my son was a pallbearer at his funeral. Sadly, that is not the only serious loss he has experienced in his young life.

We can scream at Heaven, "Life shouldn't be this hard!" But we believers do know this: One day all the hard times will be over, and all the tears will be wiped away by the hand of the one on the throne. (He himself has known much heartache.)

No more hunger, no more thirst, no more scorching heat, but instead springs of living water and the kind hand of the Father on our cheek. Are you waiting in confident hope for that day?

It's coming, and we can prepare for it even now. As the great preacher Henry Ward Beecher said, "Heaven will be inherited by every man who has heaven in his soul."

Father God, thank You for this sure word of an eternity with You. While I'm waiting, help me live as a good citizen of that far country, even as I live out my days in this vale of tears. In Jesus' name, amen.

Blessings in Death

Then I heard a voice from heaven say, "Write: Blessed are the dead who die in the Lord from now on." "Yes," says the Spirit, "they will rest from their labor, for their deeds will follow them" (Revelation 14:13).

Scripture: **Revelation 14:6-13**
Song: **"The Haven of Rest"**

Dad died suddenly of a heart attack at the age of 55. I lived in another state, and I knew my young son now wouldn't get the chance to know his godly grandfather. In my limited perspective, it seemed that God wasn't doing the best thing.

But in this verse we see Heaven's perspective. "Blessed are the dead who die in the Lord." It is a good thing to die in His hands. Now there is rest, a rest from labor forever.

My dad was a hard worker and a ready volunteer at his church. He taught a Bible class and used his accounting knowledge to help with the church budget. He had a plush garden and gave many bags of produce to families in the community. One day he will be rewarded for his labor. But now he has rest.

The weeks and months after a death can be an awkward time for friends of the grieving family. So let us consider today: How can we use the truths of Heaven to encourage those who grieve?

Dear Lord, thank You for the promise of rest from our labor some day. I know that my loved ones who have gone before me are blessed with that rest in You. I give You praise with a grateful heart, in Jesus' name. Amen.

Thunder and Hallelujah!

Then I heard what sounded like a great multitude, like the roar of rushing waters and like loud peals of thunder, shouting: "Hallelujah! For our Lord God Almighty reigns" (Revelation 19:6).

Scripture: **Revelation 19:1-8**
Song: **"Hallelujah, Our God Reigns"**

During a crashing thunderstorm, it's nice to have Dad around. I remember growing up in the Midwest and fleeing to the basement with flashlights during storm warnings. As long as Dad was along, we kids weren't overly afraid. True, the sound of the thunder was fearful, but we could look up at him and then relax.

Some days we might wonder, as we look around us at our horribly divided and suffering world, "Who is actually in charge here?" But we know: God rules the heavens, and He has already defeated the enemy who now runs free for a while on the earth. So, the enemy can thunder occasionally, but even to do that he needs permission from above. When I feel bothered by this opposing evil, I need only to look at my heavenly Father and relax.

One day Christ will come back and reign over all. Let us look for that day and say "Hallelujah!" And when the things that oppose His kingdom roar, we can look above at the face of our Father and take a deep breath.

Almighty and everlasting God, *I praise You, for You are the Lord of lords and the God of gods. I look forward to the time when You will reign over all with perfect justice and peace. In the precious name of Your Son, amen.*

Justice and Relief

God is just: He will pay back trouble to those who trouble you and give relief to you who are troubled, and to us as well. This will happen when the Lord Jesus is revealed from heaven in blazing fire with his powerful angels (2 Thessalonians 1:6, 7).

Scripture: **2 Thessalonians 1:3-12**
Song: **"The Battle Hymn of the Republic"**

Sometimes this life just isn't fair. A less deserving coworker gets the promotion because he has "connections." Or, as was the case with my father, a man of integrity who refused to compromise, we are forced into early retirement when our moral standards thwart executive plans. In Dad's situation, I wanted justice immediately. I prayed for it fervently, and I became impatient when God didn't respond according to my timetable.

In our verse today, God says He is just. After Dad's death, I was sad for months as I thought of the hard times he'd unjustly suffered. But God reassured me that His justice will ultimately unfold. Maybe not in this lifetime, though. I may not see everything played out on earth. But justice will happen when He returns, if not before. Yes, that is the wonderful thing to me: God has already written the ending of this story of the cosmos, and it is good and just.

Father God, help me trust in Your justice when I don't see it here in this world. Thank You for the promise that one day, when Your Son returns, You will accomplish perfect justice and give relief to the troubled and oppressed. All praise to You, in the name of Christ my Lord. Amen.

The Plans of the Builder

The plans of the LORD stand firm forever, the purposes of his heart through all generations (Psalm 33:11).

Scripture: **Psalm 33:4-12**
Song: **"Have Thine Own Way, Lord"**

Julia waited for 30 minutes before deciding that no one was showing up for Bible study. *Great!* she thought. *I can go home and do some laundry.* She packed up her things and headed out of the building. Just then she saw two ladies walking from the parking lot. Her emotions were swirling. Disappointment? Excitement?

Julia resolved to welcome these ladies and proceed with the study she'd prepared. When Julia left that evening, she thanked God for the women who arrived at just the right moment.

Plans change, whether we like it or not. When builders construct a house, they often make changes to adjust for unforeseen problems or the preferences of the homeowner. The blueprints are redrawn, and the plan continues from that point.

God's intervention in our lives always suits His purposes. He is the homeowner, and we obey by adjusting our perspective and following His blueprint within each situation.

Lord, You're the builder, and I'm the worker. I will put my plans for today in second place and allow Your divine purposes to rule. In Jesus' name, amen.

July 12–18. **Casey Pitts** works beside her husband, an Air Force chaplain, in ministering to military families through teaching, writing, and small group studies.

Focus Forward

Holy brothers, who share in the heavenly calling, fix your thoughts on Jesus, the apostle and high priest whom we confess (Hebrews 3:1).

Scripture: **Hebrews 3:1-6**
Song: **"Turn Your Eyes upon Jesus"**

On the wall facing the end of the balance beam was a large poster of Nadia Comaneci, the famous gymnast from Romania. Nadia's face was intense with concentration, as her perfect form posed on the balance beam.

Our instructor would encourage us to focus our attention on that poster as we moved delicately across the narrow apparatus. Looking into Nadia's eyes, we gained confidence, hoping to be just like her some day.

My gymnastics trainer knew the importance of setting our minds on something greater than the task immediately before us. She knew that when we glanced away from the face of our hero, our bodies would waver slightly.

The same is true when we focus our eyes on the Lord Jesus. Imagine walking through your life on a narrow road, with the face of Jesus as your focus. When we look to the side, we falter. When we become too engrossed in the moment, we lose sight of the goal. Then we must pause a moment to regain our perspective.

O God, teach me to walk in Your truth today. When I'm caught up in the trivial things of the moment, help me look forward into Your eyes. There I'll see the "author and perfecter of [my] faith" (Hebrews 12:2). In the name of the Father, the Son, and the Holy Spirit, I pray. Amen.

Best Recipe

The entire law is summed up in a single command: "Love your neighbor as yourself" (Galatians 5:14).

Scripture: **Galatians 5:7-14**
Song: **"They'll Know We Are Christians by Our Love"**

Mother and I looked with dismay at the flat, pock-marked slab of brownies. We had always used the boxed variety, but today we'd dared to start from scratch.

"They're ruined," I said, holding back tears. "And I so wanted brownies!" While I was disappointed, I think Mother was more embarrassed, saying, "Apparently, you can't substitute baking soda for baking powder." Thirty years later, I'm more careful about following directions.

It's true, not only in baking: Small errors can have huge impact. Our words and attitudes can convey blessing . . . or something far less attractive. In fact, a sour attitude coupled with a few choice words can spread like wild fire and do untold damage. I know of a church where one woman complained rather mildly about the music minister. Before long, the whole church was ready to fire him.

Paul cautions the Galatians that a little yeast leavens the whole loaf. What seems to be an insignificant sin can turn sweet, warm relationships into something flat and hard, just like a pan of burned brownies. God has given us the best recipe: Love your neighbors as yourself; never burn them.

Father, I yield my attitudes to You. In place of selfishness and pride, give me words of life and hope to share. Through Christ, I pray. Amen.

Free for the Hearing

God's Word is not chained (2 Timothy 2:9).

Scripture: 2 Timothy 2:8-13
Song: "You Are My All in All"

Molly, a mother of three in Asia, places her precious copy of the Bible back in her laundry bag until tomorrow. The pages were rumpled long before the book arrived in her hands. The used copy was hand-carried across the border by a friend visiting from a nearby nation. She keeps the precious book hidden during the day, opening it only in private moments.

Millions of people like Molly must hide their Bibles. Others long for a few pages of Scripture to share among an entire village. In Africa, Asia, and the Middle East, the Word of God goes forth despite valiant efforts to restrain it. Governments try to protect their people and maintain order through other belief systems, confiscating illegal Bibles and arresting missionaries. Yet, copies of the Bible abound, hidden in jars of grain and under beds.

The bigger picture goes far beyond paper copies of Truth. God's Word is preached in these "closed" nations. Even one verse of Scripture, held tight in the mind and heart of a believer, proves the gospel is not chained. Will you grasp His Word in your heart as if your life depends upon it? Molly does.

Father, guide and protect those who share Your message around the world. Open my mind to learn Your Word today. Give me opportunities to share Your truth with those in my own neighborhood. In Jesus' name, amen.

Challenged by the Word

You know that I have not hesitated to preach anything that would be helpful to you but have taught you publicly and from house to house (Acts 20:20).

Scripture: **Acts 20:17-24**
Song: **"Precious Words"**

Grace Church held a business meeting to decide whether the minister should be relieved of his position. Mr. Smith had recently preached loving, but firm, words from the pulpit. He challenged the members to evaluate their habits. Were they habits of mere tradition or habits developed by faith? He had ruffled the feathers of more than one founding family.

The people took turns speaking in this meeting, until one young girl stood. "Mr. Smith is the sixth minister we've had in three years. We've had one problem or another with each of them. Did you ever consider that the problem might be us, and not the ministers?"

Sometimes we don't want to hear what God's servants must say to us. As a rejected Jesus himself put it: "No prophet is accepted in his hometown" (Luke 4:24). So some preachers just can't get through to their own congregations.

Paul preached the Word boldly. But his hearers looked beyond the man to see and hear God's call to them.

Lord God, open my heart to Your truth, even if it is not what I want to hear. Give me the courage to take Your message to heart and to obey it, no matter the kind of messenger You use to convey it. In Jesus' name, amen.

Whom Can You Trust?

We ask you, brothers, not to become easily unsettled or alarmed by some prophecy, report or letter supposed to have come from us, saying that the day of the Lord has already come (2 Thessalonians 2:1, 2).

Scripture: **2 Thessalonians 2:1-12**
Song: **"The Clouds of Judgment Gather"**

Tabloid magazines litter the checkout line announcing shocking marriages, horrific affairs, and daily alien sightings. Occasionally the headlines try to tempt potential readers with special knowledge about the future. "Nostradamas Says World Ends Tomorrow" or "Scientists Discover End Times Secrets in DaVinci's Last Supper." We may snicker as the lady in front of us eagerly purchases several copies. How can she believe this stuff?

Reader's Digest published an article in July 2008 about how television, magazines, and the Internet had influenced court cases. The media had been able to convince the public of the guilt of a bombing suspect, for instance. After only a few days of actual scientific investigations, the media was proven wrong, but the damage was already done—people had believed a lie.

As Christians, let us be careful about where we get our knowledge of God. If we seek to know the living Word, we will find Him in the written Word that witnesses to Him.

God of all truth, I submit myself to You today. Forgive me for those times when I have strayed from Your Word. In Jesus' name, amen.

Excellent!

May our Lord Jesus Christ himself and God our Father, who loved us and by his grace gave us eternal encouragement and good hope, encourage your hearts and strengthen you in every good deed and word (2 Thessalonians 2:16, 17).

Scripture: **2 Thessalonians 2:13-17**
Song: **"Thy Word"**

"Look, Mommy!" Elie beamed. "The teacher said my paper was 'Excellent!'" She held it out for me to see.

"I am so happy for you, Elie. You've worked hard, and your teacher noticed, didn't she?"

My daughter nodded. "I'm going to work on my homework now," she said eagerly.

This small compliment carried my child through several days of school. My encouraging words helped her see that she was headed in the right direction. And her teacher gave positive reinforcement, knowing the result would be a more motivated, successful student.

Our God knows our need for encouragement. He offers grace and strength for the particular daily challenges we face. But ultimately He gives encouragement to keep us heading in the right direction overall. It's as if He says to us, "My child, you are Excellent!" Though we are unworthy of His grace, it is that same grace that will "present [us] before his glorious presence without fault" (Jude 24).

Lord Jesus, fill me with the hope and encouragement that only You can give. Strengthen me in every word and deed, and help me to know the glories of Your grace in a deeper way every day. In Christ I pray. Amen.

God Songs

I will sing of the LORD's great love forever; with my mouth I will make your faithfulness known through all generations (Psalm 89:1).

Scripture: **Psalm 89:1-8**
Song: **"Sing Away the Shadows"**

Ever heard a song in an elevator—and had that tune playing over and over in your mind throughout the rest of the day? For the psalmist, it will be a song of Scripture—and it will "play" eternally.

How can we make it a song that we too can sing forever? You see, I have a tough time memorizing mere words. Yet, for some reason I can learn a song, and it will stick in my mind forever. Consequently, I have discovered that if I learn songs that are Scripture, or at least contain Bible verses, I can memorize verses with ease.

And the Bible is full of many promises to take into our hearts and hold close. In verse 4 of our Scripture today, God promised David that his line of descendents would be established forever until Jesus' return. What other promises are written within the Scriptures? Where are the promises for me? When I find them will I be able to remember them and make them a part of what is written in my heart until I see Jesus?

Lord, help me hide Your Word in my heart so it can go with me everywhere I go. Thus may I sing of Your great love forever. In Jesus' name, amen.

July 19–25. **Becki Reiser**, of Dover, Ohio, has a part-time ministry with her husband, Jeff, that focuses on offering forgiveness to those who injure beyond words.

Even in the Hard Times

Why are you weeping and breaking my heart? I am ready not only to be bound, but also to die in Jerusalem for the name of the Lord Jesus (Acts 21:13).

Scripture: **Acts 21:1-14**
Song: **"Lord, Make Me an Instrument of Your Peace"**

When facing adversity or facing death, do we turn tail and run, or do we march straight ahead, fully knowing where our choices will take us? I think about Randy Pausch, the professor from Carnegie-Mellon University. He wrote *The Last Lecture* while suffering pancreatic cancer.

Facing a terminal illness can make a person go to bed and never get up again. Not so with Mr. Pausch. He decided he'd make his experience with a fatal disease something people could actually learn from.

Here in Acts 21, Paul must choose. If he goes to Jerusalem he will die. His attitude? He welcomed whatever would come, for his life was solidly in God's hands. Just as Randy Pausch welcomed the opportunity to teach others, even under painful circumstances, so too did Paul. He wanted every experience of his life to show forth the goodness and greatness of his Lord Jesus.

How do I face adversity? I want to have the same attitude as Paul. I want to welcome any and every opportunity for Christ's life to show through in my life—in good times and hard times.

Father, may I be an instrument of Your love. Use me to make a difference to someone listening to the concert of my life. In Jesus' name, amen.

Strong to the End

He will keep you strong to the end, so that you will be blameless on the day of our Lord Jesus Christ (1 Corinthians 1:8).

Scripture: 1 Corinthians 1:4-9
Song: "Spirit, Strength of All the Weak"

Did you ever begin a task full of energy—all the while thinking "I can do this"—and then long before the chore was finished, you felt like quitting? I think we've all been there. It's like running in a race, but we never bothered to practice first. We get weak, our legs feel like rubber, and our lungs burn for lack of oxygen . . . all within the first few blocks! We find out that we're just not equipped to run, and we never make it to the finish line.

It can happen in our walk with the Lord. We may not always be prepared to do some form of ministry that lands in our path. It might be an unplanned opportunity to lead a Bible study, to teach Sunday school, or simply to speak a word for Christ to a visiting stranger. It's not that we can't do these things. But we do need to prepare for them, to train for the race. Then we can step out in faith and use the knowledge we have already. Read, study, listen, and pray. Then let God use us as He will.

To train for this Christian race, your must warm up, start off slowly, and then pick up the pace. Soon your endurance will grow and you'll be strong to the end, because you trained properly.

Father, keep me from losing interest in this long race to please You. Let me learn at Your feet, so I'll have the confidence I need. In Jesus' name, amen.

The Promise Keeper

I will surely bless you and give you many descendents (Hebrews 6:14).

Scripture: **Hebrews 6:13-20**
Song: **"Father Abraham"**

When my 17-year-old daughter died, I thought my life had ended too. Or at least part of the *purpose* of my life: being a mother. Then God reminded me that I didn't have just one child, I had four. The other three needed me desperately. Their world had come to an abrupt halt as well as mine.

Eight weeks after Liz's death, I felt the Lord speak something to my heart. I needed to write a book about our experience. He gave me the title and the dedication page. And I could see in my mind's eye what the cover would look like.

Then the doubting began. I had never written, so how could I do this? I began to doubt what I felt God had spoken. Then I began to doubt it would ever happen.

After eight years, I now have a manuscript ready. I doubted, but God never wavered. He told me something, and He kept His word. Just as Abraham received a promise from God and waited patiently (v. 15), he finally received what was promised.

*Help me, **Father,** to learn to trust You. When You speak to me, let me listen and be obedient. Help me to have grace and endurance while I wait for the unfolding of Your plans, in Your own time and way. I pray this prayer in the name of Jesus, my merciful Savior and Lord. Amen.*

Surrounded by Hope

Let us hold unswervingly to the hope we profess, for he who promised is faithful (Hebrews 10:23).

Scripture: **Hebrews 10:19-25**
Song: **"The Solid Rock"**

Sometimes when we are in the pit of despair, we can only keep something simple in our minds. For me that was a single word: *hope.* That word was a lifeline for me after Liz died. I had a tough time concentrating, and retaining things was nearly impossible.

But loving friends and family surrounded me . . . as I held fast to *hope.* It seemed that everywhere I looked the word would turn up. It was the one thing that actually registered in my brain, despite my shock and grief.

Apparently, many people were clinging to that same beautiful word. Folks started to bring me things that displayed it. I received rings, cards, pens, and books—with *hope.* A friend from Taiwan even sent me a necklace and earrings, with the word *hope* written in Chinese.

As you can see, I was surrounded by *hope!* The few Scriptures I was able to remember seemed to contain the same message. Then I realized that my *hope* was built on Christ. Without Jesus, I would never have survived that difficult time in my life.

Father God, help me always to build my trust and confidence in Jesus Christ, to lean on Him and trust in His promises. He is my life, my salvation, and all my hope for the future. In the name of the Father and of the Son and of the Holy Spirit, I pray. Amen.

Walking in the Light

If we walk in the light, as he is in the light, we have fellowship with one another, and the blood of Jesus, his Son, purifies us from all sin (1 John 1:7).

Scripture: **1 John 1:5-10**
Song: **"Jesus Is the Light"**

It is difficult for me to see in the dark, since I suffer from night blindness, and I have astigmatism in both eyes. I cannot get my eyes to adjust very quickly. When I go to see a film, I have to stand and wait until a very bright scene comes on the screen, or I just let my husband lead me to the aisle he wants to sit in. Yet, if I would walk into the theater before the movie begins and the lights are on, I can see just fine.

And I can see pretty clearly how this works in my walk with the Lord too. When we walk in darkness, we cannot see, we are blind. But when the light of the world comes, He throws light into every shadowy corner, and it can no longer be dark. Do we let Jesus bring to light the dark areas in our lives?

Simply put, we have to stop sinning. Christ will show us where we need to clean up, and He will do the purifying, if we let Him. Come, join me on this blessed walk. We'll help each other stay on the well-lighted path.

Heavenly Father, help me to surrender the dark areas in my heart, the areas that I have not yet given over to You. I know that where there is light, darkness has to flee. In the name of Jesus, who lives and reigns with You and the Holy Spirit, one God, now and forever, amen.

Don't Rust Out!

We hear that some among you are idle. They are not busy; they are busybodies (2 Thessalonians 3:11).

Scripture: **2 Thessalonians 3:1-15**
Song: **"Language of Disciples"**

When I was a child back in the 60s, I remember once riding with Mom in the car as we got on the highway for a trip to my grandparents' house. Once we hit the on-ramp, my mother would "stomp on the gas"—and it felt to me as if we were flying! She used to tell us kids that she was "blowing out the carbon." I wasn't sure what that meant, but I knew it was fun.

Later, when I was a bit older, it was explained to me that carbon would build up in a car's engine from idling. Hence the (questionable) procedure. And just cruising around town didn't qualify for "carbon blowing." You apparently needed to reach a certain speed for a period of time. That would help the engine clear out its carbon problem. Or so I was told.

The Scripture also speaks of idling. If we're not busy with our Father's business, we may end up forgetting about our calling as the body of Christ: to be His hands, feet, and voice in the world. That ministry will demand much of us. But as an old preacher once said: "When it comes to serving our Lord, better to burn out than to rust out."

Dear Lord, they say idle hands are the devil's workshop. Keep me from a lazy approach to the command to make disciples. In Jesus' name, amen.

Obedience: a Blessing!

The Lord called to him in a vision, "Ananias!" "Yes, Lord," he answered (Acts 9:10).

Scripture: **Acts 9:10-16**
Song: **"Where He Leads Me, I Will Follow"**

When a popular evangelist held a conference in our town, I served as an usher in the large auditorium. On a Friday evening, a lone woman slipped into my third-deck section. As the worship music started, her face radiated her love for the Lord, and I sensed that she was at the conference for a specific reason.

Watching her, I felt a nudging in my spirit to give her a word of encouragement. *She doesn't know anything about me—and she'll think I'm crazy*, I thought. Nevertheless, I prayed, "Yes, Lord."

Stepping towards her, I trusted God to give me the words to say—words that soon washed over her like healing rain. Moved to tears, she thankfully embraced me.

I never learned that lady's name, but her face is forever etched in my mind. When I think of her and those precious moments, I'm reminded of the blessedness of simple obedience.

Father God, help me to hear Your still, small voice. And give me the courage to boldly answer Your call without question. I stand before You, a vessel willing to be used for righteous purposes—and thank You for using me in spite of my imperfections. In Jesus' name, amen.

July 26–31. **Jan Parrish** served as a minister and counselor before becoming caregiver to her mother-in-law. She lives in Colorado, with her husband of 27 years.

False Accusations

This is the man who teaches all men everywhere against our people and our law and this place. And besides, he has brought Greeks into the temple area and defiled this holy place (Acts 21:28).

Scripture: **Acts 21:27-36**
Song: **"Wounded for Me"**

"Lord, this is so unfair!" I cried. "I can't even defend myself." While my father-in-law lay dying of cancer, a close friend made false accusations about me to the minister and other church leaders. I was out of state and grieving the loss of a family member, which made her betrayal even more shocking. A more experienced teacher, she felt justified in trying to "take over" the women's Bible study I'd been leading.

Few things are more painful than false accusations, especially when someone questions our motives. I was angry—and worried that others would believe the reports. But the more I prayed, the greater peace I found. The Lord showed me that sometimes good people make bad decisions. Our part is to forgive and move forward.

During the next month, my hands were tied; I could do nothing about the situation but pray. Though I was deeply wounded, I continued to submit the matter to God—and the truth came to light before I returned. Because God fought the battle for me, I never had to defend myself.

Heavenly Father, help me to rest in You when circumstances spin out of my control, and I feel so powerless. In Christ's precious name, amen.

Totally Worth It

My brothers, I have fulfilled my duty to God in all good conscience to this day (Acts 23:1).

Scripture: **Acts 22:30–23:11**
Song: **"Christian, Dost Thou See Them?"**

Seventeen-year-old Cassie Bernall had no idea she'd face the decision of her life as she headed to Columbine High School on April 20, 1999. However, when two gunmen entered the school library where she was studying, she began to pray.

With a gun pointed at her face, she was asked, "Do you believe in God?"

She hesitated for only a moment before she responded, "Yes."

Cassie met her Savior with a clear conscience. She'd done everything He asked without compromise, and her one word testimony has influenced countless others with renewed faith and courage.

God prepared Cassie by speaking to her heart. "Honestly, I want to live completely for God. It's hard and scary, but totally worth it." She had written those words in a note on April 19th.

I too want to live completely for God. I know it will require setting aside my own agenda and asking God what He wants me to do throughout each day. I know it will be difficult; I'm convinced it will be totally worth it.

Father, I pray for all who must make life and death decisions in our world, all for the privilege of being called Christian. Through Christ, amen.

Standing Firm

I am now standing before Caesar's court, where I ought to be tried. I have not done any wrong to the Jews, as you yourself know very well (Acts 25:10).

Scripture: **Acts 25:1-12**
Song: **"The Storm Is Passing Over"**

Sometimes it's OK to follow the crowd, but it's certainly not the best way to parent. Our teenage son needed strong parenting and strict boundaries. We couldn't just do what "all the other moms and dads" were doing.

One particularly trying time: our young Tom "totaled" a bus bench. Because he caused his car to slide into a bus stop while he was speeding in a school zone, we made him sell his car. He lost money on the sale and was car-less for several months. Friends and family thought we were too harsh. But after much prayer, we stood firm and did what we believed God would want.

Tom faced those consequences squarely, learned a very difficult lesson, and is a better driver today. In the end, the judge was more lenient because he knew that Tom had already received significant discipline.

In our Scripture I see an apostle who seemed to stand against a whole world of contrary opinion. It didn't turn him. Paul knew his calling, and he knew his mission. More importantly, he surely relied on the living Lord who dwelt within him. May it be so for each of us today.

Father, help me remember that no matter the opposition, I can find shelter in the storm. Thank You for being my Rock. In Jesus' name, amen.

Work in Progress

Being confident of this, that he who began a good work in you will carry it on to completion until the day of Christ Jesus (Philippians 1:6).

Scripture: **Philippians 1:3-11**
Song: **"Footprints of Jesus"**

Though I've been a Christian for 40 years, I'm still a work in progress. Yet it's reassuring to know that no matter where I am in my Christian walk, God is at work, honing my character to match His.

It seems that the sins I struggled with as an immature Christian no longer plague me. But as I mature in the faith, I wrestle and seek to overcome the more subtle sins. When I'm home at last, sitting at the feet of Jesus, I'll be free from the very presence of sin. But until then, I know I'll occasionally fall. Even Billy Graham, one of the most prolific and well-known evangelists of our time, admits to sinning every day.

But Christ Jesus cannot fail! You and I are His work of art, a project in purification. As He does His cleansing work within, let us encourage one another and treat one another with the utmost patience. That is, we can remind one another regularly with this acronym that once appeared on colorful lapel buttons: PBPGINFWMY. (Please be patient, God is not finished with me yet.)

*Thank You, **Jesus,** for choosing my soul as Your workshop. I'm encouraged to know that what You have started there You will continue to completion. Do shape me into the person You created me to be. In Jesus' name, amen.*

In Chains for Christ

It has become clear throughout the whole palace guard and to everyone else that I am in chains for Christ (Philippians 1:13).

Scripture: **Philippians 1:12-18**
Song: **"A Shelter in the Time of Storm"**

Joni Erickson Tada is, in a sense, in chains for Christ. One day she was a carefree teenager, the next she was imprisoned in a quadriplegic body due to a diving accident. Yet her chains not only encouraged others but also increased her faith as she grew into more and more reliance upon Christ. Because Joni took her tragedy and gave it to God, He has used her in a mighty way.

Confined to a wheelchair, Joni creatively adapted her lifestyle and learned to paint by holding a brush in her teeth. Soon God began calling her to help others with limited abilities.

What would her life have been like if she hadn't taken that dive? Would she still have a worldwide ministry? Would she have developed the strong character and courage to move into such a ministry?

From great tragedy can come great character. Reflecting on the ministries of both Joni and the apostle Paul, I ask myself, "What are my chains? What adversity or physical infirmity can I give to Christ for His glory?"

Most merciful God, thank You for the wonderful testimonies of Paul and Joni. Thank You that You use ordinary people to do extraordinary things for You. Please examine my life and show me if there are any chains that may be used for Your purposes, now or in the future. In Jesus' name, amen.

DEVOTIONS®

Gary Allen, Editor

*T*he Son of Man did not come to be served, but to serve.

—Matthew 20:28

AUGUST

*Photo © Gino Santa Maria |
Dreamstime.com*

My Final Home

For to me, to live is Christ and to die is gain (Philippians 1:21).

Scripture: **Philippians 1:18-29**
Song: **"When We All Get to Heaven"**

For many years, I was terrified of dying. Each time I heard of a tragic accident, I became more afraid. Finally, I gave my fears to God and asked Him to give me a healthier perspective.

He reminded me of my experience in childbirth: the labor and the delivery of my first child. Though I was nervous and somewhat afraid, I could hardly wait to hold my little girl in my arms. Once she was born, I nearly forgot about the painful delivery. I could see that dying must be something like that. I don't have a full understanding of the process, but I do eagerly anticipate the moment when I will see my Savior, face to face.

And, of course, this world is not my dwelling place. Jesus is preparing that right now, and there's not a mansion on earth whose splendor can compare to the home He's building for me. No doubt that is why the apostle could declare, with all confidence, that dying would be far from a hopeless loss for him. How much he would gain!

Father, I look forward to arriving in Heaven to dwell with You. Help me keep my eye on that prize and to speak of its wonders, so others can live with great expectation too. In Christ's precious name, amen.

August 1. **Jan Parrish** served as a minister and counselor before becoming caregiver to her mother-in-law. She lives in Colorado with her husband of 27 years.

The Greatest of All

The Son of Man did not come to be served, but to serve (Matthew 20:28).

Scripture: **Matthew 20:20-28**
Song: **"I Will Serve Thee"**

Our daughter and son-in-law were relaxing on the couch when 2-year-old Grace came up and wanted to play. Tom laid aside his book, got down on the floor, and played with her for an hour or more. Then he bathed her and tucked her into bed. He does this every night after work. What a great example of a servant! Then I thought, *God does much the same for me.* He takes care of my needs, not just when it's convenient for Him, but every single time I come to Him for attention.

Sometimes the hardest work is being a servant, because we seldom see immediate results. It's messy. It's not fun. Jesus lived for years with 12 men who often didn't "get it." How frustrating that must have been. But still He lovingly washed their dirty feet, tirelessly explained God's truths to them, and patiently guided them toward maturity.

I'm a lot like those disciples. My nature is incurably self-centered. Only through the power of His Spirit can I serve others as He so patiently and lovingly serves me.

*Thank You, **Lord,** that You never give up on me. Though I am so undeserving, yet daily You shower me with Your grace, mercy, and love. I ask for the heart to serve those You bring to me. In Jesus' name I pray. Amen.*

August 2–8. **Elizabeth Nelson** spent her childhood in a fishing village on the Bering Sea before moving to Minnesota. She now resides in Aurora, Colorado.

Lord of My Rocky Life

When the son of Paul's sister heard of this plot, he went into the barracks and told Paul (Acts 23:16).

Scripture: **Acts 23:12-24**
Song: **"Rock of Ages"**

I've never had people plotting to kill me. But there have been times when life was so hard that I thought I wanted to die. I didn't know what to do, and I was desperate for answers.

The apostle Paul, hearing from a nephew of his impending assassination, must have wondered, "Why is this happening? I thought You were in control, Lord. Can't You do something?"

For any of us, life can become downright treacherous. In those rocky times, God is not absent. Not at all. When I cried out for Him to rescue my child, He was there, working behind the scenes, slowly but surely. When my house burned down and I couldn't cry out, I felt Him there, holding me up. He allows these things into my life in order to press me, once again, close to Him. To show me that I'm not in control, but He is.

I would never choose to have such trials in my life. But looking back, I know without a doubt that God was there. He was there the whole time.

Almighty and gracious Father, *thank You for being with me in every trying circumstance of my life. Thank You for lightening my load, comforting me in Your arms, answering my prayers. I love You! In the name of Jesus, Lord and Savior of all, I pray. Amen.*

Enduring Treasures

Here we do not have an enduring city, but we are looking for the city that is to come (Hebrews 13:14).

Scripture: **Hebrews 13:12-18**
Song: **"City of Gold"**

Maynard and Loraine Londborg had been married for little more than a year when they felt God calling them to the mission field in 1946. They left their families in the Midwest and traveled to a remote village in Alaska. There they would care for orphaned children.

As the years passed, they endured many hardships. After all, they lived in a frozen, forbidding landscape, with no running water and no grocery store. They raised their children in a drafty old mission house.

The Londborgs started a Christian high school for native boys and girls whose only school had been 700 air miles away. They cared lovingly for the sick. They made friends for the kingdom. When they returned from Alaska 20 years later, they left behind enduring treasures: spiritual children, believers who'd been strengthened, young people who went on to places of leadership.

God does not promise us treasures on earth, and those are fleeting anyway. But we are promised an enduring city that will never pass away. And God himself will be there. He is the greatest treasure of all.

Dear God, please keep me from grasping the things of this life as if they could somehow become enduring treasures. Show me how to lay up treasures in Heaven through selfless acts of service. In Jesus' name, amen.

Patterns

Do not conform any longer to the pattern of this world, but be transformed by the renewing of your mind (Romans 12:2).

Scripture: **Romans 12:1, 2**
Song: **"May the Mind of Christ, My Savior"**

Years ago, I signed up to help "pattern" a baby girl who was born with Down's Syndrome. I was to move her legs and arms in specific motions in order to enhance her muscular strength and coordination. If someone else were to come in and pattern her limbs incorrectly, imagine the confusion in her mind and muscles.

The world has a pattern too. The problem is, it's very attractive and promises to make us happy. When we follow the destructive pattern of the world, we suffer. But God is waiting with open arms for us to ask for His help.

We once hired a young man to hang wallpaper for us. Barry wore a headset constantly while he worked. When I asked him about it, he said that God had rescued him from an addiction to drugs, but that his mind had been affected. So hour after hour, day after day, Barry listened to and memorized Scripture. In the process, God renewed and restored his mind. I will never forget his diligence in seeking God. And I will never forget that clear testimony to God's life-transforming power.

O gracious God, open my eyes to see the patterns of the world that are harmful to me. Renew my mind and my spirit that I may serve You with every spiritual gift You've given me. In the name of the Father, the Son, and the Holy Spirit, I pray. Amen.

But Look at You!

Do everything without complaining or arguing (Philippians 2:14).

Scripture: **Philippians 2:14-18**
Song: **"Make Me a Blessing"**

Will Bowen, minister of a church in Kansas City, grew tired of the barrage of usual complaints—about the type of music, about the length of the evening service, about the Youth program, about . . . well, the list seemed endless. So in July 2006 he issued his church members a challenge. He asked them to join with him in a "No Complaints" campaign. They would all agree to cease from complaining, gossiping, or criticizing for 21 days. (Most people, including the minister himself, took months to string together 21 straight complaint-free days!)

Complaining is a problem that I slip into when things aren't going my way. A few months after I was married, I went to the Lord with what I thought was a legitimate complaint about my husband. In an instant, the Holy Spirit seemed to say, "But look at you." *Ouch!* What I saw in me was anger, pride, and unforgiveness. Not a pretty sight. To my chagrin, I had to let God work in my life, just as He would work in my husband's life. And now, when I feel like complaining, I try to remember God's greater purpose: to build His character in me.

Dear heavenly Father, *thank You for forgiving me, even when I complain. And thank You for nudging me gently back onto the path. Give me a heart of gratitude for all that You've done for me. In Jesus' name, amen.*

What's Your Focus?

Everyone looks out for his own interests, not those of Jesus Christ (Philippians 2:21).

Scripture: **Philippians 2:19-30**
Song: **"My Hope Is Built"**

We recently bought a vacation home in the mountains. After a few months of searching, then closing on the house and picking out furniture, I began to feel myself getting depressed. We'd wanted to give this place to the Lord, to use it to bless others' lives. But it was becoming a primary focus in my own life.

In my times of prayer, I felt as if the Lord was saying, "You've been thinking about 'things' for too long. Get your eyes back on me and on what's most important to me." And as I did indeed switch my focus, I also felt my depression lifting. In its place flowed a welcome peace and a fresh joy in the Lord.

God may bless us with material possessions. God may allow us lives of relative ease. But as He reminded me that day, there is never joy in the things themselves. Things will rust, decay, and disappoint. Rather, there is pure joy in growing to know the giver of all good and perfect gifts. In that process we can't help becoming more interested in His own interests.

Eternal Father, forgive me for focusing more on my own interests than on Your interests. Please grow in me a heart for things eternal, and fill me once again with the joy of my salvation. Thank You, in the precious name of Your Son, Jesus. Amen.

What Can I Do for You?

Each of you should look not only to your own interests, but also to the interests of others (Philippians 2:4).

Scripture: **Philippians 2:1-13**
Song: **"Brothers, Joining Hand to Hand"**

"I love you, Daddy," said 2-year old Brian, throwing his arms around Darren's neck and giving him a wet kiss on the cheek. Brian was placed in Darren and Ruthie's home because he needed to be part of a loving, stable family. Now they are adopting him. Right now, Brian is most concerned with having his needs met. But as time passes, Brian is growing to love the other members of his new family.

Just as Brian needs a family, so God has placed us in His family, the church, in order to help us grow in Him. Though we may contribute imperfectly with our spiritual gifts, it's important that we offer our willing, humble participation. His desire is that we mature to the point where we can see the hopes and the needs of our brothers and sisters around us.

We have a tendency to ask, "What's in it for me?" when it comes to the church, just as little Brian wonders the same with his earthly family. But isn't God pleased when we finally look at our brothers and sisters and ask what *we* can do for *them*?

Lord God, *help me to see with ever clearer vision the needs of my fellow believers in the body of Christ. Give me the desire to serve them and to consider their interests above my own. I ask this in the name of Jesus. Amen.*

The Power of Love

Dear friends, let us love one another, for love comes from God. Everyone who loves has been born of God and knows God. Whoever does not love does not know God, because God is love (1 John 4:7, 8).

Scripture: **1 John 4:7-12**
Song: **"Beloved, Let Us Love One Another"**

On Christian television I heard an elderly lady sharing an astounding story. Her son had been killed in an accident by a drunk driver, a young man who was about the same age as her boy. At first, she was distraught over the loss of her son. As time went on, she prayed that God would help her to love and forgive the young man who had caused the deadly accident. She noticed that her rage began to leave, and her heart started to fill with compassion. She reached out to the youth and offered forgiveness.

Touched by a love he'd never imagined, this boy became a Christian. And the bereaved mother visited him regularly in prison, treating him as a son.

I was deeply moved to see this unique relationship that expressed God's great love and healing power. It's easy for us to love people who love us. But how do we love those who cause us grievous harm?

Dear God, help me to truly love the unlovely. I know I can't do that by my own willpower, but by Your help and strength. In Christ's name, amen.

August 9–15. **Judy Gyde,** of Toledo, Ohio, has written for more than 40 publications. She and her husband, Bruce, have three children and seven grandchildren.

Sin Doesn't Pay

Like a partridge that hatches eggs it did not lay is the man who gains riches by unjust means. When his life is half gone, they will desert him, and in the end he will prove to be a fool (Jeremiah 17:11).

Scripture: **Jeremiah 17:7-13**
Song: **"Change Me on the Inside"**

A few years ago, a con man in our city started a money laundering business out of his home. He was a brilliant, articulate man, smooth with words and quite charming. Through his deceitful ways, he acquired several insurance companies and stole over 200 million dollars.

This bogus businessman spent the money on lavish homes, expensive cars, and a foolish, immoral lifestyle. The FBI stepped into the picture and found him living in a mansion in Europe. Then, how things changed for him! One day he was living in opulence; the next day he sat in prison—where he will remain for many years.

We can look around us and become discouraged at the apparent prosperity of countless shady characters. Unrepentant bank robbers, drug dealers, and identity thieves may think they've beaten the system. But what they don't realize is that they could never beat God's "system." There is no perfect crime, but the perfect Lord of all will bring everything to light.

*Thank You, **Lord,** for searching my heart and mind. I pray for mercy in light of the things I've done wrong. You forgive everyone who calls on Your name—so please, start with me, right now. Through Christ, amen.*

Right This Way, Folks!

If I go and prepare a place for you, I will come back and take you to be with me that you also may be where I am. You know the way to the place where I am going (John 14:3, 4).

Scripture: **John 14:1-4**
Song: **"In the Sweet By and By"**

Heaven, mansions, and complete fulfillment in the afterlife. According to the Bible, there is only one way to these blessings: "I am the way and the truth and the life. No one comes to the Father except through me" (John 14:6). Jesus said the He alone is our path to Heaven.

My friend Cathy believes there are many paths to God—like many roads leading up to the mountain peak, all arriving at the same destination—and that Jesus may be one of those ways. In other words, she thinks our Christian views are too narrow, that God will take everyone to be with Him someday, and there is no need for judgment.

We know that all truth is God's truth, and that we can find some truth in most of the world's religions. But where, in those religions, do we find a Savior who rose from the dead, just as He said He would? This same Savior prepares a place for those who believe and love Him. It's beyond our wildest imagination to understand the magnificent splendor and joy we will experience then.

Dear heavenly Father, thank You for Jesus, who died on the cross for my sin, was buried, and rose again on the third day. I am grateful for all He has done to make it possible for me to be with You forever. In His name, amen.

God Is Trustworthy

Trust in the LORD with all your heart and lean not on your own understanding; in all your ways acknowledge him, and he will make your paths straight (Proverbs 3:5, 6).

Scripture: **Proverbs 3:3-8**
Song: **"I Will Trust You, Lord"**

When my friend Donna prepared to move, she didn't know until the last minute where her family would live. Her husband had taken a new job, and their current home had sold. They frantically searched for a house, but just couldn't find the right one. In her frustration, she laughed and said, "I know God has a place for us; I just wish He would let us know where!"

Donna kept praying and trusting God for guidance. Suddenly, the realtor called and everything came together. They moved just in time, to a place with beautiful, blossoming trees and her favorite kinds of flowers. God had lovingly cared for her, even amid much anxiety.

Maybe you are in a similar situation, wondering exactly how God might lead you out of a fearsome difficulty. But if you are His child, remember that He holds you and all your circumstances in His hands. Keep your trust in Him. He will direct your paths according to His infinite wisdom, based on His desire for your growth in spiritual maturity.

Lord, *sometimes I wonder how You will work things for Your glory and my growth. Yet I trust You to do the best for me in all circumstances, even if it means helping me to learn patience and endurance. In Jesus' name, amen.*

Yielding to Him

It is we who are the circumcision, we who worship by the Spirit of God, who glory in Christ Jesus, and who put no confidence in the flesh (Philippians 3:3).

Scripture: **Philippians 3:1-6**
Song: **"Take My Life and Let It Be"**

Before I became a genuine Christian, I was a church-goer and a nice person. I believed that if my good deeds outweighed my bad ones, certainly I would be acceptable to God, and He would let me into Heaven someday. It was kind of a karmic approach to the gospel . . . and was I wrong!

My own opinions about spiritual matters kept me from knowing basic scriptural truths—until I actually began to read the Bible. I discovered that I needed to be born again, allow His indwelling Spirit to guide me, and use my spiritual gifts in the work of the church. How God changed my life!

Since 1976, I have enjoyed a rich relationship with the Lord. I love to worship Him by living my life with joy and purpose. Now my motive for good deeds is to honor Him because I love Him, not to try to earn my way to Heaven. I trust Him, not my flesh (my way of doing things), to help me live a successful Christian life.

Dear Lord, *Your ways are perfect. Help me to rely on You and Your strength, rather than my own. Show me the things You would like for me to do to please You. Thank You for Jesus' sacrifice for me, which makes me acceptable to You. In His precious name I pray. Amen.*

A Good Witness . . . or Not?

Join with others in following my example, brothers, and take note of those who live according to the pattern we gave you (Philippians 3:17).

Scripture: **Philippians 3:17-21**
Song: **"The Fruit of the Spirit"**

On Tuesdays, I work as a nurse in a medical clinic. My primary purpose there is to be a "light" to the staff—a Christian presence—by doing my job with excellence. I help my coworkers with their work whenever I have opportunity.

Interestingly, I've overheard other believers attempting to witness to the doctor. One patient spoke about Christ, but later bickered about a small mistake on her bill. Another lady wore a "Praise the Lord" T-shirt for her office visit, while telling the doctor she'd recently had an abortion in order to save her career. Another Christian man nastily refused pills the doctor prescribed.

Is it possible for Christian witnesses to subtly damage the cause for Christ? I think so. None of us is perfect, including myself, and we all make mistakes. But it is a good thing when we become more sensitive and think about how our words and actions give glory to God or not.

Dear Lord, show me the ways I may unintentionally offend the cause of Christ. Please forgive me and help me to be more sensitive in my words and actions. I need Your help and strength to be a good testimony. In the name of Jesus, my Savior, I pray. Amen.

Focus on Your Prize

Forgetting what is behind and straining toward what is ahead, I press on toward the goal to win the prize for which God has called me heavenward in Christ Jesus (Philippians 3:13, 14).

Scripture: **Philippians 3:7-16**
Song: **"Higher Ground"**

Our granddaughter Megan's softball team won two trophies this season for their excellence. These teammates found the competition challenging but worked diligently toward the prize. They trained and practiced hard. And it paid off.

God wants us to keep our eyes straight ahead on our prize. And He will direct us each step of the way as we seek Him with all of our hearts. How? By giving us insights through His Word, by speaking to us with His "gentle whisper"(1 Kings 19:12) as we listen for Him in prayer, and by bringing mature fellow believers into our lives with their words of wisdom.

When you and I keep our eyes on the Lord, determined to follow His ways and do His will, we can't go wrong. For no matter where we are, we know He stays true to His promise: "Surely I am with you always, to the very end of the age" (Matthew 28:20). And there the prize is waiting for us.

Dear heavenly Father, help me to keep my eyes on the prize, that I would follow Your ways all of my life, until the day I stand before Your Son and am like Him. Show me how to live a disciplined, successful life in Christ Jesus to that day. Thank You, in Jesus' name. Amen.

The Cutting Edge

I will hear what God the LORD will speak: for he will speak peace unto his people, and to his saints: but let them not turn again to folly (Psalms 85:8, *King James Version*).

Scripture: **Psalms 85:4-13**
Song: **"Safe in the Arms of Jesus"**

My mother had spent the day sewing, and Dad had come in from working the fields. We settled down by the woodstove for a relaxing evening. I was sitting on the floor playing with the scissors (and probably cutting up Mom's patterns), so Dad told me to put the scissors away. Not normally a defiant child, even I was surprised when the words "I ain't gonna do it" escaped from my lips.

Just as the Lord chastised His people and showed the fierceness of His anger when they disobeyed, I encountered the wrath of my father. In both cases, those who were commanded were the objects of love. And the commands were meant for protection.

Before the evening ended, I was curled up in my father's lap, his arms of forgiveness surrounding me. Yes, the Father loves us and chastens us, but He also forgives and extends mercy. As the psalmist says: "Mercy and truth are met together; righteousness and peace have kissed each other" (Psalm 85:10, *King James Version*).

Father, even as an adult, pattern me after the image of Your Son, Jesus. I know You have my best at heart, and I am grateful. In His name, amen.

August 16–22. **Janet Trabue**, a great-grandparent, is a retired insurance agent whose passion has always been writing. She lives in Thornton, Colorado.

Terror on the High Seas

Falling into a place where two seas met, they ran the ship aground; and the forepart stuck fast, and remained unmoveable, but the hinder part was broken with the violence of the waves (Acts 27:41, *King James Version*).

Scripture: Acts 27:33-44
Song: "My Anchor Holds"

The closest I ever came to relating to Paul's experience on the high seas was a white-water rafting trip in Colorado. Though my little venture pales to what Paul and his fellow cell mates endured, the fear factor surely was comparable.

I felt little comfort when our guide told us that we were entering "Widow's Curve." Soon he was straining mightily to maneuver our raft around sharp rocks and boulders. What a relief to immerge from the white water and float peacefully down the stream once again.

Have you been there—thrust into violent waves, not knowing if the winds will calm or if your vessel will make it? Yet we have a wise and all-powerful guide to take us through our stormy trials. He knows the dangers that lie ahead. We can put our trust in Him for safe passage. As the famous preacher Henry Ward Beecher once said: "Fear is a kind of bell. . . . It is the soul's signal for rallying."

Father, I know You never promised that the seas would always be calm. But You are present and steadfast when my little boat jostles wildly in the waves. So I pray: May I always be mindful of Your protecting hand. In the name of Jesus, Lord and Savior of all, amen.

Great Things

The Lord hath done great things for us; whereof we are glad (Psalms 126:3, *King James Version***).**

Scripture: **Psalms 126:1-6**
Song: **"A Gladsome Hymn of Praise We Sing"**

There I was, innocently sitting at an intersection. The traffic light turned green, but something told me not to go—just as another car speed through its red light. I thought: "God's protection is a great thing!"

If that has ever happened to you, what was your reaction to the speeding driver? (God's forgiveness is truly a "great thing" too.)

Too often we equate "great things" only with material blessings: a good job, a new car, a big bonus. Thus we take many "great things" for granted. For example, have you ever been delivered from a bad habit, ever enjoyed blessed moments in prayer, or simply stood in pouring rain after a searing drought?

The ability to rejoice in Him is a "great thing" and truly makes us glad. We can rejoice in His protection and His forgiveness. Paul summarized "great things" in 1 Corinthians 13:13, "Now abideth faith, hope, charity, these three; but the greatest of these is charity," (*King James Version*).

Dear Father in Heaven, *You touch my life in so many ways. Thank You for Your protection, forgiveness, joy, and above all, the love that You show towards me every day. Guide my thoughts, actions, and deeds that I may honor You in all that I do. In the name of Jesus, who lives and reigns with You and the Holy Spirit, one God, now and forever, amen.*

Standing Tall

Instead of the thorn shall come up the fir tree, and instead of the brier shall come up the myrtle tree: and it shall be to the Lord for a name, for an everlasting sign that shall not be cut off (Isaiah 55:13, *King James Version).*

Scripture: **Isaiah 55:6-13**
Song: **"A Mighty Fortress Is Our God"**

When we feel blown about by life's troubles, we need only to think of Joseph, the patriarch who became immovable in his devotion to the Lord after having suffered many trials. It seems he chose to view his troubles as opportunities—opportunities for God. As he said to his brothers in Genesis 50:20 (*King James Version*), "Ye thought evil against me; but God meant it unto good" .

Have you found that, when you give your life into the Lord's hands, even the thorns can be turned into strong trees? That's because our relationship with Him is all about redemption. It's not that God saves us from the bad things that happen in life. No, Christians suffer as much as others from disease, accidents, and natural disasters. The difference is that they know God can work within all situations for His glory.

In other words, when bad things happen to us, it is best to avoid asking: "Why did this happen?" The better question to keep always upon our lips is this: "How will God use this?"

Father, when it seems that my path is strewn with thorns and briers, help me to look up and see Your glory. In Jesus' name, amen.

Pay It Forward

As my Father hath sent me, even so send I you (John 20:21, *King James Version*).

Scripture: **John 20:19-23**
Song: **"So Send I You"**

My father was part of the "Pay It Forward" movement 70 years ago and wasn't even aware of it. To "pay it forward" means to pass on a good deed to another person after having been a recipient yourself. How did he do it? It may seem like a little thing, but here it is: My father always chose the chicken neck, leaving the breast, thighs, and legs for the rest of the family.

This simple gesture taught his family how to share and sacrifice for others. (By the way, his unselfishness left the entire family fighting for the chicken neck so dad could finally get his next favorite piece, the back.) Simply put, Dad taught us to "pay it forward," putting others first.

We can never repay the Son of God for the sacrifice He willingly made for us. But we can certainly "pay it forward" by sharing His gospel with others—extending His love to our friends and neighbors. After all, we never know when we might be helping a future minister, missionary, or Sunday school teacher whose own desire will be simply to "pay it forward."

Father, thank You for sending Your Son to minister to His disciples who, in turn, ministered to the multitudes and finally reached even me with Your gospel. I pray for strength and wisdom to "pay it forward" out of gratefulness for Your goodness to me. In Jesus' name, amen.

Law-abiding or Lawless?

For what the law could not do, in that it was weak through the flesh, God sending his own Son in the likeness of sinful flesh, and for sin, condemned sin in the flesh (Romans 8:3, *King James Version*).

Scripture: Romans 8:1-8
Song: "The Law Commands and Makes Us Know"

Lights flashed to warn passing motorists. A state patrolman had pulled a bright red pickup truck off to the side of the road.

Since that particular stretch of highway is notorious for speed traps, I assumed the driver and patrolman weren't just discussing the weather. The law had been broken, and justice was apparently swift. The goal of such law enforcement is to help erring motorists learn from their mistakes and take corrective action.

However, within minutes, that same vehicle passed me at lightning speed. The law of the land had little effect upon that driver; he'd refused to change his ways.

Of course, our sinful nature is no surprise to God. Thus He paid our "fine" years ago. The driver of the truck was stopped and given a warning before blood was spilled, but the blood of God's only Son was shed, and His life sacrificed, because of our lawlessness.

Dear God, help me to be mindful of sin in my own life—and turn from it. Thank You, Lord, for sending Your Son to pay the penalty for me. Help me to put away fleshly desires and submit to Your law. I know Your rules are for my own good. In Jesus' name I pray. Amen.

Falter or Altar?

I have learned, in whatsoever state I am, therewith to be content. . . . I can do all things through Christ which strengtheneth me (Philippians 4:11, 13, *King James Version*).

Scripture: **Philippians 4:1-14**
Song: **"Nothing Is Impossible"**

Our granddaughter was in the first grade and had an opportunity to go on a bus trip with the youth group from Sunday school. Being concerned grandparents, we asked, "Are you sure you want to do this?" Her reply was, "I'm scared, but I want to do it anyway." Grandpa reminded her of Philippians 4:13, which has become the tie that binds us together as a family. Years later, when this same "little girl" was trying to become a paramedic (having experienced three major surgeries in the process), Grandpa continually kept this verse before her.

How often we give in to our fears or see obstacles as insurmountable, when we could be looking to Christ for His strength. This is not to say that we will not have trials and tribulations, as Paul himself suffered. But Christ promised to be with us in every situation. And with Him, we can be content.

The bottom line? Fear will cause us to falter; lay that fear on the altar.

Lord, thank You for giving me strength when I am weak, frightened, troubled, or confused. The certainty that You are always by my side is a constant comfort. You have the answer before I even have the question. Thank You for Your guidance. In the name of Jesus, amen.

August 23

Change? Suspicious!

When he [Paul] came to Jerusalem, he tried to join the disciples, but they were all afraid of him, not believing that he really was a disciple. But Barnabas took him and brought him to the apostles (Acts 9:26, 27).

Scripture: **Acts 9:23-30**
Song: **"Amazing Grace"**

Paul was once a notorious enemy of Christians. He was traveling to Damascus to persecute them when Jesus confronted him and changed him. Instead of throwing Christians in jail, Paul would now proclaim their Christ.

No wonder, though, that when Paul tried to join the disciples in Jerusalem, he faced suspicion. Those disciples had good reason to fear. No doubt Paul had arrested many of their loved ones. It wasn't until Barnabas trusted Paul that others began to accept the new apostle.

Have you ever found it hard to trust a person who has been radically converted from darkness to light? It can be difficult because we've all heard of the proverbial "jailhouse conversion." Yet the genuine article occurs in countless lives. It happened to Paul; it may well happen to your neighbor this very day. Are you ready to encourage him and to help him grow strong in his new life in the Lord?

Lord, help me to see what You are doing in the lives around me. And give me the grace to accept change in others and myself. In Jesus' name, amen.

August 23–29. **Carolyn D. Andersen** has two grown children and enjoys living in the plains of central Nebraska.

My Fortress

The Lord Almighty is with us; the God of Jacob is our fortress (Psalm 46:7).

Scripture: **Psalm 46**
Song: **"Mighty Lord, Extend Thy Kingdom"**

I knew the storm was coming. Weathermen broke into television programming, and storm sirens were blaring. Soon our house shook as wind, rain, and hail beat against the roof and walls. As baseball-sized hail bombarded a glass door again and again, I marveled that it held.

It was the middle of the night, and I could see only a small part of the storm around my home. Throughout the night, I reminded myself, God is my fortress. He is my refuge and strength. God is faithful to provide protection for me.

In the morning, I surveyed the damage. The siding was battered. There was roof damage too, but the house had stood. As I surveyed the devastation in my neighborhood, I was thankful for God's protection—and knew I was called to help others "dig out."

When storms of change come upon me, I can recall a wonderful doctrine that theologians teach: the immutability of God. It means that God's basic character and integrity never change. If He was an almighty fortress in the days of Jacob, then He is still almighty in my own day. Thanks be to God!

Father, thank You for Your protection in all of life's storm. You are my fortress in every circumstance. All praise to You, in Christ's name. Amen.

On Duty

The LORD will keep you from all harm—he will watch over your life: the LORD will watch over your coming and going both now and forevermore (Psalm 121:7, 8).

Scripture: **Psalm 121**
Song: **"'Trust in the Promise"**

"Halt! Who goes there?" An alert sentry shouts this command when he sees movement at the edge of camp. He has his rifle at the ready and is sworn to protect his fellow soldiers. With the sentry on duty, others in camp can go about their daily tasks or rest without concern about the enemy.

Clearly, it's important that a sentry never fall asleep! In fact, to sleep on guard duty, during a time of war, is traditionally considered a capital offense.

According to the psalmist, God never sleeps. He is always aware and willing to provide all I need to grow in Him, amidst good times and bad. And by acknowledging God's protection, I can go about my daily activities and rest in confidence.

I am persuaded that God continues to be my sentry, my protection from harm. And what is the worst harm He saves me from? Jesus gives the answer: "Do not be afraid of those who kill the body but cannot kill the soul. Rather, be afraid of the One who can destroy both soul and body in hell" (Matthew 10:28).

Father, thank You for Your watchfulness over me. I know I can trust Your gracious salvation even in all of life's difficulties. In Jesus' name, amen.

A Place of Refuge

Sustain me according to your promise, and I will live; do not let my hopes be dashed. Uphold me, and I will be delivered; I will always have regard for your decrees (Psalm 119:116, 117).

Scripture: **Psalm 119:114-117**
Song: **"Because He Lives"**

Ever felt thoroughly crushed by life?

It has been over a year since I was thrust into a time of crushing. Not long after my family endured a time of financial and health-related stresses, I saw two policemen and my minister walking up to my front door. I started shaking and felt sick. How could there be more? I wanted to scream, "God, that's enough, I can't handle any more!"

They told me my husband, Sam, had been in a fatal car accident. I couldn't breathe; the news was too horrible to comprehend. I was in shock for many days. Only the hope of Heaven sustained me.

I couldn't understand why all this had happened, but I learned the only place I could go was into the arms of Jesus my Savior. As I have recovered and mourned my loss, I still keep going back to Him. He continues to sustain me, support me, and lead me as I rely on Him. I can truly say along with the psalmist, "Uphold me, and I will be delivered."

Father, I thank You that You have sustained me through great losses. I know that I can find hope in Your Word, so keep me opening it, day by day. Yes, speak, Lord, Your servant hears! In the precious name of Jesus, amen.

Detours of Life

His [Publius's] father was sick in bed, suffering from fever and dysentery. Paul went in to see him and, after prayer, placed his hands on him and healed him. When this had happened, the rest of the sick on the island came and were cured (Acts 28:8, 9).

Scripture: **Acts 28:1-15**
Song: **"Guide Me, O Thou Great Jehovah"**

I hate detours, especially when I'm racing around on a tight schedule. This summer, it seems all the routes I use to commute are under construction. That means I am constantly detoured and delayed as I attempt to get to work.

Paul was on a mission to make known the gospel to the people in Rome, to stand before Caesar, and proclaim the good news about Jesus. Instead of an easy, swift trip, Paul experienced detours. He was shipwrecked off the Island of Malta, he was thrown into a freezing cold sea . . . then he was bitten by a snake. (Talk about a bad day at work!)

Yet the great apostle took it all in stride. He simply refused to let the detours thwart his ministry to the people of Malta. In other words, God's mission was his priority. And Paul must surely have known: The hand that points the way also provides the way. (In other words, Paul was really on course the whole time.)

Lord, help me to see past the detours so I can follow Your leading without worry. Help me realize that detours are simply a part of the process of trusting Your Spirit's leading each day. I pray this prayer in the name of Jesus, my merciful Savior and Lord. Amen.

Gifts of Love

I am amply supplied, now that I have received from Epaphroditus the gifts you sent. They are a fragrant offering, an acceptable sacrifice, pleasing to God (Philippians 4:18).

Scripture: **Philippians 4:15-20**
Song: **"I Love You, Lord"**

When my son was young, he was convinced my favorite flower was the dandelion. No, it wasn't any sweet aroma of the flowers he brought me, but the sweet aroma of his love that touched my heart.

When my husband planned to spray our yard, my son ran outside and picked as many dandelions as he could. Containers of the little yellow flowers filled our home. What a sweet way for a little boy to express his love!

Out of love, the Philippians gave gifts to Paul, over and over. They supplied Paul's needs as he ministered on their behalf in the name of Christ. In return, God poured out abundance upon the Philippians.

Somehow, the perfume of our freely-given gifts rises to Heaven. Such love-gifts can be expressed through a hug, a smile, or some small kindness offered to one who's struggling. At other times, we must gear up and give at great sacrifice. In either case, God himself drinks in the aroma of our love offered to His creatures. The size of the gift doesn't matter; what matters is the heart of the giver.

O God, work in me a heart of selfless love. Let my love gifts be a sweet perfume, helpful to others and pleasing to you. In the name of Jesus, Lord and Savior of all, I pray. Amen.

Dreams of Boldness

For two whole years Paul stayed there in his own rented house and welcomed all who came to see him. Boldly and without hindrance he preached the kingdom of God and taught about the Lord Jesus Christ (Acts 28:30, 31).

Scripture: **Acts 28:16-25, 28-31**
Song: **"O for a Thousand Tongues to Sing"**

Paul's ministry to the citizens of Rome must have been much different than he had dreamed. Instead of traveling in his typical manner, with friends to help him, Paul arrived in Rome as a prisoner of the government. No doubt, he intended to preach in synagogues and market places, his usual forums. Instead, he welcomed all who came to hear the gospel, while he was under house arrest. In spite of the circumstances, Paul preached the message of salvation boldly and without hindrance.

I dream of boldly telling others about Jesus. But when reality hits, I often say nothing. I am afraid to open my mouth.

That's sad, because I'm not under house arrest! I am free to go where I want, do the things I want, yet I shrink from telling of the grace and goodness of God that I have known. But are you there too? Let us pray for one another today—that we take the first small steps towards a heavenly, apostolic boldness.

Heavenly Father, give me the kind of boldness and perseverance that Paul displayed. Help me to openly proclaim the truth of the gospel to those around me. In Christ's holy name I pray. Amen.

Journey of Hope and Purpose

Now He is not the God of the dead, but of the living; for all live to Him (Luke 20:38, *New American Standard Bible*).

Scripture: **Luke 20:34-40**
Song: **"Teach Me Thy Will, O Lord"**

It is not unusual for people to have difficulty at times dealing with their own mortality.

We review our lives and reach forward, looking for that sense of purpose, for the contribution we hope to make with our lives. As we grow older, we are more aware that our time on earth is limited. We become more sensitive to this need to find meaning in life. Sometimes our hope for finding purpose withers like the flower.

How important it is for us to remember that as children of God, we are eternal beings. A mystery unfolds before us as we accept Jesus as Lord and Savior. At that moment our eternity begins. Our lives are no longer confined to a moment in time. Jesus explains that God is not the God of the dead, but of the living. He assures us of a resurrection leading to eternal life. Never more will we experience pain, grief, or sorrow. He will wipe away our tears.

Our purpose is found in knowing God, and knowing God is found in His living Word.

Father, thank You for this life You have given me. Help me to find time each day to spend with You. Take away my anxieties, and replace them with Your peace. Let my purpose in each day become Your glory.

August 30, 31. **Jeff Short** is a military veteran with a background in social work. He enjoys the arts, fitness, and the outdoors.

The Certainty of God's Word

God is not a man, that He should lie, Nor a son of man, that He should repent; Has He said, and will He not do it? Or has He spoken, and will He not make it good? (Numbers 23:19, *New American Standard Bible*).

Scripture: **Numbers 23:18-26**
Song: **"The Bible Stands"**

After completing my time in the service, I returned home to a small town in Georgia.

I began attending a church that had been experiencing a great success in its ministry. The pastor was a young man not too long out of seminary. One of the points that he stressed to the congregation time and again was not to blindly accept his words or those of another. He reminded us of the importance of meeting with God individually, searching the Scriptures, and knowing His truth. He realized the important fact that man is fallible, even when he has the best intentions.

In an ever-changing world where we often witness injustice and suffering, let us not think for a moment that God is not in control. May we never question His love— love so great that He gave His beloved Son as a redeeming sacrifice for all humanity.

What God has said, He will certainly do. Let each of us become more intimately acquainted with Him; in doing so, we will surely learn how absolutely trustworthy He is.

Father, fill me with hope that comes from truly knowing You. Help me to stand firmly upon Your Word. Enable me to live a life that will become a light to others and a witness of Your wonderful, merciful, and certain love.

DEVOTIONS®

I urge . . . that requests, prayers, intercession and thanksgiving be made for everyone.

—1 Timothy 2:1

SEPTEMBER

Photo © JL Gutierrez | iStock

Gary Allen, Editor   **Margaret Williams,** Project Editor

DEVOTIONS® is published quarterly by Standard Publishing, Cincinnati, Ohio, www.standardpub.com.
© 2009 by Standard Publishing. All rights reserved. Topics based on the Home Daily Bible Readings,
International Sunday School Lessons. © 2007 by the Committee on the Uniform Series. Printed in the
U.S.A. All Scripture quotations, unless otherwise indicated, are taken from the HOLY BIBLE, NEW
INTERNATIONAL VERSION®. NIV®. Copyright © 1973, 1978, 1984 by International Bible Society.
Used by permission of Zondervan. All rights reserved. Where noted, Scripture quotations are from the fol-
lowing, used with permission of the copyright holders, all rights reserved: *New American Standard Bible
(NASB),* © The Lockman Foundation, 1960, 1962, 1963, 1968, 1971, 1972, 1973, 1975, 1977, 1995. *The
Revised Standard Version of the Bible* (RSV), copyrighted 1946, 1952, © 1971, 1973.

Refuge from Life's Storms

My soul, wait in silence for God only, for my hope is from Him (Psalm 62:5, *New American Standard Bible*).

Scripture: **Psalm 62:5-12**
Song: **"Be Still and Know"**

Some time ago, I heard about a man who had lived his life seeking God. To his family and friends he had been a light that reflected his faith. But as he grew older, he began to suffer from dementia. He was no longer able to function on his own or even recognize his family and friends. Yet even as he walked in silence down this final path, the gentleness of his spirit gave witness to the Savior that he so dearly loved.

At times, when we face hardships in our lives, we naturally look around us for a way to "solve our problem." We try to rely on our own perceived strengths. If it's a physical setback, we hope doctors can make a correct diagnosis and provide an effective treatment. Or in financial distress, we may seek help from church or charities.

God's desire is that we look to Him and trust in Him alone, amidst every circumstance. He is our refuge and our strength, our everlasting hope.

Father, help me remember that You are ever-present in my life. In my weakness and frailty, remind me that my strength comes from You. Regardless of my circumstances, may I be a source of comfort to those who are broken, giving witness to Your eternal love. In Jesus' name, amen.

September 1–5. **Jeff Short** is a military veteran with background in social work. Living in Georgia, he enjoys the arts, the outdoors, and the pursuit of fitness.

Childlike Approach

He who believes in the Son has eternal life; but he who does not obey the Son shall not see life, but the wrath of God abides on him (John 3:36, *New American Standard Bible*).

Scripture: John 3:31-36
Song: "Can a Little Child Like Me?"

It's amazing to watch children's excitement as they take in the world around them. Everything is larger than life. Colors are bright and vivid, stars sparkle like diamonds, and the sounds of nature rise up like symphonies.

I believe such childlike simplicity has a great reward—even for us adults. Jesus tells us that in order to receive the kingdom of God, we must come to Him as a child. That involves an open, trusting heart, a belief that issues in grateful service.

You see, God wants fellowship with us. And because He loves us and understands us, He has made this relationship possible if we'll simply believe in His beloved Son Jesus. When we come to Him by faith—faith that He provides—He seals us with His Spirit and welcomes us into His kingdom with loving and open arms.

In our world, we usually gain a reward by paying for it or earning it in some way. Perhaps that is why it's so hard for some folks to simply believe and follow the Son with childlike joy. They may think the free gift is too good to be true. But it's not. Believe. Live.

Father, help me to approach life with the simplicity and trust of a child, knowing that in Your Son Jesus I am complete. In His name, amen.

Able and Willing

Certainly I will be with you, and this shall be the sign to you that it is I who have sent you: when you have brought the people out of Egypt, you shall worship God at this mountain (Exodus 3:12, *New American Standard Bible*).

Scripture; Exodus 3:7-12
Song: **"Abide in Me, O Lord"**

There is an old saying that goes something like this: "If you are not part of the solution, you are probably part of the problem." Yet we can often find excuses why we should not act in obedience to God's call. In fact, those excuses come readily to me: I am an introvert, so I am at my best behind the scenes. I am not an effective speaker. I need more training; I have other projects to complete first. The excuses can go on and on. Nevertheless, God assures us, as He did Moses: He will go before us and prepare our way.

It's one of those paradoxes we find in Scripture. For example, the apostle Paul tells us that in our weakness we are made strong. How can that be? The apostle knew well that there is a critical ingredient in this formula: God. In our weakness and in our lack of ability, we are made complete through Him. In other words, the same hand that points the way provides the way. He is able, and He is most assuredly willing.

Father, help me view my weakness as an opportunity to be embraced and strengthened by Your Spirit. May I not dwell so much on my own inability, but on You, in whom all things are possible. In Christ's name, amen.

I'm Concerned

Say to them, "The Lᴏʀᴅ, the God of your fathers, the God of Abraham, Isaac and Jacob, has appeared to me, saying, 'I am indeed concerned about you and what has been done to you in Egypt' " (Exodus 3:16, *New American Standard Bible*).

Scripture: **Exodus 3:16-22**
Song: **"Calm Me, My God"**

Have you noticed that our lives unfold through seasons? We experience periods of barrenness, like the trees in winter that sleep for a time. Yet they are called back to new life with the blossoms of spring, the sun once more bouncing light from their leaves.

During our difficult times, we may begin to feel that God has forgotten us, left us in stark winter. But no: These barren times are often the richest, filled with revelation, brimming with experiences that bring us closer to our Savior. And those times also develop empathy and understanding within us. How can we make a difference in the world if we can't relate to the struggles of others?

The Lord says it simply and directly to His people: "I am concerned about you." And it's more than a soothing sentiment. God came down from Heaven, and He experienced suffering and sorrow in human flesh. We know that in Jesus we have an advocate who is compassionate and understanding. May we never doubt His concern for us.

Father, help me appreciate all the seasons of my life. Whether in spring or in winter may I honor You, in Christ's precious name. Amen.

True Success

Moses was pasturing the flock of Jethro his father-in-law, the priest of Midian; and he led the flock to the west side of the wilderness, and came to Horeb, the mountain of God (Exodus 3:1, *New American Standard Bible*).

Scripture: Exodus 3:1-6, 13-15
Song: "The Triumphs of the Saints"

Society tries to define success for us. And, sadly, we Christians often buy into it, judging ourselves and others based on thoroughly secular standards.

Let us embrace the truth about success, which comes to us from God's Word: It is all about daily fellowship with Him. Through that fellowship, we begin to know the mind of the Lord, and we begin to do His will more consistently. And what better definition of success could there be—simply carrying out God's will for us, each moment of our day. I see Moses as successful in just this way. In the mundane hours and the routines of the shepherd's life, as he walked along, he surely drew closer to God.

That kind of living will cause us to alter our plans regularly, though. Our plans are not always parallel with God's. Often in order for us to develop—or simply for God to get our attention—He has to take us down an unexpected pathway. This path may not fit our personal itinerary. But let us be certain that God, who gave His beloved Son for us, desires only the very best for our lives.

Father, help me be successful today through simple obedience. Refine me and make my life a testimony to Your grace. In Jesus' name, amen.

The Doable List

Your hands made me and formed me; give me understanding to learn your commands (Psalm 119:73).

Scripture: **Psalm 119:73-77**
Song: **"The Law of God Is Good and Wise"**

As a young wife I felt I could never please my husband. I cleaned house, washed clothes, took care of our children, paid bills, grew a garden, canned vegetables and fruit, sewed my own clothes, washed the family car . . . you get the idea. My list was endless, yet it was never enough.

So you can imagine my surprise when, at the prompting of a friend, I asked my husband to make a list of all the things I could do to make him feel loved. Refusing pen and paper, he simply said, "Get up and make my breakfast, send me to work with a kiss and a lunch, and be there to greet me when I return home." It was that simple, and yet I had worn myself ragged trying to meet needs he never asked me to meet.

God made and formed us. Often we run ourselves ragged trying to serve Him, yet He promises that His burden is easy and His yoke is light. With understanding we can serve Him with renewed joy and energy, day by day.

Lord, *thank You for Your Holy Spirit who gives me understanding to learn Your commands and to obey them. Please keep me from taking on more than what You have given me, for You know how weak I truly am. In the holy name of Jesus, my Lord and Savior, I pray. Amen.*

September 6–12. **Sandy Cathcart** is a freelance writer, photographer, and artist who loves the Creator and all of nature. She writes from her home in Oregon.

September 7

Exercising Happiness

Say to wisdom, "You are my sister," and call understanding your kinsman (Proverbs 7:4).

Scripture: **Proverbs 7:1-5**
Song: **"This Is the Day That the Lord Has Made"**

My friend Nelson has a perpetual smile and always finds humor in the most difficult situations. You would think he's never known real sadness. But I know better. He has weathered a difficult childhood, a beloved wife who rejected God and him, and the inability to have his own children.

Yet Nelson understands that God wants him to be content in all circumstances. So he *exercises* being happy. Here's what I mean: He gets up in the morning and tells himself, "This is going to be a good day." It doesn't matter whether the dog chews up his best pair of shoes and wets on the carpet before Nelson gets out the door. It doesn't matter what the circumstances; Nelson will give thanks within it. (Wisdom tells Nelson that if he's not exercising happiness, then he will end up exercising sadness.)

When I think about Nelson, I realize that I walk through many of my days without exercising any kind of wisdom. But what a difference seeking the Lord's mind and heart can make.

Father, please help me to seek Your wisdom, refusing to jump into my day without gaining understanding from You. Show me Your will in each decision I'll face, and let me rejoice in the midst of every situation. Thank You, in the precious name of Your Son, Jesus. Amen.

Words of Life

**"From the fullness of his grace we have all receivd one bless-
ing after another"** (John 1:16).

Scripture: **John 1:14-18**
Song: **"There's a Wideness in God's Mercy"**

My friend Robyn suffers from depression. I sometimes
look into her face and wonder where she escaped to,
because I no longer see the friend I once had. Her humor
and intelligence hide behind clouded eyes.

Recently she gave me a stack of her poems, hoping
I'd set them to music. I dug through the pile of sadness,
reading words of death and hopelessness. Then, at last, I
came to a poem she penned long ago when she first gave
her life to God. It spoke of soaring above a mountaintop
and finding refuge in God's wings, of being drawn closer
and closer to her Lord. She wrote of living waters, deep
waterfalls of God's ever-flowing love. Here were such
beautiful words of life tied to the repeated phrase, "His
love is ever-flowing on me."

"Robyn, when you wrote those words, you were hearing from the Word," I said. "Could you go back to the
beginning and fall in love with Him all over again?"
Suddenly I realized that all of our days would be brighter
if we understood this one thing: Each and every day
begins and ends with Christ.

*Father, in the beginning You spoke love to me—and, O, how my heart leapt
for joy! May I never lose the wonder of that moment. Help me to see Your
smile in the treasured moments of every day. Through Christ, amen.*

September 9

No Travel Required

The word is near you; it is in your mouth and in your heart (Romans 10:8).

Scripture: **Romans 10:5-10**
Song: **"Nearer, Still Nearer"**

When Dr. Livingstone, pioneer missionary and African explorer, had not been heard from for three years, the New York Herald sent Henry Stanley to find him. With the paper's resources, Stanley organized a small army of porters, guides, and armed escorts. Traveling was extremely difficult; two companions died and Stanley suffered severe bouts of fever. Along the way Stanley was forced to take large detours because of conflicts with African natives.

After nearly eight grueling months, Stanley finally arrived at Ujiji on Lake Tanganyika, where he was led to a pale, frail-looking man. Raising his hat Stanley spoke the now famous words: "Dr. Livingstone, I presume."

Such extraordinary efforts are sometimes necessary to find missing human beings. But no such effor is needed to find Jesus Christ. We don't have to climb to Heaven or explore the ocean depths. Jesus is always nearby and ready to be found by those who are willing to believe in Him and confess Him before others.

Lord, thank You that our salvation does not depend on our own efforts but on our faith in what Jesus did for us through His death. Help us feel His presence near us today. In Jesus' name, amen.

It's About His Name

I have been crucified with Christ and I no longer live, but Christ lives in me. The life I live in the body, I live by faith in the Son of God, who loved me and gave himself for me (Galatians 2:20).

Scripture: **Galatians 2:15-21**
Song: **"There Is a Fountain Filled with Blood"**

I sat at the kitchen table feeling less of a woman than ever before. A civic organization had wrongfully accused me for receiving money for rendered services. I knew I was in the right, yet I refused to fight or take the matter to court. Instead, I offered to give back the money.

It was what I believed God wanted me to do in this situation—though everything in me screamed at the injustice of it. And my brother-in-law only added to my shame. "All you really have in life is your name," he said. I knew he meant well, but our worldviews were worlds apart. He didn't claim to walk with God as I did.

Slinking from the table to cry alone, I felt God's presence as warm, loving arms around me. And I remembered this: It hurt to the infinite level of Christ's pain in giving up His rights for my sake. The life I now live is no longer about my name; it's about the Name that is above all names.

Almighty Lord of all, *You know I love You, yet my love falls so short of the love You've given me. You gave yourself for me. Please help me to give myself fully to You, so that it is no longer I who live, but You shining brightly through me. Through Christ I pray. Amen.*

Better Than Diamonds or Roses

You shall not covet your neighbor's house. You shall not covet your neighbor's wife, or his manservant or maidservant, his ox or donkey, or anything that belongs to your neighbor (Exodus 20:17).

Scripture: **Exodus 20:12-21**
Song: **"Give Him the Glory"**

I watched as Phil wrapped a shining diamond bracelet around my friend's thin wrist. If that wasn't enough, he had also brought her roses. Debbie's face lit up with joy as she caught her husband's loving look.

Envy filled my heart. It wasn't even Debbie's birthday, or Christmas, or *anything!* Perhaps if I were thin and pretty like Debbie, my husband would bring me gifts.

I sulked all the way home until I reached the porch steps and realized the silliness of my thoughts. My husband may not bring me flowers, but he is forever faithful. He is my best friend, willing to listen when I have a need. He provides me with a comfortable home; he is gentle and kind; he even calls from work to say that he misses me.

Greeting my husband with a long embrace, I said, "Thanks for being my husband, even if you never bring me roses." While he muttered something about not being able to understand women, I thanked God for taking away my envy. On that day I learned the value of a gift more precious than diamonds and roses.

Father, help me to nurture a thankful heart and to treasure the precious gifts You've given me. In the name of Jesus, my Savior, I pray. Amen.

Sometimes, a Painful Process

I am the Lord your God, who brought you out of Egypt, out of the land of slavery (Exodus 20:2).

Scripture: **Exodus 20:1-11**
Song: **"God Is So Good"**

I rushed my 2-year-old son into the emergency room. He was already turning blue. A doctor whisked him from my arms and barked out orders. It took three hard-muscled assistants to hold Rob steady. His little body jackknifed as he croaked in terror. I tried to calm him with soothing words, but they were lost in the echoes of his pain.

Rob believed with all his heart that his mother had abandoned him in those dark hours of sickness. I was the one who handed him over to those awful doctors who stuck a tube down his nose and into his lungs, seeming to pump the very life out of him. In truth, the doctors saved his life. But Rob wouldn't understand that truth for many years to come. His experience would have been different if he had trusted me enough not to fight.

It's like that in my own life as God leads me out of slavery to my own wilfulness. Sometimes the process is painful—and I make it more so by forgetting that He is my Lord God, always leading me to a better place.

Almighty God and Father of all, *thank You for Your gift of freedom. You have delivered me from a life of hopelessness and brought me into a land full of promise. Because You are God and there is none like You, I praise Your holy name through Jesus Christ. Amen.*

Whose Role Model Are You?

Now these things occurred as examples to keep us from setting our hearts on evil things as they did (1 Corinthians 10:6).

Scripture: 1 Corinthians 10:1-11
Song: "Be Thou My Vision"

The leader of our Bible study group posed a question that made us squirm in our seats. "Who in this group do you consider to be an example that you could follow?" Most of those named as role models blushed as they protested.

We rarely see ourselves as others perceive us. It is easy to give a false impression, either positive or negative. And some people are simply experts at masking their faults in public, while their private lives leave much to be desired. Others, as those in our group, are only too aware of their shortcomings.

The Christian's role model is Christ, our spiritual rock. As we follow Him, our actions become models for others. We do not become stamped copies of little Jesus models, but an outward demonstration of what has happened to us by His power. We become like Christ because we have been occupied with Him. So, when my heart is set on Christ, I will automatically be pointing others to Him.

Heavenly Father, *I thank You for every godly person that You have brought into my life. I pray that as I endeavor to walk with You, I too will be a good example for others, through Jesus Christ my Lord. Amen.*

September 13–19. **Penny Smith,** a native of Hazleton, Pennsylvania, enjoys a teaching and writing ministry both at home and abroad.

Run for Your Life!

My dear friends, flee from idolatry (1 Corinthians 10:14).

Scripture: **1 Corinthians 10:14-21**
Song: **"Through It All"**

Daisy, a lovable, affectionate little dog, has the temperament of a social butterfly. She refuses to be ignored as she hops on hind legs, rubbing her front paws together, her soft brown eyes pleading, "Please notice me." Daisy is so sociable that she seizes any opportunity to slip out the door to find someone—anyone—to be a playmate.

On such occasions we have found ourselves strategizing about how to corner her as she flees from yard to yard. Her little game sends us into a frantic chase, lest she run onto the road and into traffic.

We really ought to develop a "Daisy disposition" where sin is concerned—and run for our lives. Anything that comes between the Lord and us has the potential of becoming an idol. Some activities may seem innocent enough, like Daisy's desire to play. But are we running from a safe place into a danger zone? If so, we'd better run for our lives, back to the safety zone.

Let's not relegate the temptations of idolatry to the biblical days of Baal's prophets or Asherah's devotees. No, it's a very practical threat to every person and culture, even today.

*Increase my capacity for You, **O God**. May my desires be satisfied with right choices—because I no longer crave what's harmful. In the name of Jesus, Lord and Savior of all, I pray. Amen.*

September 15

Consider the Cost

Those who make [idols] will be like them, and so will all who trust in them (Psalm 135:18).

Scripture: **Psalm 135:13-18**
Song: **"Come Thou Fount of Every Blessing"**

The donated wood chips looked good when they were delivered. They would make a perfect covering for the frontage of the muddy lot we had moved onto, and I wouldn't have to mow them. But several months later when I returned from a mission trip, I was appalled to find that the side of the house was completely covered with layers of little red and black insects—and they weren't ladybugs. I learned later that these were untreated chips from an elder tree, which drew those little pests.

Our house looked like something out of a horror movie. And insect sprays did not daunt these little bugs. We were inundated. *Free wood chips indeed!* I paid dearly for their removal.

Like those bugs, sin breeds undercover until it becomes exposed. By that time it has often become overwhelming. Unless secret sin is dealt with—usually requiring an accountability relationship with a trusted friend—it eventually takes over. The good news is this: No sinful form of idolatry is beyond the power of Christ to defeat.

Almighty and gracious Father, *thank You for the gift of Your Son who paid the price of my redemption. Thank You that He destroyed the works of evil that would try to overtake me. Please keep me from anything today that would push You from the throne of my life. In my Savior's name, amen.*

It's OK to Ask

If we know that he hears us—whatever we ask—we know that we have what we asked of him (1 John 5:15).

Scripture: **1 John 5:13-21**
Song: **"Praise the Name of Jesus"**

On occasion, my friends will burst out laughing at something I've said. Usually, when I rethink a blurted pronouncement, I understand why they've laughed: It made no sense. Strangely, though, my friends know exactly what I meant because they know me.

For example, when I leave a friend's house I usually say, "See ya'!" But recently I started out the door and called over my shoulder, "See me!" Now does that make sense?

As laughter filled the room, I added to my blunder: "If you need me, I'll call!" But isn't that how the Lord works with us? The apostle John assures us that our Lord hears us. In a way, God is saying, "If you need me, I'll call." In other words, I'm here for you. It's OK to ask for help. But even if you don't, I'll step in when you need me.

When I'm threatened by my challenging circumstances, I want to remember to call out to Him, "See me!" I know that He will come to my rescue.

O God, thank You for nudging me when my feet tend to head a different direction from that which You have chosen for me. Please don't pay attention to my complaints, but do see into my heart. When I need You, come to my rescue! In the name of Jesus, who lives and reigns with You and the Holy Spirit, one God, now and forever, amen.

Tuning Up

When Joshua heard the noise of the people shouting, he said to Moses, "There is the sound of war in the camp" (Exodus 32:17).

Scripture: **Exodus 32:15-24**
Song: **"Open My Eyes, That I May See"**

Persons without sight generally have sensitive hearing. My friend Tina hears a whisper three rooms away, recognizes individual voices in a room filled with people, and detects the musical key upon hearing the very first notes. Her ear is trained.

Joshua probably didn't realize he was in training when he went up the mountain with Moses (see Exodus 24:13). It takes a spiritually tuned ear to distinguish a war cry from a song, as our Scripture verse shows, or to distinguish the sound of emotional frenzy from revival.

Aaron's state was even more critical. He not only needed a spiritual hearing aid, but spiritual eyesight as well. He initiated the act of idolatry in making a golden calf and encouraging the people to worship it. Then he lied about the whole scenario to save his skin.

When our spiritual ears are tuned to God's will, we will learn His ways. Even though our sight is limited in this life, He reveals His will through His Word. Thus we're protected from some truly ugly pitfalls.

O gracious God, help me properly discern Your voice that I may walk in Your ways today. Open my heart's eyes and ears that I may know You better down through the years. In Jesus' name I pray. Amen.

Me, Instead!

Please forgive their sin—but if not, then blot me out of the book you have written (Exodus 32:32).

Scripture: **Exodus 32:30-35**
Song: **"Burdens Are Lifted at Calvary"**

Many years ago my brother, who was three years older than I, was diagnosed with cancer in his throat. Neither of us was a Christian at the time.

When I received the news of my brother's illness, I was devastated. Because of my work, I was unable to visit him until the weekend. I clearly remember my distress as I slipped into a vacant office on my lunch hour and tearfully argued with God. I don't know where I had gotten the idea, but I prayed, "Lord, take the cancer from him and put it on me, instead." Of course, the Lord would not do such a thing, but it seemed to be the one way that I knew to express my heart.

Moses had a similar thought when he identified with the sin of the people: punish me, instead. What a foreshadowing of Jesus, who took our sins upon himself that we might receive new life.

In my brother's case, his cancer was dealt with, and it wasn't placed on me. But that is not the end of the trials we will face in this life. Yet we—all of us believers—can patiently await the day when a new Heaven and earth make sin and suffering obsolete.

Most merciful God, if I tend to argue my case before You, help me to pray the prayer that never fails—Thy will be done. In Jesus' name, amen.

Who's to Blame?

Then the LORD said to Moses, "Go down, because your people whom you brought up out of Egypt, have become corrupt" (Exodus 32:7).

Scripture: **Exodus 32:1-10**
Song: **"Wonderful Grace of Jesus"**

I live in a house that I really do not want. My intention was to downsize, but it didn't happen. The house I moved into has as much space—if not more—than the one I left. You see, I was supposed to share this space with a friend. That didn't happen either.

Now, if I mention the problem of caring for a house this size, the absent house partner responds, "It's all my fault." No, the choice to move here was mine, as well. And I'm finding my faith being stretched.

I wonder that the Lord seemingly disowned His people at Sinai. But did the people belong only to Moses as the verse suggests? Not really. But since Moses had taken up the challenge to lead this people out of Egypt, he shared a responsibility. Moses' "house partner" may have seemed to be absent at times, but He was still on board.

Are you stuck with something you didn't necessarily desire? As you reevaluate your choices in the matter, you may find the situation to be a blessing.

Heavenly Father, *thank You for helping me to endure situations that stretch my faith beyond reason. Please give me wisdom to make right choices in the future. In Your Son's precious name. Amen.*

Safest Place on Earth

I will take refuge in the shadow of your wings until the disaster has passed (Psalm 57:1).

Scripture: **Psalm 57:1-5**
Song: **"Safely, Safely, Gathered In"**

Years ago one of my children was caught shoplifting. I was so furious my insides shook. "When we get home," I said, "you will tell your father exactly what you did." All I could think was, "How could you *do* this to me?"

After a silent, 45-minute drive from the mall, we arrived home. I waited in the car, trying to calm myself, while she walked into the house. When I went in, though, the scene wasn't what I expected. There, curled up in her father's lap, was our wayward child. Instead of harsh discipline, unconditional love and forgiveness had won the day.

The scene took me back to when I was a child. No matter what I did, no matter how much and how loudly my mother yelled at me for my misdeeds, I knew my father's lap would always be open, and his arms would always wrap around me.

Some troubles are of our own making. Some are not. But remember there's a place of refuge: the Father's protective presence. It's the safest place on earth.

*Thank You, **Father God,** that through Your Son, I can cry, "Abba, Father!" I am so blessed by Your love. In Jesus' name, amen.*

September 20–26. **Michele Huey** serves up a cup of inspiration with *God, Me & a Cup of Tea,* her weekly newspaper column and daily radio program.

My Portion

"The Lord is my portion," says my soul, "therefore I will hope in him" (Lamentations 3:24, *Revised Standard Version*).

Scripture: **Lamentations 3:22-26**
Song: **"Give Thanks to God the Lord"**

As I write this, I'm staring at a $502 heating oil bill, which is due the same month as the real estate taxes and the car insurance. I don't know where the money will come from. Our income barely meets our outgo.

I remember another time when money was low, the bills were high, and I didn't know how we'd pay for the heating oil. Taking God at His Word—specifically, Matthew 6:33 and Malachi 3:10—I trusted that if I did my part, He would do His. Soon we received a check from an unexpected source that was exactly the amount we needed for the heating oil.

That was 27 years ago. Since then, I have learned that His faithfulness is as sure as the sunrise. As I look around at my beautiful home, which we built ourselves, and enjoy the pictures of my children and grandchildren, I know that He truly has been my portion, the perfectly reliable object of my hope.

Yes, our every need has been supplied down through the years. And He will supply *this* need too. (In fact, He just gave me a great idea!)

*As I recall Your faithfulness, **Lord**, I am humbled, thankful, and awed. You truly are my portion, and I can safely hope in You. I pray through my deliverer, Jesus. Amen.*

Use Praise Fuel

Praise the LORD, O my soul; all my inmost being, praise his holy name. Praise the LORD, O my soul, and forget not all his benefits (Psalm 103:1, 2).

Scripture: Psalm 103:1-5
Song: "Just a Little Talk with Jesus"

I was driving to visit my son at his college when I heard what sounded like stones hitting the inside of the hood. When I pulled over and walked around the car, the noise abated, then quit. So I hopped back in and proceeded on my way.

When I got home that evening, my husband popped the hood and then came to get me. "Look," he said, pointing to a belt that was split lengthwise, half of it hanging down uselessly. "I don't know how you made it home. You were running on a prayer."

We had a furnace once that we jokingly said ran on prayer. It lasted for 25 years. Not bad for running on prayer—sometimes, probably, just the *fumes* of prayer!

Come to think of it, running on prayer is a pretty good idea. It's the secret to making it through life's rough spots, isn't it? When I've tried everything and nothing is working, I remember the psalmist's words: "Call upon me in the day of trouble; I will deliver you" (Psalm 50:15).

When I'm all out of options, the best one is left: The heartfelt prayer of praise.

*How wonderful to know, **Lord,** that I'm never out of options. Thank You for hearing me and answering when I call. Through Christ, amen.*

Surprising Party

He will not always accuse, nor will he harbor his anger forever; he does not treat us as our sins deserve or repay us according to our iniquities (Psalm 103:9, 10).

Scripture: **Psalm 103:6-10**
Song: **"Grace Greater Than Our Sin"**

When I was in third grade, I invited my entire class to my house for my birthday party—but didn't tell my mother. (All the kids always had birthday parties. Why did my mother always say "no" when I asked?) So that year I took matters into my own hands.

Walking home from town the day of the party, I dragged my feet. I still hadn't told Mom. *She'll kill me!* I thought. I'd just have to confess and face her wrath, which I'd rather deal with than the jeers of my classmates.

When I stepped into the dining room, though, a decorated cake waited on the table, decked out for more than a family get-together.

"How did you find out?" I gasped.

"Vivian's mother called and asked what time the party started," Mom said, giving me her warning look.

I figured the hammer would fall when it was over. But Mom surprised me. All I got was a gentle "talking to." Grace and mercy were the real presents I received that day. (Those are gifts that I still need and receive, no matter how old I am.)

Father God, thank You that Your grace is greater than all my sin. And You never treat me as I deserve. Through Christ my Lord, amen.

Big Love!

As high as the heavens are above the earth, so great is his love for those who fear him (Psalm 103:11).

Scripture: **Psalm 103:11-16**
Song: **"Abiding Love"**

Although I've felt God's loving touch on many occasions in my life, two times in particular stand out in my mind. The first was when I was in the hospital after giving birth by C-section to my second child. Feeling low, I huddled under the covers and wept silently, longing for a bowl of my mother's homemade chicken soup. A few days after I got home, my best friend brought supper: homemade chicken soup.

The second time was years later on my birthday. After I put my three small children to bed, I dropped down on the sofa, feeling sorry for myself. No cards came in the mail that day. No one had called to wish me "Happy Birthday." My husband was still at work, putting in another of his 12-hour days. My father was dead; my mother was suffering the later stages of Alzheimer's.

"Lord," I whispered, "I need something special from You today." I opened my Bible to the day's reading, Romans 8:35-39, and smiled. "For I am convinced . . . [nothing] will be able to separate us from the love of God that is in Christ Jesus."

Lord, You are the maker of Heaven and earth. Yet You took time to answer a prayer for chicken soup. And You bent down to embrace a tired, lonely homemaker with Your words of love. Thank You, in Christ's name. Amen.

Looking Up

Praise the LORD, all his works everywhere in his dominion. Praise the LORD, O my soul (Psalm 103:22).

Scripture: **Psalm 103:17-22**
Song: **"From All That Dwells Below the Skies"**

I'm a sky watcher. From fiery sunsets, to misty mauve mornings, to the sparkling, diamond-studded canopy of a cold winter night—I savor them all.

"The heavens declare the glory of God," David the psalmist wrote. "The skies proclaim the works of his hands" (Psalm 19:1). As the great scientist and educator George Washington Carver once put it: "I love to think of nature as an unlimited broadcasting station, through which God speaks to us every hour, if we only will tune in."

In other words, how can anyone view the splendor overhead and not see God? Yet "The fool says in his heart, 'There is no God'" (Psalm 14:1). But perhaps the fool doesn't look up, so all he sees is dirt.

I too have a choice. I can focus on the mud and bemoan my lot. Or I can lift up my eyes and view God's handiwork. I can open my ears and hear it shouting His praises. I can open my mouth and join the heavenly song.

Today, won't you join me in looking to the skies? Let us lift up our voices and join the heavenly chorus that praises eternally: "Holy, holy, holy is the Lord God Almighty, who was, and is, and is to come" (Revelation 4:8).

*Thank You, **Lord,** for surrounding me with evidence of Your reality and love. Let praise be my song all through this day. In Christ's name, amen.*

A Visit from God

The LORD came down in the cloud and stood there with him and proclaimed his name, the LORD (Exodus 34:5).

Scripture: **Exodus 34:1-10**
Song: **"The Name of Jesus"**

Watching my father die from cancer was one of the hardest things I've ever done. I was, after all, Daddy's girl. I couldn't believe he would leave us without saying good-bye, but in his last hours he was quite medicated. For two days afterward, I stayed in the house, hoping for some special form of comfort—but nothing.

But that chaned on the day of his funeral, my 20th birthday. Before I even opened my eyes that morning, I felt it. A presence in the house, a peace so strong yet soft and comforting. It permeated every molecule in the air around me and every fiber of my being—body, heart, mind, and soul. Joy filled me.

I believe it was God himself, giving me a little taste of Heaven. A little taste that carried me through the tough times I faced in the years that followed. Those peaceful moments often reminded me that what awaits me goes far beyond all I could ask or imagine, according to His power that is at work within me (see Ephesians 3:20).

Dear Heavenly Father, *thank You for the gift of Your Son so long ago. You wanted to come down and be with us! And thanks for keeping Your promise never to leave me or forsake me. Grant me an increasing awareness of Your abiding presence in my life through Your Holy Spirit. In the name of the Father, the Son, and the Holy Spirit, I pray. Amen.*

What a Name!

If you suffer as a Christian, do not be ashamed, but praise God that you bear that name (1 Peter 4:16).

Scripture: **1 Peter 4:12-19**
Song: **"There's Something About That Name"**

With pen in hand, Peter remembers. He recalls the mountaintop where Jesus glowed white in glorious rapture and talked with spiritual giants. He recollects the small room tucked away in the family house where a young girl returned to life and got her future back. He remembers an after-breakfast walk along the rock-strewn beach of a familiar lake . . . and the softly spoken words of hope and trust.

As Peter calls to mind the highlights of his days with Jesus, he puts pen to scroll and urges those who read his letter to remember. They must not forget the name by which they are known. Remembering that name, God raises them above their troubles. Jesus saves them, as His name promises He will do.

We have no portraits of our Lord, but we have His name. The name of one who rises up in the pages of history more formidably than any Gibraltar up out of the sea. Great men and women come and go, but Jesus came and stayed. He is the centerpiece of the masterpiece.

Jesus, with Your name I am blessed, and by Your name I am called. It is in Your name I am sent, and it is for Your name I go. Praise to You! Amen.

September 27–30. **Phillip Barnhart** is a retired minister living in Florida who occasionally serves as an interim. He has written several books and many articles.

What a God!

Woe to him who quarrels with his Maker . . . Does the clay say to the potter, "What are you making?" Does your work say, "He has no hands"? (Isaiah 45:9).

Scripture: **Isaiah 45:9-13**
Song: **"All Praise Be to God"**

As Uzziah's reign drew to a close, a tranquil interlude for the nation ended. Isaiah understood the potential political turmoil and urged the country to stand on firm theological principle. The people must affirm the sovereignty and supremacy of God. They must know God is in charge.

Before the battle of Waterloo, Napoleon said to his staff, "We will place the infantry here, the cavalry here, and the artillery here." A member of his staff spoke up, "Shouldn't we pray about this, sir?" Napoleon stood to his full stature and responded, "It is Napoleon who proposes and disposes." From that moment on, the battle of Waterloo was lost. The rain came in torrents and bogged down infantry, cavalry, and artillery.

While attempting to explain the role of president of the United States to her 4-year-old son, a mother said the president was the boss of the country. Using his newly acquired Sunday school wisdom, the little guy exclaimed, "No, Mommy, that's not true. God is the boss."

Dear God, my past, present, and future are in Your hands. All the tenses of my life are under Your sovereignty. You know where I am, and You know who I am. So, please, direct my steps today. In the name of Jesus, amen.

What a Praise!

Now, our God, we give you thanks, and praise your glorious name (1 Chronicles 29:13).

Scripture: **1 Chronicles 29:10-16**
Song: **"Praise to the Lord, the Almighty"**

The people have given, and the offering plates are full. The building project is adequately financed, and a proper residence for God can be built. It is fitting that the king kneels and gives praise to God. "David praised the Lord in the presence of the whole assembly" (v. 10). David takes time to give thanks.

It is always time to give thanks. As someone has said, we should always be praising God, because God is always blessing us.

A minister had just started his Sunday sermon when it began storming outside. With thunder and lightning, rain poured down in wild torrents. "God is wonderful!" the minister told the congregation. "While we're sitting here dry and comfortable, God's out there in the parking lot washing our cars for us!"

God's blessings do rain down on us every day, in every way. We only have to hold the hand of one we love or watch a child at play on the sidewalk or lift a juicy apple to our lips to know that. We only have to take a breath to know it is time to give thanks.

Father, You so are good to me. You are generous beyond measure, so I cannot count high enough to itemize my blessings. I sit at Your table and eat my fill—then You offer even more. Thank You, in Jesus' name. Amen.

What a Beginning!

Remember also your Creator in the days of your youth, before the evil days come, and the years draw nigh, when you will say, "I have no pleasure in them" (Ecclesiastes 12:1, *Revised Standard Version*).

Scripture: **Ecclesiastes 12:1-8**
Song: **"The Year Is Swiftly Waning"**

The book of Ecclesiastes relates Solomon's futile attempt to produce meaning in life. He's cynical about the human situation, and his writing hardly fosters hope. Failing to find the meaning of life in science, philosophy, or pleasure, the king concludes that nothing makes much sense.

Ecclesiastes is an autobiography of someone out of fellowship with God; it shows us the emptiness that it brings. However, give Solomon credit: he knows his condition and wants others to avoid it. He encourages people to remember God when they are young. Ecclesiastes, interestingly enough, closes by calling young people to faith.

I was blessed with immediate exposure to the Christian faith. Born on Wednesday and taken to church the following Sunday, I have been there ever since. All through my childhood, faith was nurtured in me. Precepts and principles flowed into me, and my relationship with God guided the steps I took in life. For over 70 years I have stood firm on that foundation.

O God, Creator of Heaven and earth, thank You for being with me in all stages and ages of life. May I encourage young people to find You early, talk to You often, and love You always. In Christ's holy name I pray. Amen.

My Prayer Notes

_____

_____

_____

_____

_____

_____

_____

_____

_____

_____

_____

_____

_____

_____

_____

_____

_____

_____

_____

_____

DEVOTIONS®

*L*ook, at the birds of the air . . . Are you not much more valuable than they?

—Matthew 6:26

OCTOBER

Photo © Liquid Library

Gary Allen, Editor   **Margaret Williams,** Project Editor

DEVOTIONS® is published quarterly by Standard Publishing, Cincinnati, Ohio, www.standardpub.com. © 2009 by Standard Publishing. All rights reserved. Topics based on the Home Daily Bible Readings, International Sunday School Lessons. © 2007 by the Committee on the Uniform Series. Printed in the U.S.A. All Scripture quotations, unless otherwise indicated, are taken from the HOLY BIBLE, NEW INTERNATIONAL VERSION®. NIV®. Copyright © 1973, 1978, 1984 by International Bible Society. Used by permission of Zondervan. All rights reserved.

What a Blessing!

The LORD is good to all; he has compassion on all he has made (Psalm 145:9).

Scripture: **Psalm 145:8-13**
Song: **"Count Your Blessings"**

Three-year-old Bridgett went forward to the altar with her grandmother when the Lord's Supper was celebrated. The minister placed his hands on Bridgett's head as she knelt there. Returning to her seat, she asked, "Grandma, why did the minister put his hand on my head?" Bridgett's grandmother responded, "To bless you, dear."

"Why?" Bridgett replied, "I didn't sneeze."

But God blesses us all the time—when we sneeze and when we don't. King David, the psalmist, must have known he was blessed that way. He surely knew God's bounty, counted and recounted His benefits. He knew God gave him great favor all the time.

A young novice, eating the best bread he'd ever tasted, asked one of the brothers at the monastery, "Did we make this bread, or was it given to us?" The brother smiled and answered, "Yes."

*Sometimes I am embarrassed by my riches, **Father**. The fatted calf and best robe, for me? Unspeakable joy and peace that exceeds understanding, for me? I live in the promised land every day, and I am so thankful for every blessing that comes from Your hand. In the name of Jesus, who lives and reigns with You and the Holy Spirit, one God, now and forever, amen.*

October 1–3. **Phillip Barnhart** is a retired minister living in Florida who occasionally serves as an interim. He has written several books and many articles.

What a Responsibility!

God said, "Let us make man in our image, in our likeness, and let them rule over the fish of the sea and the birds of the air, over the livestock, over all the earth, and over all the creatures that move along the ground" (Genesis 1:26).

Scripture: **Genesis 1:26-31**
Song: **"All Creatures of Our God and King"**

Appoint me creator of the world, and I'd come up with a better maintenance plan. Place angels and archangels in charge. Devise an automatically renewable ecological system. A lot of divine intervention, not much human participation. But that's not the way God wants it. He wants us to be in charge . . . for now. He will reign from Heaven, but He wants us to rule on earth until Christ returns.

So, working for clean air and clear water is simply creation care, and the best ecology is a good theology. In this vein, writer Thomas Merton urges us to have an "unspeakable reverence for the holiness of created things." And why not? What God makes, He makes good. Therefore, we ought to appreciate it to its fullest.

Creation is God's first act of grace, a wonderful gift to us, but packaged with great responsibility. Little Donna wrote a letter: "Dear God, in school we read that Thomas Edison made light. But in Sunday school they said You did it. I bet he stole your idea." It is God's idea of creation for which we are responsible.

Father, *I see Your glorious handwriting everywhere; You've put Your signature on everything. What a good giver You are! Through Christ, amen.*

One of a Kind

When I consider your heavens, the work of your fingers, the moon and the stars, which you have set in place, what is man that you are mindful of him, the son of man that you care for him? (Psalm 8:3, 4).

Scripture: **Psalm 8**
Song: **"Joyful, Joyful, We Adore Thee"**

Michelangelo explained his theology of art to a friend. "Why do you think I've given my life to creating a race of glorious creatures in marble and paint? Because I see human beauty as God's most divine attribute." As great as God's work is in sun, moon, and stars, it is greater still in the creation of human life. We top the list of what God makes. Answering the psalmist's question: *that* is why God is mindful of us.

We are handcrafted, not mass produced. We are not churned out on an assembly line where each looks like all the others. An acquaintance of mine wrote a musical play in which is the song, "There Are No Cookie Cutters in Heaven." God makes only originals, no copies.

When God made you, He had His mind on His business. When God made your friend, He was having a good day. When God made me, He knew what He was doing. When we were made, God stamped "one of a kind" on each of us.

Creator God, thank You that I am carefully and wonderfully made. And since nobody has my DNA, You honor me with a marvelous uniqueness. May I live today worthy of creaturehood. In the name of Christ. Amen.

Glimpses of God's Majesty

The heavens declare the glory of God; the skies proclaim the work of his hands (Psalm 19:1).

Scripture: **Psalm 19:1-6**
Song: **"For the Beauty of the Earth"**

As a girl I loved spending early mornings with Grandma. Before others awoke I heard the song of the mockingbird, and I listened to her stories. We smelled the roses and found beauty in the lush grass and trees, the fresh air and blue skies. I remember other times when I played in the summer rain, splashing my feet in warm water puddles. And when thunder and lightning forced me inside, I felt safely close to God.

Our Scripture reminds me that the heavens and earth declare God's majesty. All creation magnifies the Lord in a language all its own. It gives me glimpses of Heaven, eternity with God, where someday I will see Him face to face.

I do long to walk with Him in the cool of the day as Adam and Eve did—and perhaps I will smell the roses and listen to the mockingbird with Grandma again. Until that glorious day, I will tell others of God's love and the wonderful work of His hands.

Father in Heaven, thank You for reminders of greatness in Your creation of the earth and sky. Thank You for the love and care You bring through Your presence and the presence of the ones I love. Through Christ, amen.

October 4–10. **Sue Tornai** is a writer and Sunday school teacher in Carmichael, California. She and her husband have 6 children and 13 grandchildren.

Wheelchair Proclamation

Give thanks to the Lord, call on his name; make known among the nations what he has done (Psalm 105:1).

Scripture: **Psalm 105:1-11**
Song: **"Go, Tell It on the Mountain"**

A friendly spousal tennis match between Peter and Peggy is unique, because Peter plays tennis from a wheelchair. His easy smile and deeply tanned skin reflect his career in coaching people for wheelchair sports.

Peter played baseball for the United States Air Force, but his athletic life changed directions when he suffered a serious auto accident in 1959. Yet he has a sparkle in his eye and a willingness to share his hope in Christ.

He uses wheelchair sports to inspire and motivate people to do things they never dreamed they could do. "Something good happens when people with disabilities switch from their ordinary wheelchairs to sports wheelchairs," says Peter. This is so important to Peter that he founded an organization that sends sports wheelchairs around the world to health clubs. In other words, through the unique medium of wheelchairs and sports, this dedicated Christian is making known among the nations what God has done and is doing.

Almighty and most merciful God, *thank You for all the ways You bless me. And help me, like Peter, to make known to others what You have done. Show me how to reach out to people with Your love, and equip me to do it with winsomeness and grace. I pray this prayer in the name of Jesus, my Savior and Lord. Amen.*

Open Her Eyes

They went off and worshiped other gods and bowed down to them . . . Therefore the LORD's anger burned against this land, so that he brought on it all the curses written in this book (Deuteronomy 29:26, 27).

Scripture: **Deuteronomy 29:25-29**
Song: **"Our Heavenly Father Calls"**

A gentle breeze carried the scent of jasmine and brought music to the wind chimes when I visited Carolyn, my flower-child friend. She saw my eyes fall on the angel I'd given her at Christmas.

"I love her song," she said as she turned the switch that played "Ode to Joy." With childlike enthusiasm Carolyn showed me her other treasures. "And this is my beautiful Indian goddess," she said, caressing a polished wooden statue. "I pray to her every day."

Astonished, I tried to keep calm. "As lovely as she is, Carolyn, she has no power to help you in tough times."

"But I can see her and touch her," she replied.

My heart fell. I can't help thinking of the effect of idolatry on my friend's life. By praying to a stick of wood with no power to hear her or answer her prayers, Carolyn will miss the opportunity to praise the Lord of all.

Carolyn has moved away, and I don't see her anymore. But I pray that God will open her eyes and that she will experience His great love for her.

Lord, *I pray for all who trust only in the things they can see and touch. Reach out with Your love and touch them. In Jesus' name, amen.*

The Joy of His Delight

The LORD will again delight in you and make you prosperous, just as he delighted in your fathers, if you obey the LORD your God and keep his commands and decrees that are written in this Book of the Law and turn to the LORD your God with all your heart and with all your soul (Deuteronomy 30:9, 10).

Scripture: **Deuteronomy 30:1-10**
Song: **"Amazing Love, How Can It Be?"**

On a rainy day with my first-grade class, we spent our recess time in the gym. Our teacher told us not to run on the bleachers, but I did. And I fell on my face. By the time I got home, my eyes were swollen nearly shut.

As a child I learned that when I didn't obey my parents and teachers, besides getting into trouble, I often got hurt. Later I made choices that led me away from God. Trapped in guilt and sin, I became lonely, longing to feel God's love the way I'd felt it before.

Then a minister reminded me that Jesus died for my sins. He said, "You can accept what Jesus did for you on the cross and experience forgiveness, or you can keep beating up on yourself." I chose to accept God's forgiveness. Day by day I learned to surrender my heart to Him, and I began thanking Him for loving me. As I trusted Him more, I learned that He delighted in me. I began living with the joy of it—the joy of the Lord's delight.

Heavenly Father, *thank You for not giving up on me. As You restored Israel, You restored my life and gave me hope. You are my refuge; I will bless Your name forever. In Christ's name I pray. Amen.*

Pray Like This!

Be strong and courageous, for you will bring the Israelites into the land I promised them on oath, and I myself will be with you (Deuteronomy 31:23).

Scripture: **Deuteronomy 31:19-26**
Song: **"You Are My Strength When I Am Weak"**

Dr. Felipe, a missionary doctor, was ready to perform an emergency Caesarean section. First, though, he and his surgical team prayed for the woman, her baby, and for God's guiding hand. Skillfully they went to work. When Dr. Felipe lifted the lifeless baby from the womb, he said, "I think we lost him."

"No, no, we prayed for him," the nurse said. "The baby is in God's hands. We don't worry." Inspired, Dr. Felipe began resuscitation efforts. And soon a piercing cry filled the room—the sweetest sound!

The team rejoiced and praised God. These believers in Central Africa sought God and depended on Him for everything. They found that, as Joshua needed all his courage and strength to lead Israel into the promised land, they required the same kind of courage and strength to meet the challenges of every day.

I am encouraged by the simple faith of these people—"I prayed, this is in God's hands, and I don't need to worry." Can I pray that way? *Will* I pray that way today? May God give me the courage to do so.

Lord God, *keep me from growing weary in my routines, and help me draw on Your power in the most impossible situations. In Jesus' name, amen.*

It's About Relationship

"This is the covenant I will make with the house of Israel after that time," declares the LORD. "I will put my law in their minds and write it on their hearts. I will be their God and they will be my people" (Jeremiah 31:33).

Scripture: **Jeremiah 31:31-37**
Song: **"Jesus, Lover of My Soul"**

I obeyed my parents, followed the rules, and tried hard to please God. But I was not happy. I read my Bible, sang in the choir, and taught Sunday school. Yet something was missing. I began to choose my ways over God's ways, and I found more emptiness and despair. By this time I had been through divorce, and my children were grown and gone. I was alone and lonely.

"I don't want to go on anymore," I cried out to God.

"Could you make it today if I promise to stay with you?" God's Spirit seemed to whisper to me.

"I guess so." My tears flowed as I sensed that God could really love me. I began trusting Him by reading my Bible and spending time in prayer each day. Trusting God made me feel even more loved and blessed.

I think I began learning what God meant by the new covenant—"I will put my law in their minds and write it on their hearts. I will be their God and they will be my people." He meant relationship.

*Thank You, **Father,** for Your love and faithfulness. Thank You for putting Your law in my mind and writing it on my heart. Help me live in a love relationship with You and others each day. In Jesus' name, amen.*

Great Treasure: Found!

May the words of my mouth and the meditation of my heart be pleasing in your sight, O Lord, my Rock and my Redeemer (Psalm 19:14).

Scripture: **Psalm 19:7-14**
Song: **"Worthy, You Are Worthy"**

In Matthew 13, Jesus told a story about a man who found hidden treasure in a field. He sold everything he had to buy that treasure-filled field. I have found that treasure in knowing Jesus as my Lord and Savior.

You see, nothing in my life is more important than Him. Nothing brings me more pleasure. It is nearly more than I can conceive to know that He actually died for my sins so I could live with Him forever.

But He didn't leave me at the cross to figure things out for myself. In His mercy He gave me His Spirit to guide me and lead me into wisdom and joy. And His scriptural precepts, more than chains that bind, are a light to my path. In fact, they've become an anchor in life's storms.

Yes, I find security in the boundaries God has set for me. Although at times I've wandered outside and chosen my ways over His ways, He has reached out to me and forgiven me. He has blessed me and given me hope.

*Thank You, **Lord and Savior,** for the treasure of knowing You, Your forgiveness and Your laws that guide me and keep me close to You. May the words of my mouth and the meditations of my heart be pleasing in Your sight today . . . and forever. In the name of the Father, the Son, and the Holy Spirit, I pray. Amen.*

This Is Not All There Is

The grass withers and the flowers fall, but the word of our God stands forever (Isaiah 40:8).

Scripture: **Isaiah 40:6-11**
Song: **"Eternal Source of Joys Divine"**

Each spring my husband sows tiny summer poinsettia seeds in the ground around our lamppost. Soon twin blades break the soil, and by the end of summer, robust stalks stand three to four feet tall. The flowers' real beauty unfolds as the days shorten and the stalks' leaves turn brilliant shades of red, pink, and yellow. Surely, we might think, this hardy-looking plant will once again sprout next year. But that is not to be. The flower blooms for a season, then droops and dies.

We, too, bloom for a season. I become more conscious of that with each birthday. And, in fact, all creation suffers the effects of time. Health fails. The values of investments rise and fall. Cars and clothes wear out and must be replaced. But behind a fragile creation stands a God whose word remains true. He regulates the tides. He governs the seasons. And He invites us to spend eternity with Him.

Heavenly Father, *thank You that when circumstances pull me down I can look for You at work behind the scenes. Open my eyes to enjoy the earthly beauty around me—but to live always with eternity in view. In the name of Your Son, my Savior, I pray. Amen.*

October 11–17. **Shirley Brosius** lives with her husband, Bill, in Millersburg, Pennsylvania. She enjoys playing board games with five grandchildren.

I Take Thee As Lord

Know therefore that the LORD your God is God; he is the faithful God, keeping his covenant of love (Deuteronomy 7:9).

Scripture: **Deuteronomy 7:7-11**
Song: **"Tell Me the Stories of Jesus"**

The dedication of children forms a covenant among the child, the parents, and the congregation. Parents promise to nurture the child in the Lord, and members of the congregation declare they will provide teaching and model godly Christian lifestyles for him or her. This creates a community of faith in which the child may grow into spiritual maturity.

Special bonds develop between children and those in the church who know them, even as early as the nursery years. But what happens if parents fail to bring children into the church fellowship? The covenant remains in force on the part of the church, but if parents do not uphold their vows to nurture their children within a community of faith, the children may drift from spiritual moorings.

God offers us a covenant of love when we profess faith in His Son, the Lord Jesus Christ, as our Savior. He places us in a community of faith. And living in obedience to His commands keeps us from drifting from our own spiritual moorings.

Dear Heavenly Father, *thank You for never reneging on Your covenant with us. Motivate me to remain faithful, as well, and to do my part to nurture the children in my own community of faith. I pray this prayer in the name of Jesus, my merciful Savior and Lord. Amen.*

Find a Fellow Struggler

[God] comforts us in all our troubles, so that we can comfort those in any trouble with the comfort we ourselves have received from God (2 Corinthians 1:4).

*Scripture: **2 Corinthians 1:3-7***
*Song: **"Comfort, Comfort Ye My People"***

A friend of mine suffers from an anxiety disorder. As she speaks at women's retreats, she often shares how God helps her handle her fear of public speaking and of even walking into a roomful of strangers. She is always surprised by the number of women who express appreciation. Many suffer from similar disorders, yet they've been too embarrassed to tell anyone: Wouldn't they appear to be weak Christians? My friend's testimony offers them hope; she has found God's grace to be sufficient.

We live in an imperfect world where we deal with illness, death, and myriad family and societal problems. Yet as we survive by God's grace, we become living monuments to His power. Our individual stories may be as varied as our fingerprints, but they point to the same mighty God who can redeem the most difficult situations. That includes our personal weaknesses.

What story might you share with someone today as a testimony of God's love? How might your own struggles encourage a fellow struggler?

Father, thank You for using difficult experiences in my life to bring glory to Your name. Give me courage to share what You have done for me with someone who might be encouraged by my story. In Jesus' name, amen.

Counting on My Prayers

Then many will give thanks on our behalf for the gracious favor granted us in answer to the prayers of many (2 Corinthians 1:11).

Scripture: **2 Corinthians 1:8-11**
Song: **"Praying Always"**

Scottish minister Robert Murray McCheyne once said, "If the veil of the world's machinery were lifted off, how much we could find is done in answer to the prayers of God's children."

Many results are already known. When the table had been set but there was no food to serve, 19th-century evangelist George Mueller prayed for provisions to run his orphanage—and a baker soon showed up with bread for breakfast. Augustine, an early church father, credited his mother's prayers for his conversion after he'd led a promiscuous life as a youth. At the Christian community of Herrnhut in the 1700s, believers took hour-long turns praying around the clock. Their prayer meeting lasted over 100 years. During that time more than 300 missionaries went forth from there.

Our prayers are vital to the well being of others and to the propagation of the gospel. If we fail to pray, someone somewhere may be let down. So, are you adding your prayers to the "prayers of many" today?

Heavenly Father, I know Your hands respond to my prayers. Ministers, missionaries, and church teachers see positive results as I support them. May I help to uphold them by continuing to pray. In Jesus' name, amen.

Pedicure, Anyone?

How beautiful on the mountains are the feet of those who bring good news, who proclaim peace, who bring good tidings, who proclaim salvation, who say to Zion, "Your God reigns" (Isaiah 52:7).

Scripture: **Isaiah 52:7-12**
Song: **"Since I Have Been Redeemed"**

Faces and fingernails might be considered beautiful. But feet? Feet come with bunions, calluses, and hammer toes. Isaiah, however, describes as "beautiful" the feet of those who bring salvation.

This morning I called a terminally ill friend to encourage her to meditate on the 23rd Psalm. I shared with her how, at a women's retreat, we participated in a scavenger hunt based on that Scripture. On a lawn, we rested on blankets in "green pastures." At a gazebo we dipped our hands and feet in the "still waters" of a tub. We skipped down a "path of righteousness" and crawled through an obstacle course to ponder "the valley of the shadow of death." Our activity ended around "a table prepared for us" to celebrate the Lord's Supper. I thought my friend might benefit from such calming and peaceful thoughts.

Whenever we plant seeds of faith in another, we're part of the army that crosses mountains to proclaim peace. We need no pedicure. Our feet are already gorgeous.

Heavenly Father, bring to mind words of faith to share with those I meet today. May I remind them of who You are and how You care for them. Through Christ, my Lord and Savior. Amen.

Tasty Memories of Home

God sets the lonely in families (Psalm 68:6).

Scripture: **Psalm 68:4-10**
Song: **"Homeward Bound"**

I grew up with four much-older brothers and sisters. As they married and moved away, they returned home to visit my parents on Sunday afternoons. On winter days, the men went down to a meadow creek, chopped ice, and used it to crank up a batch of vanilla ice cream. It was always served with homegrown strawberries that my mother had crushed, sweetened, and frozen. We were a family. As we ate, we rejoiced over upcoming births and shared the challenges we faced at school or work.

Now we live in different times. It's hard for my sons and their families to visit on a Sunday afternoon because their children have so many social activities—sport events, birthday parties.

Some people are separated from their birth families by hundreds of miles. So, in this day and age, our church families become increasingly important. We need fellow believers to rejoice with us when we're up, encourage us when we're down, and walk beside us through the daily challenges of life.

Almighty and gracious Father, thank You for the brothers and sisters in my church family. Help me to get to know them so that I can truly mourn with those who mourn and rejoice with those who rejoice—especially with those whose birth families are out of touch. In the name of the Father, the Son, and the Holy Spirit, I pray. Amen.

Invitation for Meditation

God is our refuge and strength, an ever-present help in trouble (Psalm 46:1).

Scripture: **Psalm 46:1-7**
Song: **"The Quiet Hour"**

A church near my home offers a quiet setting for outdoor meditation. At the corner of a parking lot, a park bench faces a tiny plot of ground that holds an angel statue, a birdhouse, and a decorative flag from which chickadees proclaim: "The whole earth is full of God's glory." A small tree and a cluster of morning glories complete the peaceful setting.

But as I take daily walks by the bench, I have yet to see anyone seated there. Nor do I myself pause to enjoy the solitude. I may have appointments, or I simply decline to stop in the middle of my busy day. So the peace and quiet offered by that bench goes largely ignored by those of us who pass by.

So too God offers himself as our refuge and strength, an ever-present help—but do we accept or ignore the offer? Do we have appointments that prevent us from spending time with Him? Are we unwilling to take the time to seek Him? If we fail to spend time with God, we may miss the opportunity of receiving His strength.

Almighty and everlasting God, *thank You for being my daily refuge and strength. Help me remember that I must accept the offer if I don't want to miss the blessing. As I walk through my days, may I learn to pause and hear Your call: "Be still, and know that I am God." In Jesus' name, amen.*

Shall We Bow?

The LORD is the true God; he is the living God, the eternal King. When he is angry, the earth trembles; the nations cannot endure his wrath (Jeremiah 10:10).

Scripture: **Jeremiah 10:6-10**
Song: **"Praise to the Living God"**

Last summer I went on a "Steps of St. Paul" tour with a group from my church. As we toured the ruins of ancient cities, I was amazed by the broken pieces of statuary littered on the ground. These broken stone idols represented the gods that were worshiped in Jesus' time. Today most people don't even know their names or what they represented. They are the remnants of dead religions.

But the apostle Paul spread Christianity throughout these lands by preaching the good news of Christ. Over two thousand years later our Bible, the story of God's love for mankind, still tops best-seller lists.

Unlike statues that crumble, our beliefs have withstood the test of time. Our God is alive. He dwells within us to guide us in all our ways. Our Lord is the one true God, the eternal king of the universe. He is loving, but not safe, so let us bow to Him today. He is more than worthy of our worship.

O God, creator of Heaven and earth, please let Your word be a lamp unto my feet and a light unto my path. Thus may I show others the way to the true, living, and loving God. In the name of Jesus, amen.

October 18–24. **Georgeanne Gaulden-Falstrom** lives with her husband and two terriers in Irving, Texas. Retired, she has led a ministry of writing for her church.

Family Shame

All who worship idols are put to shame (Psalm 97:7).

Scripture: **Psalm 97**
Song: **"Restore in Us, O God"**

All of Sara's family are Hummel collectors. You've probably seen these colorful figurines, for they appear everywhere in gift shops. They are delightful pieces of ceramic art, based on the drawings of a Franciscan nun, Maria Inocentia Hummel, born in Bavaria in 1909.

Sara's favorite aunt had gathered the largest collection in her family, over 100 pieces. When this aunt died, Sara had expected her cousins to give her at least one of the figurines as a remembrance. But neither she nor her mother were offered any of the collection. Although extremely disappointed, neither said anything to the cousins.

When Sara's mother became terminally ill and discussed her wishes, she expressly said, "Don't give anything to your nieces." She described them as selfish. She warned Sara not to get too involved with her cousins or expect anything from them. Sara was shocked because her mother had always been very close to her family. She was their example of a loving and forgiving Christian.

What a shame that this family put more emphasis on a collection of figurines than on generous and loving relationships. In this case, innocent figurines had apparently become destructive idols.

O God, please look into my heart and help me see if any form of idolatry is damaging my relationship with You or Your people. In Jesus' name, amen.

S. O. S.

If calamity comes upon us, whether the sword of judgment, or plague or famine, we will stand in your presence before this temple that bears your Name and will cry out to you in our distress, and you will hear us and save us (2 Chronicles 20:9).

Scripture: 2 Chronicles 20:5-12
Song: "Praise God, for He Is Kind"

Recently the national news showed evacuees returning to what had been their homes on Galveston Island. Devastation was everywhere. Standing in her home that was damaged beyond repair, a woman in her 70s told the newscaster that she didn't know what she would do. Nevertheless, she believed God would take care of her.

In today's Scripture passage, Judah's ruler, Jehoshaphat, had been warned that the enemy was coming to wage war. His response to the approaching crisis was to call on the people to join together in fasting and prayer. Firmly believing that the Lord would hear them and save them, his army went into battle, singing praises to God. The Lord responded favorably to them.

The story gives me pause to consider: When I receive warning that a disaster is on it's way, will I be prepared? What's in my emergency response kit? Is it filled with only medical supplies and a flashlight—or have I included prayer and praise to God?

Heavenly Father, *You have assured me that I can lean on You in any crisis. Please answer my cry for help and save me from harm. Comfort me and give me Your peace. In the holy name of Jesus, amen.*

Deliverance

From the LORD comes deliverance. May your blessing be on your people (Psalm 3:8).

Scripture: **Psalm 3**
Song: **"The Battle Belongs to the Lord"**

Lord Byron once said: "Adversity is the first path to truth." But when King David was surrounded by adversity, he found his pathway leading to *the* Truth, God himself. David poured out his fears to the Lord, believing that God would deliver him from distress. He also asked God to bless the people.

We are God's people if we are indwelt by His Spirit. God has promised to hear our prayers and answer them. Sometimes the answer is "no," of course, and we must look for the lesson to be learned. If the answer is "yes," we'll naturally lift up thankful hearts of praise. Either way, we can trust that God's answer flows from His love and concern for us. (And if the answer is "wait," we can learn patience and perseverance as our faith grows.)

Being able to turn our fears and troubles over to God is, in itself, a great blessing. Have you tried "letting go and letting God" fight your battles for you? Will you and I let Him bless us into comfort and peace?

O God, king of glory, You have promised to hear my prayer. You know the needs of my family and the problems I am facing. Only You can fight this battle for me, so please send Your favor and blessing in this time of trouble. I do seek Your wisdom and peace. In the name of Jesus, who lives and reigns with You and the Holy Spirit, one God, now and forever, amen.

Through the Storm

The eternal God is your refuge (Deuteronomy 33:27).

Scripture: **Deuteronomy 33:26-29**
Song: **"I Want Jesus to Walk with Me"**

Storm clouds had been gathering since we left Colorado Springs. And as we crossed into New Mexico, the sky was becoming ever more eerie.

As the rain began to pour down on us, I could soon see nothing past the windshield wipers. Yet I feared pulling over, thinking someone might plow into us from behind.

Our only place of refuge? Prayer. Both Liz, in the back seat, and Patti, beside me, were praying with me as hard as the rain was falling.

You see, we believe that God is trustworthy and keeps His promises. We've been promised that He is our refuge in times of trouble, and we feel His presence with us in the scariest of times. (In about 45 minutes the rain stopped. Our fears were relieved, and we praised God for bringing us safely through the storm.)

There will always be storms and challenges in our lives. But I like how 19th-century Scottish novelist Henry Mackenzie summarized the key to coming through them: "It is only from the belief of the goodness and wisdom of a supreme being, that our calamities can be borne in the manner which becomes a human being."

Lord, *those storm clouds are again rolling into my life, and I may be getting lost again. Please reach out Your hand to me and bring me safely to refuge, shielded by Your grace. Through Christ I pray. Amen.*

Let God Reign

Great is the LORD in Zion; he is exalted over all the nations (Psalm 99:2).

Scripture: **Psalm 99**
Song: **"Gathered Here in That Great Presence"**

Today's news can be pretty discouraging. Besides local and world political crises, there are financial crises, job layoffs, wars, threats of war, and devastating natural disasters. We live in a time of constant uneasiness. Yet there's little we can do about most of the headlines, except to pray.

God listens, hears, and answers our prayers. And I believe that He is the mighty king and just ruler of all nations on earth. Yet He wants to be a part of our lives. Through prayer we can lift up our concerns about what is happening in the world today. And praying for God's leadership and wisdom in all situations is, in a sense, praising His power. It is recognizing His omnipresence and omnipotence.

When you hear or read the news, do you pray about your concerns, or spend your time worrying about how you will be affected? Knowing that God is in control is the best way to gain peace in a world filled with chaos.

Gracious God, ruler of the universe, please calm my fears as I listen to today's news headlines. Give the leaders of our country wisdom and guidance in the decisions they must make about our country's welfare. We praise You for Your just rule and undying love. In the name of the Father, the Son, and the Holy Spirit I pray. Amen.

Victory in Jesus

Clap your hands, all you nations; shout to God with cries of joy (Psalm 47:1).

Scripture: **Psalm 47**
Song: **"We Shall See the King"**

It's Friday night anywhere in Texas. Fans pour into the high school stadium for this week's big football game, and the air buzzes with anticipation.

The band plays the school fight song as the home team runs out onto the field, led by pom-pom waving cheerleaders. Everyone applauds the school colors as they rise to their feet cheering and clapping, shouting for victory.

The coaches discuss last-minute changes to the game plan. One team will taste victory and the other defeat. But what will victory cost?

Our psalm describes a similar scene. Instead of honoring a team of athletes, it is a celebration honoring and praising the Lord Most High. But the mood and anticipation of victory is the same. The game plan is already in play.

What is different about this celebration? We are already *assured* of victory. It came to us at the cross, the atoning sacrifice that produced eternal salvation for all who believe. It was not an easy victory, though; the price was the precious blood of the incarnate God. What greater reason to celebrate than our victory in Jesus? *Alleluia!*

Father, *I praise You for Your victory over sin at Calvary. Wash me clean with the atoning blood of Your Son! Through His name I pray. Amen.*

What Love!

Then the man and his wife heard the sound of the Lord God as he was walking in the garden in the cool of the day, and they hid from the Lord God among the trees (Genesis 3:8).

Scripture: **Genesis 3:1-8**
Song: **"Hide Me in Your Holiness"**

My husband works for the telephone company and has encountered sundry service problems over the years: cut cables, water in the lines, inefficient splices. Sometimes the problems stem from the environment. Beaver and prairie dogs gnaw lines, woodpeckers peck holes in cables, and cutter bees pack alfalfa around cable pairs causing them to attract moisture. Steve's most recent culprit was Frosted Pops cereal. A customer's toddler had pushed a piece of the cereal into a telephone jack, making it useless. It was an act of innocence and ignorance.

After Adam and Eve sinned, they hid themselves from God because they were neither innocent nor ignorant. They deliberately broke their intimate connection with God. Thus no longer were they clothed in righteousness, enjoying perfect communication with their creator. They could not abide His presence anymore, so they hid. Yet God, in the cool of that day, hotly pursued them in love. And by His grace, He hid them in His holiness.

Father, thanks for hiding me in Your Son. When I blow it and don't want to admit my wrongdoing, You still welcome me. Through Christ, amen.

October 25–31. **Vicki Hodges** lives in the Rocky Mountains of western Colorado with her family. She teaches high school Spanish and loves to travel.

Go with Plan A

He answered, "I am a Hebrew and I worship the LORD, the God of heaven, who made the sea and the land." This terrified them and they asked, "What have you done?" (Jonah 1:9, 10).

Scripture: **Jonah 1:1-10**
Song: **"Do You Tremble?"**

I sat silent, completely shocked as I watched the newsreel play repeatedly. The "Breaking News" line that streamed across the bottom of the TV screen informed viewers that a commercial airplane had flown into the World Trade Center in New York. Terrorists had attacked America. Over the next few days, more details emerged, and I realized how little I had ever worried about terrorists. The word had never been included in my everyday vocabulary. Yet now it permeated various aspects of my life. I joined millions of innocent victims.

The shipmates on Jonah's boat had a similar experience when Jonah revealed who he was and whom he worshiped. In the storm-tossed boat, they experienced some "collateral damage" from God's displeasure toward the stubborn prophet. In a sense, they were innocent victims.

Now God is certainly no terrorist, but He is powerful and just. He had commissioned Jonah for a job, but Jonah refused. (Jonah intended to live on Plan B.) Therefore, God pursued him in order to accomplish His perfect plans for the salvation of the people He loved.

Lord, help me remember that You are the all-powerful creator. Teach me to have a heart of reverent fear before You. Through Christ I pray. Amen.

Joyful Celebrations

The mountains skipped like rams, the hills like lambs (Psalm 114:4).

Scripture: **Psalm 114**
Song: **"Victory in Jesus"**

Susann had prayed for Denzel's salvation throughout their 40 years of marriage, despite his lack of interest in Christianity. But in recent years, Denzel began attending church services with her. Week after week, he sat through sermons sporting his customary scowl.

Four months ago, Denzel's daughter committed suicide. As any parent would, Denzel grieved deeply. Amazingly, one day he told Susann that he had been praying, and he finally understood what Christianity meant. He declared to her, and to his family and friends, that he had committed his life to Christ and was a "new man" at age 73.

Scripture tells us there is rejoicing in Heaven when one sinner repents. Each time a person enters the waters of baptism, there is cause for heartfelt worship.

As Psalm 114:4 indicates, there is a sense in which all of creation shares in joyful celebrations. Today's passage informs us that the Israelites remembered all of God's miraculous provisions, and they made a point of praising Him regularly. Even for us today, there is no room for a joyless worship.

Heavenly Father, thank You that all of creation rejoices in Your great work of salvation. Keep me joyfully devoted to praying and working for Your kingdom's growth. In the precious name of Jesus I pray. Amen.

Sheep in the Hood

Know that the LORD is God. It is he who made us, and we are his; we are his people, the sheep of his pasture (Psalm 100:3).

Scripture: **Psalm 100**
Song: **"Savior, Like a Shepherd Lead Us"**

When I was a little girl, my parents drove our family to a sheep ranch during lambing season so we could watch the birthing process. Watching all those new bleating lives was a highlight of my childhood. Years later in high school, I joined the Future Farmers of America. Among other things, we studied crops, machinery, and livestock.

Several members and I traveled to a local sheep ranch during shearing season. Observing expert shearers adeptly removing wool from the sheep, I realized this: sheep are needy; they demand constant attention, and they require lots of work! Yet shepherds truly love their sheep, protect them, and know exactly what is best for them.

Throughout Scripture, God refers to himself as a shepherd and consistently compares us to sheep. What an accurate association! We wander, we follow the crowd, we are basically helpless, and we're vulnerable to various perils. The Lord, the greatest Shepherd of all, faithfully guides, protects, provides, and cares for us, His sheep, in each season of life.

Lord, help me abandon my own desires and plans. Give me a heart to follow You and to trust Your protection and provision. I yearn for Your caring, loving, wise voice, Lord. Thank You for knowing what is best for me. In the name of Jesus, Lord and Savior of all, I pray. Amen.

Missing the Mark

Repent, then, and turn to God, so that your sins may be wiped out, that times of refreshing may come from the Lord (Acts 3:19).

Scripture: Acts 3:17-26
Song: "Forgive Them, O My Father"

When I caught Blaise cheating on a unit test, she yelled at me, threw her backpack, and stomped out of class. After school, I noticed that someone had hit the windshield of my car with a rock. I immediately thought of Blaise.

The police advised me to privately confront any suspects. And if that proved futile, I should talk with each of my classes and ask for leads. If the guilty person confessed, I would not have to press charges.

Well, Blaise refused to acknowledge her guilt . . . and for good reason. You see, after a few days, one of the quietest students in our school admitted he had heaved the rock. He had aimed at one of the wild turkeys roaming on our school grounds and had missed. But he'd been too embarrassed to tell anyone. When I assured him that my husband and I were more interested in his integrity than in payment—and that we were dropping the matter—he was tremendously grateful.

When Jesus wipes out our sins, we have every reason to be grateful, eternally grateful. A clean, forgiven life revitalizes us for victory and service.

Father, thanks for desiring a relationship with me. When I repent of my sin, You restore me and bring refreshment to my spirit. In Jesus' name, amen.

Better Than a GPS

In my distress I called to the LORD; I called out to my God. From his temple he heard my voice; my cry came to his ears (2 Samuel 22:7).

Scripture: 2 Samuel 22:2-7
Song: "Lead Me Higher"

My husband is more familiar with the mountains in our area than anyone I know. When he hikes, backpacks, or hunts deer and elk, he doesn't get lost. Along with his innate sense of direction, he also knows how to focus on landmarks to mentally mark his way. Even at night, he navigates by the North Star.

This summer we bought him a GPS for his birthday, not because we felt he needed it, but because it's a trendy gadget just now. We thought he might have fun with it. He's used it several times and has found it accurate. When he's in the mountains, he locks onto a satellite signal, marks his starting point, and roams around. He's gaining the confidence of knowing that, as long as he has fresh batteries, the GPS will guide him back to his campsite.

David frequently needed God to deliver him from multiple perils and to return him to safety. Every time he called for help, God faithfully came to his rescue.

Almighty and gracious Father, many times I need to lock onto Your signal to deliver me from messes I create for myself and to liberate me from those who want to make my life miserable. I'm grateful that You hear my pleas for help and that You delight in rescuing me. All praise to You, in the name of the Father and of the Son and of the Holy Spirit. Amen.

Hand in Hand

My soul clings to you; your right hand upholds me (Psalm 63:8).

Scripture: **Psalm 63**
Song: **"God of Almighty Love"**

Two hours before our flight departed from Quito, Ecuador, the airport's announcer paged my friend Amy and me. When we reported to our gate, Amy grabbed my hand as an armed guard whisked us downstairs and out of the airport. We accompanied him and two soldiers into the rainy night, past the drug-sniffing dog, and onto the edge of the tarmac.

Our grips tightened as the officers deposited us in front of a dozen suitcases and asked us to identify ours. One soldier rested his hand on his semi-automatic while a colleague pulled each item from our luggage. While apparently routine for the officials, it was terrifying for us. Eventually, satisfied we were not transporting contraband, they released us in time to catch our flight.

Most of the challenges in my life are less dramatic than this. However, each time I feel feeble and ill-equipped to face a given situation, I reach for the Lord's hand. Like David, I am able to say that His right hand upholds me. Often the situation doesn't change, but His presence calms me just the same.

Dear God, You know how difficult life can be at times. When I'm facing suffocating circumstances, Lord, help me remember that no crisis takes You by surprise. Thank You, in Jesus' name. Amen.

DEVOTIONS®

*T*ake care to follow the commands, decrees and laws I give you today.

—Deuteronomy 7:11

NOVEMBER

Photo © digitalskillet's | iStock

Gary Allen, Editor   **Margaret Williams,** Project Editor

DEVOTIONS® is published quarterly by Standard Publishing, Cincinnati, Ohio, www.standardpub.com. © 2009 by Standard Publishing. All rights reserved. Topics based on the Home Daily Bible Readings, International Sunday School Lessons. © 2007 by the Committee on the Uniform Series. Printed in the U.S.A. All Scripture quotations, unless otherwise indicated, are taken from the HOLY BIBLE, NEW INTERNATIONAL VERSION®. NIV®. Copyright © 1973, 1978, 1984 by International Bible Society. Used by permission of Zondervan. All rights reserved. Where noted, Scripture quotations are from the following, used with permission of the copyright holders, all rights reserved: *The New King James Version.* Copyright © 1982 by Thomas Nelson, Inc. *Holy Bible, New Living Translation* (NLT), © 1996. Tyndale House Publishers.

Idle Idols

The LORD said to the children of Israel, "Did I not deliver you from the Egyptians and from the Amorites and from the people of Ammon and from the Philistines?" (Judges 10:11, *New King James Version*).

Scripture: **Judges 10:10-16**
Song: **"Thou Lovely Source of True Delight"**

Sometimes I want to question the Israelites' sanity in even considering worshiping other gods. I mean, they saw God perform mighty miracles on their behalf, time and again. How could they worship idols of stone when they knew the creator of the universe was on their side?

I wonder these things until I think of my own little idolatries. I don't make graven images, but I can easily fill my days with work, family, hobbies, even an idleness that leaves no time for worshiping the Lord. Yet He has been every bit as faithful to me as He was to the Israelites.

And when trouble comes, it's just as if God says to me, as He did to His children of ancient times, "Lori, did I not deliver you in the past, and will I not help you in the future? Turn back to me. Give me your time and energy and love."

O God, creator of Heaven and earth, all too often I put other things before You: my job, my family, my hobbies. Help me to put You at the center of my life and let nothing else push You from supremacy there. In the holy name of Jesus, my Lord and Savior, I pray. Amen.

November 1–7. **Lori Poppinga**, a minister's wife in northwest Iowa and mother of eight children, encourages others through her writing and speaking ministries.

For Crying Out Loud

So the children of Israel said to Samuel, "Do not cease to cry out to the LORD our God for us, that He may save us from the hand of the Philistines" (1 Samuel 7:8, *New King James Version*).

Scripture: **1 Samuel 7:3-13**
Song: **"Cry Out to Jesus"**

The singing congregation covered the cries of my 2-year-old for her big sister. I jiggled her, shushed her, and threatened her, hoping beyond hope she would cease her incessant screaming of "KeeeeKeeeee, KeeeeeKeeeeee" before the singing ended.

However, as the music stopped, and her screaming didn't, I hoisted her to my hip and marched out for a little attitude adjustment. Her allegiance quickly changed as she realized my intent, and her cries changed to "Mommy! Mommy!" She knew her sister could no longer help her, and she appealed to the only one who could stop the coming chastisement.

The Israelites worshiped other gods until they saw the fierce and mighty Philistines coming against them. Samuel told them exactly what to do to receive help: turn from their foreign gods and turn back to the one true God. That's just what they did. They put away their idols and asked Samuel to continue crying out to God for help. They knew their only hope rested in the Lord.

Lord God Almighty, *thank You for being the Lord God, my helper. I cry out to You for goodness, mercy, and salvation. I pray this prayer in the name of Jesus, my Savior and Lord. Amen.*

Big Problems? Bigger God!

The LORD, who delivered me from the paw of the lion and from the paw of the bear, He will deliver me from the hand of this Philistine (1 Samuel 17:37, *New King James Version*).

Scripture: **1 Samuel 17:31-37**
Song: **"My Deliverer Is Coming"**

Someone once said, "Don't tell God how big your problems are; tell your problems how big your God is." Very often my problems can look huge, giant-like.

For example, several years ago, my husband was forced to resign from a ministry. He was bi-vocational, and we needed both incomes to meet our needs. At that time, I stayed home with our seven children and homeschooled the oldest six. We had also recently found out we would be adding another member to our family in about seven months.

Now that seems like a big problem situation, right? However, within a week God had shown us another ministry opportunity, and within four months we had moved into a *seven-bedroom* parsonage in a small town close to both of our families! To top it all off, Jeff no longer had to be bi-vocational. The church wanted him fully devoted to ministry and was able to provide the financial support.

The same God who delivered David from the lion, the bear, and the Philistine can deliver us from our problems as well—even if the solution requires seven bedrooms.

Lord, my problems often seem overwhelming. Remind me of Your deliverance in the past so I can look for it in my future. In Christ I pray. Amen.

Stuck in the Mud

He also brought me up out of a horrible pit, out of the miry clay, and set my feet upon a rock and established my steps (Psalm 40:2, *New King James Version*).

Scripture: **Psalm 40:1-5**
Song: **"Lift Thy Face to the Light!"**

As a child growing up on the farm, I had many occasions to play in the mud. I loved to make mud pies, adding in a few twigs and fresh grass for texture. While mud pies were easy enough to handle, mud puddles could get a little sticky.

On more than one occasion, I would blithely stomp through mud puddles, splashing dirty water all over the place. The problem occurred when my boot refused to come out of the mud. The more I struggled, the more stuck I became. And there I stood, stuck in miry mud until my dad came along, pulled me out, and set my feet upon the rocky ground.

Today I don't stomp in literal mud puddles. But I often find myself mired down in figurative ones. I sink into the mire of worry, doubt, confusion, envy, pride, or depression—and the more I struggle, the deeper I sink into the pit of trouble. Thankfully, my heavenly Father is ready to bring me out of the pit, set my feet on the rock, and direct my steps.

Almighty and most merciful God, I easily sink into the mud of life. Bring me out of the pit, set my feet upon the rock, and guide me on Your path. In Christ's holy name I pray. Amen.

Just Fold the Socks

If I regard iniquity in my heart, the LORD will not hear (Psalm 66:18, *New King James Version*).

Scripture: **Psalm 66:13-20**
Song: **"Sin, When Viewed by Scripture Light"**

I recently assigned my daughter Tirzah to the household laundry chores. In a family of 10 people, it's a big job. I usually help her with it by doing the occasional load while she's at school, but she still has her share to do.

We often face a laundry basket full of clean, unmatched socks. Tirzah hates to fold socks and will do anything to get out of it. So even if I specifically tell her, "Just fold the socks," she will find some way to avoid the task.

The surprising thing is this: Even though she doesn't do what I ask her to do, when I ask her to do it, she still wants me to grant her a night out with her friends or a later curfew or more time on the computer. I tell her, "If you had just folded the socks, you would have had some privileges."

Similarly, if I deliberately sin, "the Lord will not hear." Oh, He knows my needs, and He's aware of my pleas. But in light of the psalmist's words, my sin apparently creates a barrier to my close fellowship with the Lord. In other words, I just need to fold the socks—do what I know God wants me to do. Then I can enjoy once again all the privileges of a child of the king.

Father, it is so easy to avoid Your still, small voice calling me to obey. But today help me avoid sin and walk in Your love. In Jesus' name, amen.

Who Rules?

Dominion belongs to the LORD and he rules over the nations (Psalm 22:28).

Scripture: **Psalm 22:19-28**
Song: **"We Bow Down"**

As I write this, another election year is upon us. I have to make a decision for whom I will vote. Or should I even vote? Will my vote make a difference?

I often wonder if the vote I cast will make a difference in the leadership of our state and our country. Will the person I vote for, if elected, hold true to the promises he or she has made during the campaign? Will the person I vote for stay strong in the midst of political turmoil? (By the time you read this, I'll have some of those answers!)

One thing for me to remember is that no human form of government is perfect; they are all flawed. Thus, since I am a citizen of Heaven, I can seek the best for my society on earth while working hard for the values of the heavenly kingdom. When I remember these things, I'm also reminded that the Lord is ruler of all nations. As the apostle Paul put it: "There is no authority except that which God has established. The authorities that exist have been established by God" (Romans 13:1).

Christ cannot be voted out, and He cannot be impeached. He can be ignored for a time, but ultimately every knee will bow and every tongue will confess that He is Lord.

Lord, give me wisdom in my voting decisions, and give our leaders wisdom to rule this country under Your authority. In the name of Jesus, amen.

See This Awesome Lord!

Come and see the works of God; He is awesome in His doing toward the sons of men (Psalm 66:5, *New King James Version*).

Scripture: **Psalm 66:1-12**
Song: **"Awesome God"**

Living on the plains, I find that checking the weather is as simple as stepping out on my porch and scanning the horizon. Sometimes I see a thunderstorm piling up in the west. Then gorgeous colors play out on the grass as clouds meet the sun and refract light into stunning shades of green, yellow, and blue.

God speaks to me in the vastness of the plains of His unending love. I understand worship through the solitary trees reaching bare branches in petition to the heavens. The racing clouds and threatening thunderheads reveal God's power and majesty. The endless miles of unblemished snow-covered fields tell of His marvelous forgiveness.

Come and see the works of God: in the smile of your child, the enduring love of your parents, the beauty of nature all around you. Or consider the vastness of the ocean, the encouragement of fellow believers, the joy in the simple things of life. All of it tells the endless wonder contained in the heavens. He is awesome!

O God, creator of Heaven and earth, it is all too easy to take for granted Your wondrous works. Open my eyes to Your awesome displays all around me. And cause me to lift my heart in thanksgiving many times throughout this day. In the mighty name of Jesus I pray. Amen.

The Patience of God

I was shown mercy so that in me, the worst of sinners, Christ Jesus might display his unlimited patience as an example for those who would believe on him and receive eternal life (1 Timothy 1:16).

Scripture: **1 Timothy 1:12-17**
Song: **"Eternal Depth of Love Divine"**

I am blessed to be the father of six young children, four boys and two girls, ranging in age from 11 years old to newborn. Each day fills me with wonder as I watch my children discover their way in this world. But some of this exciting "discovery" includes making very poor choices in relating to parents and siblings. Especially after a long day, I can grow impatient with their arguing—and the subtle stretching of our house rules.

But once the house is quiet, God has a way of reminding me how much I am like my own children. I think of how I constantly push the limits of boundaries for me, and how I too so often need mercy. I am humbled by His "unlimited patience" with me, and this humility creates a genuine desire to offer the same kind of patience to those I love the most. In other words, God gently reminds me that I am an example of His love towards everyone I spend time with, especially my children.

God, today I'm reminded of Your merciful and patient heart towards me. Help me to extend Your mercy to others today. In Jesus' name, amen.

November 8–14. **Mark Williams** is a minister, college professor, and writer living with his wife, Kelley, and their six children near Nashville, Tennessee.

The Passion of Renewal

They stood where they were and read from the Book of the Law of the Lord their God for a quarter of the day, and spent another quarter in confession and in worshiping the Lord their God (Nehemiah 9:3).

Scripture: **Nehemiah 9:1-5**
Song: **"Stand Up, Stand Up for Jesus"**

I recently attended a traditional wedding in the Smoky Mountains of eastern Tennessee. The groomsmen wore tuxedoes, and the bridesmaids all wore beautiful gowns. Everything was perfectly in place, and the attendees anxiously awaited the bride's appearance. When the wedding march finally began, we stood to our feet to get a glimpse of the bride and her father. After some initial comments from the minister, we all sat back down in comfortable padded chairs.

We stayed seated for the rest of the rather brief service. In contrast, I am inspired and challenged when I read how the Israelites stood for hours hearing the Word of God. And they spent hours in confession and worship. What a renewal of heart this would bring!

Deep in my soul, I long for such passion for Scripture and worship. I long for my daily time of Bible reading and prayer to transform me, to turn my heart with firm commitment towards God's will each moment of my day.

Almighty and gracious Father, may my life this day reflect the transforming power of undiluted time spent with You. By Your spirit, please do a new work in my heart. I pray in the name of Jesus. Amen.

No Fear with This Father

In him and through faith in him we may approach God with freedom and confidence (Ephesians 3:12).

Scripture: **Ephesians 3:7-13**
Song: **"Blessed Assurance"**

Whenever I got in trouble at school growing up, my mother would tell me, "Just wait until your father comes home." When my father eventually came home from work, I'd avoid talking to him for as long as possible. As soon as he discovered my misdeeds, I expected disapproval and punishment. So I tried to make myself scarce. In fact, I'd hope Mom could talk with him first—to walk him through his initial anger.

Thankfully, when I place my trust in Christ, He makes it possible for me to approach God the Father freely, in spite of my sin and shame. Because He has shouldered my punishment and has paid the penalty for my sin, I can rest in the power of God's love and forgiveness. Whereas my earthly mother interceded for me with my earthly father, Jesus intercedes for me with the Heavenly Father.

Does that mean I'm not sorry—or that temporal consequences won't unfold? Hardly. For contrition is an important part of my approach to the Lord as I seek His forgiveness. And I may well damage relationships with my sin. Yet I know that, like a child, I can sit in my Heavenly Father's lap without fear, thanks to the cross.

God, thank You for Your mercy and grace given through Jesus Christ. Through His sacrifice, I have abundant life in You. In His name, amen.

God's Private Office

Since the creation of the world God's invisible qualities—his eternal power and divine nature—have been clearly seen, being understood from what has been made, so that men are without excuse (Romans 1:20).

Scripture: Romans 1:18-24
Song: "This Is My Father's World"

A number of years ago, I visited the Grand Canyon while speaking at a retreat in Arizona. As we made the drive up from Prescott, I pictured in my mind what the "big hole" would look like. I'd seen pictures and heard stories, but I was excited to finally see for myself. My wife and I caught our first glimpse as we rounded a corner and approached the southern rim of the canyon.

We were speechless. After parking and walking up to the edge of the canyon, we stood in silence as we took it all in.

Later that day, as the sun set over the canyon and the painted desert stretched out in the distance, my heart filled with praise for the creator of such unspeakable beauty. I couldn't help thinking: It would be hard to deny the existence of God standing at the edge of such glory. I drove away that day feeling as if I had just met with God in His private office.

O Father, creator of all things, remind me each day of Your unfailing love through the simple beauty of Your creation. In each sunrise and sunset, river and stream, songbird and sonnet, let me find You in all of Your glory. In the name of Your Son, my Savior, I pray. Amen.

Fixated Today?

So we fix our eyes not on what is seen, but on what is unseen. For what is seen is temporary, but what is unseen is eternal (2 Corinthians 4:18).

Scripture: **2 Corinthians 4:13-18**
Song: **"Turn Your Eyes upon Jesus"**

In 2003, when I lived in Florida, three major hurricanes passed over our small town in just under six weeks. Houses were damaged, trees were downed, and the power remained out for almost two weeks.

The worst part of those weeks was the waiting and watching. As each storm approached, our community would rush to the gas pumps and grocery stores to stock up for the potential hardships ahead. Then we'd watch the weather forecast and wait . . . sometimes for days . . . for the storm to hit. As we focused on the coming storm, it was easy to lose perspective, imagine the worst, and lose heart.

Even our "normal" routine days can work a number on our hearts. If we choose to focus—"fix our eyes"—on our troubles and problems, we'll surely begin feeling some despair. So why not fix our eyes on Jesus? He promises to walk with us through the storms of our life. As we cast our cares on Him, even in the howling winds, He renews our spirit with a peace that passes understanding.

Jesus, help me today to fix my eyes on You instead of the momentary troubles of my life. When the storms seem to overwhelm me, renew my heart with Your love and grace. In the precious name of Jesus I pray. Amen.

Jogging with God

Satisfy us in the morning with your unfailing love, that we may sing for joy and be glad all our days (Psalm 90:14).

Scripture: **Psalm 90:13-17**
Song: **"Sweet Hour of Prayer"**

Several mornings a week, I wake up early and crawl out of bed, put on my running shoes, stretch my tired muscles, and head out for a jog. My main motivation is to attempt to stay in shape and to control my expanding waistline.

Being the father of six children, some mornings I wake up quite tired and consider just sleeping in. (Some days I do just that!) Yet, most of the time, another motivating factor leads me out of my garage door and onto the sidewalk.

In the cool of the morning, I know God is waiting for me to come and talk with Him. Like the rhythm of my feet on the pavement, there is a rhythm to the way He invades my thoughts and prayers. He speaks to me deep in my heart and renews my spirit—all for the purpose of helping me live for His glory each day. As I drive to work on these mornings, I have a strong sense that my heart is satisfied in God's unfailing love.

Almighty and everlasting God, may my heart be satisfied in Your unfailing love this morning. Fill me with songs of joy and praise for Your Holy name, and give me the courage to meet You on the mornings when I am the most tired. For You alone are my strength. In the name of Jesus, who lives and reigns with You and the Holy Spirit, now and forever, amen.

Learning to Trust God's Timing

For a thousand years in your sight are like a day that has just gone by, or like a watch in the night (Psalm 90:4).

Scripture: **Psalm 90:1-12**
Song: **"Time, by Moments, Steals Away"**

As a child, I loved the Christmas season. I loved decorating the tree, driving to see the lights, singing carols, and watching the Christmas specials on television. The one thing I didn't like: waiting, waiting, waiting . . . for Christmas finally to arrive.

Weeks seemed to pass like years as my brother and I waited for Christmas morning. We'd wake before the dawn and beg our parents to come to the tree so we could open our presents. The rest of the day we played with the toys we'd been dreaming of for so long.

Now that I'm grown and have wide-eyed dreamers of my own, I've learned that waiting is part of life, especially in my walk with God. I have to remind myself often that God does not work according to my schedule.

Nor does He count the days the way I do. What seems like a long period of waiting for me is merely perfect timing with God. So when I grow impatient, I am learning to trust that God is working out all things according to His plan and in His good time.

Father in Heaven, *teach me to trust that You are working out all things according to Your will and in Your perfect timing. As I wait for You to move in my life, grant my heart patience and contentment in every circumstance. In the holy name of Jesus, my Lord and Savior, I pray. Amen.*

Winds of Adversity

He heard me from his sanctuary; my cry reached his ears (Psalm 18:6, *New Living Translation*).

Scripture: **Psalm 18:1-6**
Song: **"A Cry, as of Pain"**

When hurricane Charley blasted through Florida in 2004, I felt 80-mph winds buffet my house. And I prayed like crazy. The wild wind, strong enough to uproot small trees in my yard, bombarded our city for hours and left us without power for three days. Thankfully, our neighborhood remained intact, and no friends were injured.

The next day, my family decided to drive inland to check neighboring towns. Heading east, we began to notice downed trees and leaning telephone poles. We were soon startled at the sight of telephone poles snapped in half, their ragged edges a visual reminder of Charley's wrath. As we drove on, my son soon pointed out that telephone poles were . . . simply gone. They had vanished from the edge of the road, flung to obscure places. It would be months before phone lines could be restored.

Whether we experience blizzards, tornadoes, or floods, we can be grateful that communication with the Lord does not require intact telephone lines.

Thank You, **Lord,** *for hearing me when I cry out to You for help. I trust You when storms come, knowing that Your ears are turned to me. You are my strength and my protection in every situation. In Jesus' name, amen.*

November 15–21. **Julie Gillies** is passionate about encouraging Christians through her writing. A grandmother of three, she lives in Bradenton, Florida.

Heavenly Perspective

The LORD looks down from heaven on the sons of men to see if there are any who understand, any who seek God (Psalm 14:2).

Scripture: **Psalm 14**
Song: **"I'll Fly Away"**

One of my favorite coffee-table books is *America from the Air*. It overflows with stunning photographs of small towns, big cities, and everything in between, all taken from the sky. I find the pictures irresistible because I get to see things from a completely different point of view. Things aren't always what they seem on the ground.

I like to pray along those lines as well. When I ask the Lord to change my perspective about a problem, He doesn't always give me a bird's-eye view. But I am usually able to remember that I'm seeing things from "down here." That means I see with limited vision, while God sees the big picture. I can relax and trust Him.

In the midst of our busy lives, it can be tough to discern how God is leading us. Difficulties can obscure our vision of His goodness and grace. Yet God longs for us to seek Him amidst all circumstances. He longs to give us a divine perspective from the vantage point of His heavenly kingdom.

Dear Lord, I'm so grateful that You can grant me Your heavenly perspective today. Please give me the wisdom and courage to fulfill Your purposes today in all I do and say. Help me to see through the eyes of Your heart. In Jesus' wonderful name I pray. Amen.

Peace in the Battle

O LORD, you are my God; I will exalt you and praise your name, for in perfect faithfulness you have done marvelous things, things planned long ago (Isaiah 25:1).

Scripture: **Isaiah 25:1-5**
Song: **"To God Be the Glory"**

In March 2003, America stood on the brink of war. And I stood in my family room, tears welling. My eldest son was hunkered down in a desert, 50 miles south of Baghdad, ready to surge into the city with the 3rd Infantry Division—a frightening scenario for any parent.

Fear gripped me. Eating and sleeping became challenges. How could I sit down to a home-cooked meal when my boy was eating a cold M.R.E. in a sandstorm? How could I rest my head on a soft pillow in my safe, air-conditioned bedroom, when my son faced constant danger?

Finally, during a time of worship, I felt joy again, and God removed my fears. Gratitude flooded my heart as I realized that the Lord held my son in the palm of His protective hand.

When we face staggering fear, we can run to the one who hears the cry of our hearts. God is indeed a refuge for the needy, and He is able to do marvelous things.

Almighty Father, the king of glory, You are my ever-present help in time of trouble, and my strength and protection in the midst of every battle. Thank You for removing fear from my heart and flooding me with Your peace in every situation. In the name of Jesus, who lives and reigns with You and the Holy Spirit, one God, now and forever, amen.

How Does Your Garden Grow?

All hard work brings a profit, but mere talk leads only to poverty (Proverbs 14:23).

Scripture: **Proverbs 14:22-27**
Song: **"Better Than Life"**

My daughter-in-law planted a vegetable garden for the first time this spring—no small task given her tiny back-yard at a military base. Many days of preparation left her exhausted. A wooden border structure had to be built to separate and contain the plot. Next, rich soil replaced red clay, and then she sprinkled fertilizer into the mix. Finally, the happy day arrived: she planted the very first seeds.

Soon she was able to e-mail pictures showcasing tiny carrot sprigs and broccoli buds. Months later, when I visited my grandkids, I stepped outside to a lush, full garden brimming with vegetables. Many weeks of weed-pulling, watering, and careful tending had at last begun to pay off. (And we enjoyed fresh tomatoes, carrots, and green beans with our dinner that very night.)

Sometimes the task ahead of us seems too arduous, the wait for results too long. Yet if we are faithful and diligent in our part and trust God to do His part, our efforts will be rewarded. And we can enjoy the fruits (and vegetables) of a job well done.

Lord God of Heaven and earth, help me to be a diligent worker who walks in Your strength. Plant Your dreams and purposes deep into the soil of my heart, and allow them to blossom forth, beginning this very day. I pray through my precious Savior, Jesus. Amen.

How Will God Work?

There I will teach them—this time I will teach them my power and might. Then they will know that my name is the LORD (Jeremiah 16:21).

Scripture: **Jeremiah 16:14-21**
Song: **"All the Power You Need"**

Initially diagnosed with gestational diabetes in 1987, my friend endured painful insulin shots during all three of her pregnancies. Sadly, after her third child was born, her blood sugar levels never returned to normal. The disease progressed, and daily insulin injections remained necessary.

Several years later, my friend felt certain she'd been healed by God of her diabetes. The next morning, when the time came for her usual insulin injection, she vacillated. Fear welled up in her. Without the medication she had lived on for three years, she could become very ill or even die.

"Should I take the medicine or take a giant step of faith?" In other words, would she be legitimately trusting God . . . or would this be a dangerous act of presuming upon God? She asked her husband as she held the familiar vial in her hand.

Father, I know You care about my physical health, and I know You promise to be with me in every difficulty. What I don't know is: when You will choose to heal by your power, and when You will heal through doctors and medicines, and when You will say "no" to healing. In each case, I trust You to do the best thing for my spiritual growth. In Jesus' name, amen.

Our Protector

Deliver me from my enemies, O God; protect me from those who rise up against me (Psalm 59:1).

Scripture: **Psalm 59:1-10**
Song: **"A Shield About Me"**

One moment I slumbered comfortably in my cozy bed. The next moment, a deafening noise catapulted me onto the carpet. I frantically fumbled my way to a nearby key-pad and punched in the magic numbers that would end the assault on my ears. Our sweet daughter had inadvertently set off the alarm system when she opened the back door to let the dog outside. Again! So much for sleeping in on a Saturday morning.

Originally installed for peace-of-mind while my husband traveled, the alarm system had been a blessing (in spite of its nerve-wracking potential). Climbing crime rates and a nearby home robbery convinced us of its necessity. Yet there is one whose protection is free—and peacefully quiet.

Some cities have high crime rates, some are blissfully peaceful. Watching the evening news or driving through crime-ridden areas can make us acutely aware of our need for God's protection. Whether we live in a tough neighborhood or a gated community, we can rest assured that nothing happens on this earth unless God allows it.

Father, I pray for Your Son to come soon, that the pain and suffering on this earth may be shortened. But until then, protect us, guide us, make us shining witnesses to Your love and care. In Jesus' name, amen.

Where Do We Dwell?

He who dwells in the shelter of the Most High will rest in the shadow of the Almighty (Psalm 91:1).

Scripture: **Psalm 91:1-6, 9-16**
Song: **"Dwelling Places"**

One of my daughter's schoolbooks this year is *Children Just Like Me.* It's a fascinating picture book focusing on different cultures around the world, and one of our favorite parts is the picture of each featured child's home. Some live in tiny thatched huts. Some live in high-rise apartment buildings, and some in humble adobe dwellings.

Interestingly, the childrens' clothing is always appropriate to their dwelling places. Those who live in the jungle wear only a pair of shorts. The high-rise children wear modern, fashionable clothes, and the kids in modest homes tend to wear mismatched hand-me-downs.

Similarly, we clothe ourselves according to where our minds dwell. If we dwell in anxiety, we clothe ourselves with worry. If we dwell in a negative mind-set, we clothe ourselves with pessimism. If we dwell on the bad things happening to us, we clothe ourselves in resentment.

Of course, we can't always control where we live geographically. But with God's help, we can control where our minds dwell. By the power of the Holy Spirit, we can clothe ourselves with love, joy, and peace.

Dear Lord, *help me to resist allowing my mind to dwell on things that grieve You. Help me to dwell in Your Word and in Your presence, and clothe myself in a wardrobe that pleases You. In Christ's holy name, amen.*

The Focus Factor

And when you pray, do not keep on babbling like pagans, for they think they will be heard because of their many words (Matthew 6:7).

Scripture: **Matthew 6:1-8**
Song: **"Teach Me to Pray"**

Saying the same prayer over and over without it getting monotonous might seem next to impossible. There's a tendency to switch to autopilot, and our minds start to wander. (*Did I set the DVR to record before we left? . . . I hope there's enough chicken for dinner . . . I need to stop by the pharmacy after church . . . etc.*)

It's especially a challenge when we say the model prayer in unison week after week, year after year, at our church. I've found it helpful to concentrate on each of the phrases, and then see what stands out to me afterward. I then try to briefly consider that word or phrase, like silently thanking God for providing my daily bread this week, bringing to mind anyone I need to forgive, or asking for continued protection from temptation.

In prayer we have the opportunity not only to address the living God but to sense what the Holy Spirit might be prompting within us. These brief periods of reflection can help sharpen our focus and responsiveness to the Lord.

Lord, *create in me ears that are willing to hear Your wisdom and truth—and a heart that is willing to respond in obedience. In Jesus' name, amen.*

November 22–28. **Greg Johnson** lives in Simi Valley, California, where he's a technical writer and his wife, Jan, is a writer and speaker. They have two children.

Putting Out the Fire

A gentle answer turns away wrath, but a harsh word stirs up anger (Proverbs 15:1).

Scripture: **Proverbs 15:1-7**
Song: **"Pass It On"**

I grew up hearing Smokey Bear say, "Only you can prevent forest fires." And when I read today's verse I thought it was primarily concerned with my putting out the fire of another person's anger. It gradually dawned on me that a gentle answer is a two-way street—it also throws water on the fire of *my* anger.

I learned this lesson firsthand after two of my coworkers quit because of verbal harassment from our manager. After their departure, the guns were turned on me, and I started looking for a new job. But the job never came, so over the next three years I repeatedly said in a calm voice, "I'm not going to let you talk to me that way" and then left the room. Surprisingly, over time the verbal attacks lessened and then finally stopped.

A gentle answer can make a difference with our mate, with our children, in the church, or out in our community. It might not always turn out the way we want or expect, but we can trust in God for the final outcome.

Lord God of All, *Your thoughts are higher than our thoughts and Your ways higher than our ways. Please give me the courage, wisdom, and grace to refuse to answer fire with fire or anger with anger. Instead, help me be a messenger of peace in all situations through what I say and do. I pray this prayer in the name of Jesus, my Savior and Lord. Amen.*

God Is Good

He knows the way that I take; when he has tested me, I will come forth as gold (Job 23:10).

Scripture: **Job 23:8-13**
Song: **"Create in Me a Clean Heart"**

The conference speaker shouted out several times, "God is good," and the crowd responded, "All the time!" In today's verse, Job proclaims that God is good and would do good by him: "I will come forth as gold."

When I was 29, a lump appeared on my neck. Because of its rapid growth, I was checked into a hospital and subjected to a barrage of tests. The lump was doubling in size every few days, and I honestly didn't know if I would live or die.

On that hospital bed I was angry and depressed but finally decided that, whether I lived or died, God could be trusted and would do good by me. Two weeks later, doctors removed a large nonmalignant tumor from my neck. I eventually experienced a complete recovery.

God is our good shepherd, even if our health or finances are failing, or whether we have lost a job or even a house. I hope that we can come to say with Job: God is trustworthy and good, and we will come forth as gold.

Almighty and gracious Father, You know the end from the beginning and everything that concerns my life. You are the good shepherd who can be trusted, no matter what the outward circumstances look like. Help me to believe that all things will work together for good in the lives of those who love You. In the name of Jesus, amen.

Light Out of Darkness

Even the darkness will not be dark to you; the night will shine like the day, for darkness is as light to you (Psalm 139:12).

Scripture: **Psalm 139:7-12**
Song: **"The Light of the World Is Jesus"**

Solitary confinement can seem daunting to even the boldest prisoner. One time I stepped into a solitary confinement cell on Alcatraz, and the door was slammed shut. There was no light, no sound, nothing. After a few minutes the tour guide opened the door—much to my relief!

The darkness in a prison cell, however, is nothing compared to the darkness that can invade a person's soul. Jonathan grew up as a preacher's kid, but he said the turning point came when he lit up his first cigarette in sixth grade. The cigarettes led to alcohol, and then marijuana, and eventually to crack cocaine. This in turn led to the loss of two marriages, countless jobs, and virtually all hope in his life.

Jonathan said that during his darkest days he still felt God was reaching out to him. And when he got sick and tired of being sick and tired, he entered a recovery center and today is attending a Christian college. If you know someone who's walking in darkness, keep praying that the light of God will break through to shine like the day.

Lord, I know the Scriptures say that You are light, and in You there is no darkness. May I be constantly drawn to Your light and turn away from the spiritual darkness that surrounds me every day. Through Christ, amen.

A Heavenly Mystery

He determines the number of the stars and calls them each by name (Psalm 147:4).

Scripture: **Psalm 147:1-6**
Song: **"Creation's Lord, We Give Thee Thanks"**

I like a good mystery as much as the next person, especially the ones that keep me guessing to the very end. There had been a bit of a mystery surrounding Jeremiah 33:22—which says the stars in the sky are as immeasurable as the sand on the seashore. You see, until the last century, most people thought they could figure out how many stars there were by stepping outside, looking up, and counting. But if that were the case, how could Jeremiah 33:22 be true?

It's only been since the emergence of deep space exploration that the mystery surrounding this verse has been explained. With the discovery of galaxy after galaxy unfolding into seeming infinity, it is now accepted that the number of stars—and even the number of galaxies—could never begin to be counted.

There is one, however, who knows the exact number of stars and has even given each one a name. This same mighty God, creator of the universe and creator of you and me, knows my name and is concerned about my world and daily needs. What a marvelous Lord!

Lord, *You are the almighty creator of an infinite universe and the Lord of all creation. Help me to find my place in this world that You created as You open doors of ministry and opportunity to me. In Christ I pray. Amen.*

Here's an Example

If only you would slay the wicked, O God! Away from me, you bloodthirsty men! (Psalm 139:19).

Scripture: **Psalm 139:17-21**
Song: **"Though Troubles Assail Us"**

The 1960s television series *The Fugitive* featured weekly glimpses into how an innocent man creatively avoided arrest while attempting to prove his innocence. King David had to be the original fugitive. Even though he'd been anointed as God's chosen leader, he spent years on the run fleeing for his life.

King Saul was apparently tormented by David's popularity and tried, on at least two occasions, to skewer him with a spear. And when David fled for his life, Saul released the hounds and relentlessly tracked him down. Amazingly, David had at least two chances to take the life of his persecutor. But on both occasions he soundly rejected the opportunity to put King Saul to the sword.

While we can't change the bad things that happen to us, we can be honest with God about our disappointment or anger. And we can also ask God for the grace and courage to face a difficult situation or person in a way that will bring Him glory. That was the way of David, and he serves us still as an excellent example.

Father, help me to remember that I can bring all of my anger, hurts, and disappointments to You, and You will always understand. Please give me the confident knowledge that You are my strong tower. Therefore, I never need to be afraid of anything others can do to me. In Jesus' name, amen.

Wonderfully Made

I praise you because I am fearfully and wonderfully made; your works are wonderful, I know that full well (Psalm 139:14).

Scripture: **Psalm 139: 1-6, 13-16, 23, 24**
Song: **"He Knows My Name"**

The saying "Familiarity breeds contempt" could be restated as "Familiarity breeds disinterest" when it comes to our bodies. We typically have no concept of the capability of this incredible "machine" that we were assigned at birth.

Science gives us some clues as to the magnitude of what our bodies are capable of: Our heart beats about 100,000 times every 24 hours, our six courts of blood make up to 5,000 trips throughout the body every day, our digestive system converts the food we eat into blood, bone, and cell tissue. In addition, over 4 million pores regulate our temperature, and tiny fibers in our ears help us maintain perfect balance.

Our bodies are made up of over 75 trillion cells that work together in total harmony. But the amazing thing is that our most brilliant scientists can't explain how a cell actually works. Let's look in the mirror today and thank God that we are, indeed, wonderfully made.

Lord, I thank You that I am fearfully and wonderfully made. And I confess that I only pay attention to my body when it hurts or is sick. Please help me be thankful for this wonderful gift, and let me use it to bring You honor and glory. Through the name of Jesus I pray. Amen.

What a Prayer Partner!

Go near and listen to all that the LORD our God says. Then tell us whatever the LORD our God tells you. We will listen and obey (Deuteronomy 5:27).

Scripture: **Deuteronomy 5:22-27**
Song: **"In the Hour of Trial"**

Have you ever known someone who seemed to walk very close to the Lord—perhaps as close as you would like to walk someday? That is a person you can certainly ask to pray for you. And you will no doubt want to listen closely to him or her for words of guidance too.

Moses was a person like that for the people of Israel. When he went up to the mountain, he entered an awesome space, ablaze with the fire of God's holiness. But God had called Moses to be there, to receive the commandments, and to help lead the people to know Him.

The people seemed to realize something important, already, though: They'd been blessed to survive hearing the voice of God . . . once. They weren't ready to risk it again. So, they asked Moses to intercede for them.

Yes, we can ask mature people of God for their prayers and their wisdom when we seek guidance. God is gracious in putting such folks onto our pathways in life.

Lord, thank You for those human intercessors who can go "up to the mountain" to meet the Lord on my behalf. May I also be willing to lift up prayers for others this day. In Jesus' name, amen.

November 29, 30. **Gary Wilde,** a former book editor, is now a minister living with his wife, Carol, in Moultrie, Georgia. They have twin adult sons, Tim and Dan.

Beautiful Worship

Give unto the LORD the glory due unto his name: bring an offering, and come before him: worship the LORD in the beauty of holiness (1 Chronicles 16:29, *King James Version*).

Scripture: 1 Chronicles 16:28-34
Song: "O for a Thousand Tongues to Sing"

In our church we have a special committee to help make sure the worship space is as beautiful as it can be. This involves many of the ladies in such things as arranging flowers, polishing brass, and laying out those special items we use in worship and in the Lord's Supper. They work hard so that everything will be "just right."

One of these ladies once said to me, half jokingly, "This is a great ministry for me; I've always been a little bit obsessive-compulsive anyway." Well, I knew she wasn't mentally ill in the least. But she did indeed enjoy making things beautiful—"just right"—for the Lord's day of worship.

It's an important distinction, isn't it? If we actually obsess about our attempts at beautiful perfection, we will keep all the focus on the job we're doing. But if we focus on the beauty and holiness of the Lord—and then let that beauty fill our hearts with love for Him—we'll likely want to make His worship lovely too.

Father, I know that, in worship, my heart attitude is the key. Help me to worship You well because I am overwhelmed by how well You love me. Let King David be my example—with his beautiful psalm of thanksgiving to You. I pray in the lovely name of Jesus, my Lord. Amen.

My Prayer Notes

_____

_____

_____

_____

_____

_____

_____

_____

_____

_____

_____

_____

_____

_____

_____

_____

_____

_____

_____

DEVOTIONS®

*L*et the heavens rejoice, . . . let them say . . . "The LORD reigns!"

—1 Chronicles 16:31

DECEMBER

Photo © Liquid Library

Gary Allen, Editor   **Margaret K. Williams,** Project Editor

DEVOTIONS® is published quarterly by Standard Publishing, Cincinnati, Ohio, www.standardpub.com.
© 2009 by Standard Publishing. All rights reserved. Topics based on the Home Daily Bible Readings,
International Sunday School Lessons. © 2007 by the Committee on the Uniform Series. Printed in the
U.S.A. All Scripture quotations, unless otherwise indicated, are taken from the HOLY BIBLE, NEW
INTERNATIONAL VERSION®. NIV®. Copyright © 1973, 1978, 1984 by International Bible Society.
Used by permission of Zondervan. All rights reserved. Where noted, Scripture quotations are from the
following, used with permission of the copyright holders, all rights reserved: *King James Version
(KJV)*, public domain.

Derailed by His Glory

The priests could not perform their service because of the cloud, for the glory of the LORD filled the temple of God (2 Chronicles 5:14).

Scripture: **2 Chronicles 5:11-14**
Song: **"I See the Lord"**

I'm a scheduling freak. In addition to being obsessed with checking my e-mail calendar at work, I keep a personal electronic calendar of my household chores and appointments. I perform a specific chore on the same day of the week, each week. And I grow a bit upset when I swerve off track. Nothing must stand in the way of my household schedule!

Well, almost nothing. If I have a long meeting at work or a tight writing deadline, I rearrange my personal schedule. Work is important, right? I don't want to keep clients waiting.

If only I had the same commitment to my devotional time each morning. Today's Bible passage describes priests who couldn't perform their service because of the glory of the Lord. Can you imagine not being able to perform your tasks because of the overwhelming "distraction" of God's presence?

I want to let the call to enjoy God's presence derail my personal schedules. How about you? May we all seek His presence and let it fill the temple of our hearts.

Dear Father, *help me to praise You, to know and enjoy Your presence. May I keep my time with You a priority. In Jesus' name, amen.*

December 1–5. **Lisa Earl** is a technical and freelance writer based in western Pennsylvania. She also teaches an online writing course. Lisa enjoys figure skating and spending time with her husband, Josh.

Met by Mercy

Do not hold against us the sins of the fathers; may your mercy come quickly to meet us, for we are in desperate need (Psalm 79:8).

Scripture: **Psalm 79:5-10**
Song: **"Mercy Is Boundless and Free"**

Several years ago I was going through a tough time. I was working long hours and felt that I'd neglected my personal relationships with friends and family. I'd lost touch with a lot of old friends and extended family members, and I felt guilty about that. I tried to make up for it by volunteering long hours at church and in the community.

Between working long hours and taking care of my home and husband, I finally realized that I couldn't do it all. I was overwhelmed—reached a breaking point—and ended up quitting all of my volunteer work. I even switched churches!

It was then that I realized the depth of God's grace. I began to realize that God doesn't hold our past mistakes against us. We don't have to look far and wide, striving to find mercy and forgiveness. Rather, Mercy himself meets us in the Lord Jesus Christ.

Yes, Jesus is mercy personified. The Bible says that while we were still sinners, Christ died for us (see Romans 5:8). Thankfully, we can allow mercy to meet us in the person of Jesus Christ.

Lord God of Heaven and earth, *thank You for meeting me in times of darkness. Thank You for coming to me when I'm too weak to seek You. Thank You for being mercy incarnate in Your Son, Jesus. Help me to rest in Your goodness always. I pray this prayer in the name of Jesus. Amen.*

December 3

Only a Portion

Who has measured the waters in the hollow of his hand, or with the breadth of his hand marked off the heavens? Who has held the dust of the earth in a basket, or weighed the mountains on the scales and the hills in a balance? (Isaiah 40:12).

Scripture: **Isaiah 40:12-17**
Song: **"Immanuel, We Sing Thy Praise"**

Living in landlocked western Pennsylvania sometimes makes me long to be near water. Most of my vacations have been to the coast.

A few years ago my husband and I visited the rocky beaches of Prince Edward Island, Canada. Because we'd be there on a Sunday, we decided to have our own worship service on the rocks near the beach. The expanse of water overwhelmed us and reminded us of God's power and glory.

Yet today's Scripture says that God's glory is greater than we can fathom. Human intelligence and imagination just can't comprehend His power. We were amazed at one small part of God's creation—yet the depth of what He has done is so much greater than what we can see and touch.

The Bible refers to the finger of God sending plagues on Egypt and even driving out demons (see Exodus 8:19 and Luke 11:20). Yet things that seem huge to us are a fraction of what God can do. So . . . what obstacle do you face today? What impossible challenge? Can God meet your need?

Dear Father, *Your creation reminds me of how great You are. Yet keep me mindful that what I see of Your work is only a small part of what You can do. Thank You, in the name of Jesus. Amen.*

Tangible Treasure

To whom, then, will you compare God? What image will you compare him to? As for an idol, a craftsman casts it, and a goldsmith overlays it with gold and fashions silver chains for it (Isaiah 40:18, 19).

Scripture: **Isaiah 40:18-24**
Song: **"More Precious Than Silver"**

In tough economic times, precious metals increase in value. Signs in front of jewelry stores with the words "we buy gold" emblazoned on them tempt travelers to cash in their valuables. Why the gold craze? People see value in holding something real and weighty, something solid to back up their intangible faith in the economy.

Jesus is like that. Jesus is God in the flesh. He's solid. Tangible. Real. While God is invisible, He sent us living proof that He exists, that He understands our weaknesses and temptations. Jesus is so real that He was even tempted in every way as we are, yet without sin (see Hebrews 4:15).

God also sent the Holy Spirit to live in all who believe in His Son. The reality of His presence is with us, day by day.

In tough times, we have someone real to believe in; someone who understands what we're going through; someone even more precious than gold. Poet Emily Dickinson once said, "They say that God is everywhere, and yet we always think of Him as somewhat of a recluse." But we know better: God has visited us in His Son, Jesus.

Dear Lord, when I doubt, let me trust in the reality of You. Forgive me for placing my trust in so many things that will not last. In Jesus' name, I pray.

Slow and Steady

He gives strength to the weary and increases the power of the weak. Even youths grow tired and weary, and young men stumble and fall; but those who hope in the LORD will renew their strength (Isaiah 40:29-31).

Scripture: **Isaiah 40:1-8, 25, 26, 29-31**
Song: **"Spirit, Strength of All the Weak"**

For the past few years, I've been ice skating several days a week. And I've been going to the same rink long enough to observe some patterns. But these are not just the patterns formed from blades carving the ice. I've started to notice life patterns, as well, as I observe the other people there with me.

Often kids come blasting out of the gate without warming up. They shoot back and forth across the rink four or five times, and then they go sit down.

Several adults skate regularly, and many of us take lessons. Some of the best skaters are in their 60s. They're well trained. They warm up and have built endurance. They can stay on the ice for up to an hour at a time.

Isn't that like faith? It takes practice, time, and trust. If we try to rush God, to get Him to do our will, we may stumble, fall, or just get worn out. We need to trust God daily to take us steadily across the rink of life. That way, we can "[skate] and not grow weary . . . walk and not be faint."

Dear God, help me to trust You in tough times. May I follow the principles of Your Word that I may build spiritual endurance. And please do forgive me for rushing You, for trying to do things my own way before seeking Your wisdom. All of this I pray in the precious name of Jesus. Amen.

I Want to Look Like Him

We know that we live in him and he in us, because he has given us of his Spirit. And we have seen and testify that the Father has sent his Son to be the Savior of the world (1 John 4:13, 14).

Scripture: **1 John 4:13-19**
Song: **"I Am Yours"**

I found my 4-year-old daughter with her face intently pressed up against a mirror. After a few minutes I surprised her by asking what she was doing. "I'm counting my freckles, Mommy. That's how I know I belong to you. You have freckles just like me." That was her tangible proof that she was, indeed, my daughter.

And how proud I always was when people would comment on how much she looked like me. A few years later she asked Jesus into her heart. There were no physical markings to indicate that she belonged to Him, but she knew it was true. Even at a young age, she felt she had instant access to Jesus.

That little girl with freckles is now a teenager who doesn't look so much like me anymore. But that's fine with me. I pray every day that, as she faces difficult decisions, she'll be led by the Holy Spirit dwelling in her. That way, she'll always look like Christ to everyone she meets.

*Thank You, **Dear Father,** for sending me your Spirit. I am comforted by the confidence that You dwell within me and that I belong to You. In the name of the Father, the Son, and the Holy Spirit, I pray. Amen.*

December 6–12. **Carla Edmisten** is a freelance writer who lives in Fredericksburg, Virginia, with her husband, Jeff, and children, Shelby and Logan.

It's Not What You Say

If you return to the LORD, then your brothers and your children will be shown compassion by their captors and will come back to this land, for the LORD your God is gracious and compassionate. He will not turn his face from you if you return to him (2 Chronicles 30:9).

Scripture: **2 Chronicles 30:6-9**
Song: **"Prayer Is the Soul's Sincere Desire"**

As I was growing up, I promised myself I would never repeat to my children many of the things my parents had constantly said to me. But, of course, I say those same things to them all the time. One stellar sentence that never goes out of style is: "It's not what you say, it's how you say it."

Like most brothers and sisters, my son and daughter argue over the silliest of things. Once they reach the point of needing a referee, they're forced to apologize to each other.

Yet the level of heartfelt sincerity in those apologies is often quite minimal. The tone tells it all. There is no remorse, no repentance. I could make them say it again and again until it sounded authentic, but if there is no repentance in their hearts, it won't matter.

I've been in those shoes with God, just as the Israelites were, so often, in Bible times. I can say the right words but remain unwilling to turn in the right direction. So, it's both good news and bad: He always knows when I mean it.

Heavenly Father, when I lift my heart to You, may You see a sincere desire to grow closer to You and to follow obediently in the steps of Your Son, Jesus. In His name I pray. Amen.

Exactly Who Is the Spoiled Child?

They refused to listen and failed to remember the miracles you performed among them. They became stiff-necked and in their rebellion appointed a leader in order to return to their slavery (Nehemiah 9:17).

Scripture: **Nehemiah 9:16-21**
Song: **"Rebels Who Had Dared to Show"**

If parenting is a "thankless job," then I believe parenting a teenager brings it to a whole new level. Most parents of teens know how demanding they can be at times.

I've noticed, for instance, that a teen's memory often seems to be lacking. I can take my daughter to the mall and spend a couple of hundred dollars on her. But within a week she'll be complaining that she has nothing to wear. Or we'll agree to let her spend the weekend with a friend—or give her money to go to an amusement park—and before we know it, she's complaining that she never gets to do anything.

I know God often thinks I'm just as ungrateful. He'll answer prayers, and protect my family from dangers we aren't even aware of. But inevitably, before I know it, I find myself questioning why He has allowed something difficult into my life. When will He deliver me from this uncomfortable situation? At that point, haven't I become a bit "stiff-necked" too in my rather adolescent rebellion?

O Lord, thank You for putting up with my spoiled, selfish behaviors. I thank You for Your forbearing mercy. I know I can come to You for forgiveness, finding new hope and healing in Your arms. Through Christ I pray. Amen.

Home Sweet Home

Be my rock of refuge, to which I can always go; give the command to save me, for you are my rock and my fortress (Psalm 71:3).

Scripture: **Psalm 71:1-6**
Song: **"I'll Lead You Home"**

I could hardly stand to see the auctioneer's truck backed up to the door. They were removing the last of the contents of my father's house after his death.

It wasn't just my father's house, though. It had been my home too, even though I hadn't lived there for almost 20 years. No matter how long I'd been away, coming through the front door always meant coming home.

Even after my mother had passed away, the memories of her there were so strong that it brought great comfort to me. Things never looked quite so bad from inside those walls looking out, and I always felt safe there. Even now, after the house has been sold, I drive by and feel I could walk in and everything would be the same. I feel that I'd still find the old safety and love, that it is still my house, my refuge.

I am sure that God designed families and homes with that sense of refuge in mind. But mere earthly dwellings cannot protect from all dangers. Thankfully, God is our ultimate refuge, our rock and fortress. And—greatest blessing of all—His door is always open.

*Thank You, **Lord,** for being my constant refuge. Despite how challenging my earthly circumstances may be, You are my unchanging helper and comforter. I thank You that nothing comes to me without first going through Your office and being stamped "Approved." In Jesus' name, amen.*

No Surprise to Him

Who has done this and carried it through, calling forth the generations from the beginning? I, the LORD—with the first of them and with the last—I am he (Isaiah 41:4).

Scripture: **Isaiah 41:1-7**
Song: **"God Is in Control"**

The real estate market was great. It seemed the perfect time for my husband to make the career switch he so badly needed to make. And wow, what a good life we had! I continued being a stay-at-home mom, my children were in Christian school, and we were enjoying a comfortable lifestyle.

Fast-forward four years and I'm back at work, my husband is mowing lawns just to earn grocery money, and we're avoiding phone calls from bill collectors. We eventually stopped asking ourselves "How much worse could it get?" because every time we did, another expense popped up.

It was a humbling learning experience to realize how much confidence we had placed in our checkbook. Our pride was stripped away as God brought help into our lives that we never dreamed we would have to accept.

This time of trial came unexpectedly, but it was no surprise to God. From generation to generation, He knows what is in store for us—and how He is going to use tough times to glorify His name.

Lord, I am comforted that You know the beginning and ending of my trials. When my circumstances take me by surprise, You are in control. When I begin to despair, You remind me of Your all-surpassing power. Keep me in the palm of Your hand this day. In Jesus' name I pray. Amen.

The Battle Is His

I am the LORD, your God, who takes hold of your right hand, and says to you, Do not fear; I will help you (Isaiah 41:13).

Scripture: **Isaiah 41:11-16**
Song: **"God Will Lift Up Your Head"**

My new job seemed too good to be true. I had flexibility with my schedule, the pay was good, the work was interesting—and sometimes even fun. Best of all, the staff made me feel so welcome. However . . . let's just say that it wasn't too long before the "honeymoon" was over.

The deception, the backstabbing, the feelings of inadequacy were all making me into someone I didn't like very much. I wanted to fight. I wanted to scream, "You are lying!" in the middle of the office. But I couldn't; I was trapped.

Jobs were hard to come by, and we needed my income. So I spent a lot of time praying: "God, when will You deliver me from this?"

He hasn't delivered me yet. I'm still at that job. I've seen three employees leave in a year, but I got a promotion. Apparently God wanted me to stick around so I'd learn that He would do the fighting for me.

Is there something in your life right now that seems too difficult to face any longer? Will you let the Lord your God take your hand today? He will indeed help you.

Lord, I'm glad that You are my protector and that You will carry me through all of life's situations. I don't expect You to change my circumstances; instead, fulfill Your promise to transform me—to make me more like Jesus through every situation that comes my way. In His name I pray. Amen.

Even Me

I took you from the ends of the earth, from its farthest corners I called you. I said, "You are my servant"; I have chosen you and have not rejected you (Isaiah 41:9).

Scripture: **Isaiah 41:8-10, 17-20; 42:1-4, 9**
Song: **"Brave"**

"That's not for me to do. Someone better than me should do that." Ever had that feeling?

I used to find myself thinking that I couldn't do certain things at church because of my past. I believed the lie that I wasn't good enough to serve because of my past sins. Everyone else in church was, I was sure, much better than me.

I kept ignoring the pull I felt to start a ministry for women who had made the same kinds of mistakes that I had. I kept telling God I couldn't do it, I'd be thrown out of the church, I'd lose all my friends.

When I could finally resist no longer, the support I received from the church was amazing. Other women who had experienced the same kinds of shame flocked to me. "We're so grateful," they said. "Now we know that we're not the only ones."

God turned what was ugly and sinful in my past into something that brought honor to His name. He used me to share truth with others, allowing them to be free from shame. He used me in spite of my past and . . . even *because* of my past.

Father God, thank You for equipping me to serve You, even when I was sure I could never be worthy. May I always be open to Your promptings to service. In Jesus I pray. Amen.

Cheerful in Giving

Macedonia and Achaia were pleased to make a contribution for the poor among the saints in Jerusalem. They were pleased to do it (Romans 15:26, 27a).

Scripture: **Romans 15:25-33**
Song: **"We Give Thee but Thine Own"**

Growing up in postwar Europe, my refugee family depended on others for the basic necessities of life. With the help of the American Red Cross—and with relatives sending food and clothing—we were able to survive. After we immigrated to Canada, God supplied more than all my needs. It was then the Lord showed me I was to be a steward of God's provisions, and it was now my turn to give. Being blessed abundantly by God, I not only needed to share more with others, but I was also to do so willingly and with joy.

There was a time when the Jewish Christians at Jerusalem had given to those in need. It was also through Paul and his fellow Jewish believers that the Gentiles in Macedonia and Achaia received the gospel. These Gentile Christians felt deeply indebted to the Jewish church at Jerusalem, so they shared what they had, willingly and with joy. The saints in Jerusalem had shown mercy. Now, in their own time of need, they obtained mercy from their Gentile brothers and sisters.

Father in Heaven, may I do my part in joyfully sharing my blessings with othrs. Everything I have comes from Your hand. In the name of Jesus, amen.

December 13–19. **Ingrid Shelton** is a retired teacher/librarian and a freelance writer. She lives in White Rock, British Columbia, and enjoys gardening, reading, and playing handbells at church.

Winning the War

Put on the full armor of God, so that when the day of evil comes, you may be able to stand your ground, and after you have done everything, to stand (Ephesians 6:13).

Scripture: **Ephesians 6:13-17**
Song: **"Soldiers of Christ Arise"**

A lady at church was baptized and was thrilled to be part of the family of God. But a few months later she stopped associating with other believers. She indicated that the hardships and trials she faced made following Christ too difficult. She simply gave up the struggle.

It's not easy to follow our Lord wholeheartedly, as the early Christians learned. Their lives swirled with trials. They no doubt often suffered from discouragement.

That's why Paul gave his instructions to "fight the good fight of faith" (1 Timothy 6:12). After all, we are at war—not against human armies—but against the enemy of our souls. The only way to win the battle is God's way, protected by His armor. God's Word is our weapon. We can be bold for truth, yet act in a spirit of peace and gentleness.

Every day we face challenges and struggles, but if we are clothed in God's armor, we can overcome fear and defeat. A key is to be ever vigilant. As ancient storyteller Aesop put the warning: "We often give our enemies the means to our own destruction." May it never be so of us Christians!

Everlasting God, I desire always to be vigilant, always to be clothed with the armor You provide. I know that with Your help I can be victorious in all things. In the name of Jesus, I pray. Amen.

Rejoicing in Suffering?

We also rejoice in our sufferings, because we know that suffering produces perseverance; perseverance, character; and character, hope (Romans 5:3, 4).

Scripture: **Romans 5:1-5**
Song: **"The Joy of the Lord"**

When my husband died, I was so devastated that I thought my own life was over. However, at that time the Lord began to work in my life, teaching me to persevere in my loneliness, molding my character, assuring me of the hope of eternal life.

As I went through that time, the things on earth lost much of their value as my eyes focused more on spiritual things. My hope in Christ became clearer and dearer to me. God showed me that adversity is temporary and part of life, and that He wants me to focus on Him instead of becoming entangled in fears and worries.

The apostle Paul reminds us that the early Christians suffered much. Even though they were persecuted for their faith, they rejoiced amidst their tribulations because they had set their eyes on the hope of eternal life. Even in times of trial, God showers us with unconditional love as He draws us closer to Him, imprinting eternal values on our hearts. That is our hope, and in that we can rejoice.

O God, thank You for the joys and the challenges You bring into my life. Please help me to persevere in times of trouble, knowing that Your love is sufficient. Give me more perseverance, more Christlike character, and an ever-deepening hope. I pray in the name of Jesus. Amen.

My Source of Peace

Peace I leave with you; my peace I give you. I do not give to you as the world gives. Do not let your hearts be troubled and do not be afraid (John 14:27).

Scripture: **John 14:25-31**
Song: **"Wonderful Peace"**

A fellow teacher seemed to have achieved his life's goals: personal success, financial security, and social acceptance by people he valued. But when he was unexpectedly stopped in his pursuits by a heart attack, fear about the future gripped his soul. It was then that he began seriously seeking the ultimate meaning of his life. And he soon came to faith in Jesus, the only one who could grant him peace and freedom from fear.

How anxious the disciples must have felt when Jesus told them of His imminent departure to return to His Father. What did the future hold for them without their beloved master?

Yet Jesus told them not to be afraid. He assured them that they would receive an inner peace from Him that was far superior to any peace they could find in this world. With this promise, the disciples were able to overcome fear and confusion. They now looked with hope to the future.

Today, all of us need the peace that Jesus offers. It is a supernatural gift, far more valuable than the purest gold. Yet it is perfectly free. Have you asked for it today?

Lord Jesus, *help me to know the peace You have promised to all Your disciples. May that peace radiate within me so that others will want to know You as well. I pray, in Your precious name. Amen.*

In Search of Christmas

For to us a child is born, to us a son is given, and the government will be on his shoulders (Isaiah 9:6a).

Scripture: **Isaiah 9:1-6**
Song: **"Come, Thou Long Expected Jesus"**

Philip, a young man, was walking along the Christmas-lit streets of Victoria, British Columbia, when an older gentleman stopped him at a street corner. "Are you a Christian?" he asked.

Astonished, Philip looked at the man closely before he answered, "I'm as much a Christian as anyone." However, as he continued on, the question lingered in Philip's mind. Determined to find the real answer, he bought a Bible, which he read diligently. He soon realized the truth: The child born in a manger so long ago was the Son of God. Therefore, this young man joyfully opened his heart to the light of the gospel.

Many Israelites must have rejoiced in Isaiah's prophecy. God had promised them a child who would deliver them from the oppressive bondage of their enemies. This news surely filled them with hope. Sadly, today, many people, both Jew and Gentile, still do not recognize that Jesus Christ is the promised Prince of Peace. He came to deliver us from the oppressive bondage of sin and to give us eternal life in His own unending kingdom.

O God, I praise You for sending Jesus to be my Savior. Help me to share this joyful message of salvation with those who have not yet recognized Your Son as their Savior and Lord. In His name I pray. Amen.

Our Part

Go and make disciples of all nations, baptizing them in the name of the Father and of the Son and of the Holy Spirit, and teaching them to obey everything I have commanded you (Matthew 28:19, 20a).

Scripture: **Matthew 28:16-20**
Song: **"I'll Go Where You Want Me to Go"**

What an inspiration Hudson Taylor was to the Christian world! Born in England, he received Jesus as his Savior at 17 years old. Constrained by the love of Christ, the young Taylor obeyed the call of Jesus to preach the gospel to China's millions. Even the most difficult of physical hardships, persecutions, conflicts, and poor health didn't deter him. For Hudson Taylor believed he couldn't do enough for Jesus, his precious Savior, who had done so much for him.

After the resurrection of Christ, Jesus met his disciples on a mountainside in Galilee. There He gave them the mandate to preach the good news of salvation, not only to the Jews but also to the entire Gentile world. The key to their success was to abide in His authority and remember that He was present with them always.

The Great Commission is meant for every believer, and Jesus is still with us 24-7. We are simply asked to share what Christ has done in our lives—and what He can do for all those who are willing to receive Him.

*I praise You, **Lord**, that You put a mission field right in my neighborhood. May I be faithful in sharing Your message of love with those who don't know You. In Your name, amen.*

My Counselor

And he will be called Wonderful Counselor, Mighty God, Everlasting Father, Prince of Peace (Isaiah 9:6b).

Scripture: **Isaiah 9:6b, 7; 11:1-8**
Song: **"Jesus, I Will Trust Thee"**

I had always turned to my husband for advice and guidance. When the Lord took him to Heaven, I was devastated. Now I had no one to turn to—or so I thought. Then during the Christmas season, while hearing Isaiah 9 being read in church, I clearly heard the word *counselor*. I realized God not only desired to be my God and Savior, He also wanted to be my counselor, one to whom I could go at any time for guidance and comfort. I could trust Him to lead me through the maze of life.

Just as God promises to guide me, so the Lord through the prophet Isaiah promised the oppressed people of Israel a wonderful counselor and Savior, giving them hope for the future. The Messiah, to come from the house of David, would reign in righteousness, turn their gloom into joy, and bring peace. This glorious prophecy of the birth of the Messiah told the Israelites that the Messiah would not only be the eternal Son of God but also their guide. He would lead them in a straight path to victory. For each of us today, that victory simply means journeying through life by depending on God.

Father, I thank You that You are the God of promise. Guide me in every decision today. Thank You for the assurance that You can bring good out of grief and joy out of sorrow. I pray this prayer in the name of Jesus. Amen.

How About Some Good News?

I will mention the lovingkindnesses of the LORD, and the praises of the LORD, according to all that the LORD hath bestowed on us, and the great goodness toward the house of Israel, which he hath bestowed on them according to his mercies, and according to the multitude of his lovingkindnesses. (Isaiah 63:7, *King James Version*).

Scripture: **Isaiah 63:7-14**
Song: **"Glorify Thy Name"**

I often wonder why news agencies rarely report any good news. Every newspaper I read, every newscast I watch, and every Web site I visit, all tell me about the terrible things that are happening in my community and the world. Do I really need to know about all of the tragedies of the past 24 hours? Does the average person really want to hear about all the bad? I know some of these stories are important, but why not focus on the good in our world?

In a way, Isaiah was a news reporter as well. While he reported some tragic news at times, he always returned to his central news flash: God is good. His writings have served to report to many generations, for thousands of years, that God has done great things for us because of His kind and compassionate nature. God is worthy of our praise and our worship as we live our lives to bring glory to His name.

Father, I celebrate Your goodness. Thank You for the good things You have done in my life. Help me to bring glory to Your name. In Jesus' name, amen.

December 20–26. **Mark Williams** is an associate minister, professor, and freelance writer who lives with his wife, Kelly, and their six children near Nashville, Tennessee.

What Have I Missed?

Lead out those who have eyes but are blind, who have ears but are deaf (Isaiah 43:8).

Scripture: **Isaiah 43:8-10**
Song: **"Open Our Eyes, Lord"**

Late in my junior year, my father took me to a college information night hosted by my high school. As we gathered catalogues and applications, my father encouraged me to talk to the representative from MIT. I declined, stating that I wasn't interested in attending a "trade school." In my youthful ignorance, I mistook one of the finest colleges in the nation for a local technology program.

Jesus was born in a stable in the town of Bethlehem. Wise men traveled from the East to see the new king. The Jewish religious leaders wouldn't trouble themselves to walk the few miles from Jerusalem to see the Savior for themselves.

Rather than embracing the long-awaited Messiah, they mistook the baby Jesus as a threat to their power and their way of life. Later, they would treat him like an outlaw and execute Him on a criminal's cross.

They had eyes to see and ears to hear. But they completely missed it when God came near and dwelt among them. And so I have to ask myself: What is it about the Lord in my own world that I may be missing? And what of His still, small voice am I failing to hear these days?

God, give me eyes to see Your hand at work and ears to hear Your voice so that I will not miss how You are at work all around me. In Jesus' name, amen.

God's Compassionate Choice

I, even I, am he who blots out your transgressions, for my own sake, and remembers your sins no more (Isaiah 43:25).

Scripture: **Isaiah 43:22-28**
Song: **"Father, Forgive, the Savior Said"**

One Friday night when I was in high school, some of my friends and I were out driving around with nothing planned. Before the night was over, we had wrecked the car, been involved in a big fight, and damaged some property.

Needless to say, I got in trouble with my parents—big trouble. I had violated their trust, and I knew it would take a long time to gain it back. Months later, after all of the damages were paid off, my parents returned my car and let me out of the house again. They rarely mentioned that night, but I knew they had not forgotten. Out of love, they simply chose not to hold it against me any longer.

In the same way, God chooses not to remember our sins or hold our failures against us. In His grace and mercy, He forgives us when we mess up and deserve to be punished.

How can He do this? It's because He has already "paid the damages" for our mistakes. On the cross, Jesus took every one of our sins—past, present, and future—and atoned for them forever. In effect, He became our scapegoat, the one who takes the blame for someone else's wrongdoing. Now we are free to live a life of service that honors His awesome gift to us.

God, *thank You for choosing not to hold my sins and failures against me. Help me to live in the freedom of Your mercy and grace today. I pray in the name of Jesus. Amen.*

No Dogs Allowed!

Do not be afraid of the king of Babylon, whom you now fear. Do not be afraid of him, declares the LORD, for I am with you and will save you and deliver you from his hands (Jeremiah 42:11).

Scripture: **Jeremiah 42:7-17**
Song: **"Fear Not, O Little Flock"**

My first job was delivering the afternoon newspaper when I was 10 years old. Each day after school, I would fold my papers, load my bag, and make my deliveries by bicycle. However, I had one big problem . . . I was terrified of dogs.

On my route, there were dogs that would chase me, biting at my tires and pulling at my newspaper bag. I was so afraid that my parents would often have to drive me around for my deliveries. Eventually, I quit the job—to avoid the dogs.

The Israelites who were left behind after the siege and destruction of Jerusalem were paralyzed by fear of the mighty Babylonian king. The majority of their countrymen had been killed or carried into exile. Those left were afraid they would be next. They felt they would be safer in Egypt, but God was commanding them to stay in Jerusalem. Sadly, due to their fear, many disobeyed the Lord and traveled to Egypt. They forfeited a chance to see God work among them. Why? They were simply too afraid to trust Him.

Gracious Father, help me to overcome the fears that hold me back from serving You. Teach me to trust Your plans and Your direction for my life. Help me to remember Your upholding presence, even when danger seems to lurk in my path. Amen.

His Constant Presence

Then Haggai, the LORD's messenger, gave this message of the LORD to the people: "I am with you," declares the LORD (Haggai 1:13).

Scripture: Haggai 1:7-15
Song: "What Child Is This?"

During the Civil War, no general had a greater impact on his soldiers than the general Robert E. Lee. It is said that the mere sight of him riding in the front lines caused the confederate soldiers to give the "rebel yell" and surge forward into the fight.

Lee demonstrated to his men that he was with them with his constant presence on the battlefield. Because of Lee's leadership, the Confederate army won a number of significant battles throughout the war, even though they were badly outnumbered and out resourced.

In our darkest days—our greatest challenges, our loneliest moments, or our greatest disappointments—it is encouraging to know that God is with us every step of the way. Just as the Confederate soldiers were encouraged by the sight of General Lee riding his famous horse, Traveller, we can find comfort in a God who knows everything and has everything under His control.

May we come to understand that God is with us. May we remember that His presence brings us supernatural peace.

Father, help me to sense Your presence with me in everything that I do. Lead me according to Your will and give me a peace that passes my own human understanding. In the name of Jesus, now and forever, amen.

Benefits of Obedience

When Joseph woke up, he did what the angel of the Lord had commanded him and took Mary home as his wife (Matthew 1:24).

Scripture: **Matthew 1:18-25**
Song: **"O Little Town of Bethlehem"**

In our high-tech society, we have little use for miracles anymore. Advances in medical care allow us to find cures for most illnesses. Advances in astronomy have helped us to identify far-off galaxies, comets, and stars, and advances in all areas of science enable us to explain what was formerly inexplicable. When we see or experience something we don't understand, we just surf the Web to find out more about it. It is rare that we will commit to something unless we have all the implications laid out before us.

When Joseph discovered in a dream that Mary was pregnant by the Holy Spirit, he didn't consult a medical Web site to research virgin births. Nor did he contact his lawyer to discuss contingency plans. Joseph simply trusted God to work out the unbelievable—to make the impossible a reality.

In complete obedience to God's command, Joseph took Mary home as his wife, in spite of the absurdity of the situation. As a result of his obedience, he was blessed with the opportunity to help raise the Savior. Talk about the benefits of obeying God! What is He asking you to do today?

Jesus, grant me faith to believe that with You anything is possible. You left us to continue Your work here on earth, bringing Your kingdom values into play wherever we can. Help us make You proud, Lord. In Your name, amen.

The Real Thing

"I, even I, am the LORD, and apart from me there is no savior. I have revealed and saved and proclaimed—I, and not some foreign god among you. You are my witnesses," declares the LORD, "that I am God" (Isaiah 43:11, 12).

Scripture: **Isaiah 43:1-7, 10-12**
Song: **"I'd Rather Have Jesus"**

The other night I fell asleep on the couch and woke up to the world of television infomercials. I was amazed that virtually every channel was showing paid programming. One show promised I could become a millionaire working just 10 hours a week. Another promised I could lose inches from my flabby midsection instantly, while yet another promised that I could get a college degree from home in just weeks. I couldn't help but wonder how many people were out there falling for these quick-fix scams.

It occurred to me that we often try to find shortcuts in our spiritual lives as well. We make so many things the entire focus of our lives—like making money, furthering our careers, or raising our children. Yet we still hope our relationship with God will naturally grow strong and healthy.

But there are no shortcuts in developing a deep relationship with the one true God. In time, we learn that there is nothing in this world that can satisfy our souls like Jesus.

Merciful Father, so often I make plans and go my own way. I ignore Your presence and guidance. Today forgive me for not making You the central focus of my life. Remind me that You are the only real God, and You are the one who can bring peace to my heart. In the name of Your Son, I pray. Amen.

I Will See God

After my skin has been destroyed, yet in my flesh I will see God; I myself will see him with my own eyes—I, and not another (Job 19:26, 27).

Scripture: **Job 19:23-27**
Song: **"I Am on My Way to Heaven"**

I wrestled in the tall grass with my son one afternoon. The ice was heavy on the trees and thick on every blade of grass. I rolled over Andrew and came straight down on a blade of ice. It cut me very near to my eye, and I winced at the pain. We went to the doctor, and everything is fine now, but that was not a comfortable moment.

Every living person has experienced things that they did not enjoy. Amy Grant has a song that reminds us that we will soon be with the Father. Paul talks about not being able to decide if he wants to stay on earth or die so that he can go to be with Jesus. I hear people at funerals say things like, "He's in a better place now." It's true.

God is good all the time, but in this world we will have challenges and bad times and stress. Job knows some of that pain and suffering in today's Scripture. Yet he says, "I will see God." He believes that it will all end well. Do you know that too?

Dear Father, thank You for offering me Your peace. But help me learn to accept that peace—which only comes through a relationship with Your Son—even in times of difficult struggles. I pray this in His precious name. Amen.

December 27–31. **John H. Boys** has been many things, including a tree-trimmer in Colorado and a tour-bus guide in Montana. He and his wife, Janet, and two children, live in Cassville, Missouri.

Immanuel: God with Us

When Jacob awoke from his sleep, he thought, "Surely the LORD is in this place, and I was not aware of it" (Genesis 28:16).

Scripture: **Genesis 28:10-17**
Song: **"Choose the Living Way"**

When I was much younger, I enjoyed pressing down on the gas pedal in my car. God was always with me. He let me drive as fast as I wanted to, but He was with me. Yes, He whispered to my conscience to slow down, but He didn't make my decisions for me; He left the choice to me. Yes, He spoke to me—and if I chose not to listen—then I was the one to blame for any consequences of my dangerous driving. I like the way Dr. Seuss put it in his book, *Oh, the Places You'll Go:*

You have brains in your head.

You have feet in your shoes.

You can steer yourself any direction you choose.

Anyway, I drove home from college one weekend, years ago, driving at high speed. I came around a wide, slow curve . . . going fast . . . and the next oncoming vehicle was shooting me with his police radar gun! I got a speeding ticket, having been clocked at the fastest speed I'd ever driven in my entire life. God was with me then, but He never took away my freedom of choice. A comforting but scary thought.

Immanuel, *thank You for this day. Thank You for Your presence in my life. Help me to listen so that I can better live for You today and every day. In Jesus' precious name I pray. Amen.*

Blessings Amidst the Troubles

I will pour water on the thirsty land, and streams on the dry ground; I will pour out my Spirit on your offspring, and my blessing on your descendants (Isaiah 44:3).

Scripture: Isaiah 44:1-5
Song: "Standing on the Promises"

When I was 2-years-old, my family went to my grandparents' house for a visit. I walked into the backyard, alone and continued walking until I stood upon the cover over the deep end of the swimming pool. My legs broke through the plastic, and I dangled over the water, unaware of any danger.

Thankfully, my dad just happened to walk by a window, and he saw me there. He saved me, which was, obviously, a great blessing to me.

Similarly, Isaiah tells us that God pours out His blessing on His people and their descendants. That involves watching over them, of course. Yet it is not a promise of no harm ever coming to them. We know that, even today, we enjoy God's blessings, but we also constantly keep before us the words of our Savior: "In this world you will have trouble" (John 16:33). He also called each of His disciples to take up their crosses and follow Him.

Yet I hold fast to this "follow-up" statement from Jesus: "But take heart! I have overcome the world" (John 16:33). In all such pronouncements, the God-man Jesus prophetically echoes the greatest of the human prophets.

Dear Heavenly Father, *help me to feel Your peace and joy so completely that others see You when they're looking at me. I pray. Amen.*

Always and All Ways

Praise be to the LORD, the God of Israel, from everlasting to everlasting. Let all the people say, "Amen!" Praise the LORD (Psalm 106:48).

Scripture: **Psalm 106:40-48**
Song: **"Majesty"**

Every good thing is from God. And when we receive those good things, we naturally want to say, "Thank You"—or "Amen! Praise the Lord!"

The psalmist expresses, this desire to praise the one who is so good to us. And in the New Testament, the apostle Paul continues the theme in Philippians 4:4: "Rejoice in the Lord always," he tells the members of the church in Philippi.

Please note that he didn't say to rejoice only if everything is going well for you. The Bible doesn't say to rejoice only when the weather is to your liking. It doesn't say to praise the Lord only if it's sunny.

What the Bible says, essentially, is that we should rejoice even if we're in the storm shelter while our house is getting blown apart. It says we should rejoice, even if the storm shelter is leaking water and our flashlight batteries are all dying out. In other words: Rejoice in the Lord. Always.

I would like to learn that lesson better. So much of my life involves trying to get the circumstances into a kind of peaceful harmony, so I can be happy and thankful. But suppose I were to simply be happy and thankful, no matter what?

Loving Father, help me to rejoice in all things—to thank You for the things I don't always see as good. Remind me that You are good, all the time, and in all situations. In Jesus' precious name I pray. Amen.

Still an Heir

Because you are sons, God sent the Spirit of his Son into our hearts, the Spirit who calls out, "Abba, Father." So you are no longer a slave, but a son; and since you are a son, God has made you also an heir (Galatians 4:6, 7).

Scripture: **Galatians 4:1-7**
Song: **"Adopted"**

Several years ago I was digging on a project near a pond on the property of my parents. I was driving a skid steer loader with a scoop bucket on the front. One of my nephews was on the pond in a canoe. I stopped working and looked up to tease him—and soon unwittingly drove into the edge of the pond with the loader! The water became deep faster than I expected, and I got the machine good and stuck. My dad had to bring home another machine to pull me out of the muddy water.

But he wasn't even mad at me. He was only worried for my safety. I'd certainly acted foolishly, but my father still loved and cared for my welfare, and he definitely didn't sit down right then to cut me out of his will.

It's the same with my Father in Heaven. Just as I'm an heir to everything my earthly father owns, so I'm an heir to all the spiritual riches promised me in the Son of the eternal Father.

God is my "Father," and He does not die. But when I die, I will inherit His kingdom, and the joys there will never end.

Creator of all, thank You for loving me, even when I act foolishly. Thank You for Jesus, by whose precious blood I have entrance into eternal life. I look forward to the day when I see Him, face to face! In His name I pray. Amen.